ENGINEER DEPARTMENT, U. S. ARMY.

REPORT

UPON

UNITED STATES GEOGRAPHICAL SURVEYS

WEST OF THE ONE HUNDREDTH MERIDIAN,

IN CHARGE OF

CAPT. GEO. M. WHEELER,
CORPS OF ENGINEERS, U. S. ARMY,

UNDER THE DIRECTION OF

THE CHIEF OF ENGINEERS, U. S. ARMY.

PUBLISHED BY AUTHORITY OF THE HONORABLE THE SECRETARY OF WAR,

IN ACCORDANCE WITH ACTS OF CONGRESS OF JUNE 23, 1874, AND FEBRUARY 15, 1875.

IN SEVEN VOLUMES AND ONE SUPPLEMENT, ACCOMPANIED BY ONE TOPOGRAPHIC AND ONE GEOLOGIC ATLAS.

APPENDIX F.—MEMOIR OF EXPLORATIONS AND SURVEYS, ETC.

VOL. I.—GEOGRAPHICAL REPORT.

WASHINGTON:
GOVERNMENT PRINTING OFFICE.
1889.

APPENDIX F.

MEMOIR UPON THE VOYAGES, DISCOVERIES, EXPLORATIONS, AND SURVEYS TO AND AT THE WEST COAST OF NORTH AMERICA AND INTERIOR OF THE UNITED STATES WEST OF THE MISSISSIPPI RIVER, BETWEEN 1500 AND 1880, INCLUDING LATER BIBLIOGRAPHICAL AND OTHER REFERENCES TO DETERMINED LATITUDES, LONGITUDES, AND ALTITUDES AVAILABLE FOR THE BASIS OF THE PERMANENT OFFICIAL TOPOGRAPHIC ATLAS OF THE UNITED STATES.

GENERAL TABLE.

PART I.

GEOGRAPHICAL DISCOVERY AND EXPLORATION, WEST COAST AND INTERIOR, 1500 TO 1800.

This period of exploration is alluded to in a brief paragraph in Warren's Memoir, and was evidently considered of no particular importance as regards latitudes and longitudes from which to compile the map of the territory west of the Mississippi that was constructed after the completion of the Pacific railroad surveys. It is mentioned occasionally in the Coast Survey Reports,* while in that for 1884 appears an article, regarding the various explorations, by Dr. J. G. Kohl, whose complete

* See Coast Survey Report, 1857, Appendix No. 52.

manuscript fell into my hands through the courtesy of the geographical society of Bremen. It is doubtless true that there has been no permanent use of the latitudes and longitudes of these early explorers, but the Coast Survey have been assisted by them to some extent during their early reconnaissances, and indirectly, also, parties engaged in the interior. However, if the discoveries in the Western Ocean had not been made, there would have been no requirement for the early voyages of discovery and exploration, whether their geographic positions were the best or not.

The necessities of the time, whether dictated by war or conquest, commerce or defense, demanded information, exterior and interior, of the new found lands, and little by little the Indian rawhide and bark sketches and traditional itineraries gave place to the actual travels, investigations, reconnaissances, and finally instrumental surveys, until ultimately the Government expeditions, equipped with the best instruments in vogue at the time, carried their examinations more into detail, especially on the west coast and occasionally in the interior, until there resulted a series of sketches, maps, and charts, the outgrowth of these undertakings, descriptions of which were prepared with great fullness by the late Dr. J. G. Kohl, but which have scarcely been treated upon in the literature of the country.

He also gathered a large collection of maps (mostly copies) relating to this subject while an official of the State Department, within the archives of which these still remain. They have not been availed of, except that Mr. Justin Winsor has published in the Harvard University Bibliographical Contributions, No. 19, an annotated calendar for the use of scholars, entitled "The Kohl Collection of Early Maps," prior to which I had selected, somewhat at random, a number of the most intelligible specimens that were most easily found in the then condition of arrangement of the maps, of which reproductions are herewith found listed in the table of contents and described separately.

PRIOR TO 1500.

Geographical knowledge, confined to a learned few among the ancients, consisted, at the close of the fourth century, in a surmise only of the sphericity of the earth, with vague and diminutive conception of its size, while the positive knowledge of Europeans was limited to a parallelogram, north-west and south-east in direction, about 120 degrees east and west and 50 degrees north and south, being an area bordering on the Atlantic and Indian Oceans, including the Mediterranean, parts of southern, southwestern, and central Europe, Arabia, Persia, India, and northern Africa. There were various theories concerning the shape of southern Africa; a *mare oceanum*, stretching westward to unknown Asiatic shores, with hypothetical islands intervening, opinions that this sea was navigable, and that India might possibly be reached by sailing westward. The popular mind only grasped the idea of sphericity long after the first circumnavigation in the sixteenth century. From the fifth to the fifteenth century cosmographical and all other knowledge lay almost entirely dormant. It seems probable that the American continent may have several times been reached prior to the discoveries by Columbus, but the following appears to be the only authentic published information now extant:*

In 986, Biarne, sailing southwest from Iceland, came within sight of land, believed to have been America, and conjectured by Kohl to have been Cape Cod, Nova Scotia, and Newfoundland.

In 1000, Leif, son of Eric the Red, sailed southwest from Greenland in search of lands seen by Biarne, and made a settlement at some point on Narragansett Bay. Columbus made his first voyage in 1492,† but did not reach the main-land. Cabral reached the coast of Brazil in about latitude 10 degrees north in 1500, and was the first of the navigators of this period to reach the continent.‡

FROM 1500 TO 1800.

There were eleven nationalities engaged in the discovery and exploration of the west coast and interior of the United States between the years 1500 and 1800. The chronological statement that follows gives more than one hundred and fifty separate expeditions, endeavors, or attempts in this direction, and comprises all those of importance known to me. Of these

---

* See De Costa, B. F. The Pre-Columbian Discovery of America, Albany, 1868.

† It has not been proven that Prince Henry, Toscanelli, or Columbus had any knowledge of the discoveries by the Norsemen.

‡ See Bancroft's History of Central America, vol. I, pp. 67 *et seq.*

several voyages and explorations seventy-six were Spanish, twenty-three English, twenty-one French, fifteen (at least) by the Jesuits and Franciscans, six Russian, four American, three German, two Italian, two Danish, one Portuguese, and one Hungarian.

The first voyage of Columbus gave to all Western Europe the earliest impulse for western voyages of discovery. The King of England, also rich merchants, among them Italians, became interested and favored the idea of finding a direct westerly route to China and Japan.

Hence, with the single exception of the Russians, who came from the west, all the early European discoverers and explorers of America set out from the east. They found the North American continent as a barrier, and sailed along its entire eastern coast. This coast was comparatively well known twenty years before the western or Pacific was discovered. The latter was discovered by Balboa, at the Isthmus of Panama, in 1513, and the Strait of Magellan by this navigator in 1519. Those who immediately followed these discoveries occupied themselves with the South American coast, hoping to find water communication between the Atlantic and Pacific, when subsequently, and for a similar purpose, Cortez and his captains in 1530 commenced to turn the direction of discovery from Central America to the northwest. During forty years (1492 to 1532) the east and west coasts of South America were explored and made known, as well as the east coast of North America as far north and beyond the St. Lawrence, and a portion of this river, while fully one-fourth of the two Americas, the west coast of North America, remained unknown. This led to many and varying speculations by cosmographers. Some thought there was no American continent but only a succession of islands, but the principal belief was that North America was a large peninsula joined to Asia, while Columbus died ignorant of having discovered a new continent.

Expeditions for discovery along the northwest coast expected the close proximity of Japan and China. After the Isthmus and Cape Horn were discovered, theoretically a supposed northwest passage promised shorter water communication to the above countries and possibly Cathay. Hence the expeditions along the east and west coast often took the form of a search for this passage.

In various relations, connected also with arctic explorations, these undertakings continued, until in October, 1850, Captain McClure, of the English navy, from Behring Strait reached the waters of "Winter Harbor," where Parry had come from the east in 1820, and whence he was relieved by Lieutenant Kellett's sledge party across the intervening ice space, thus proving a northwest water communication for North America, ice locked for a short distance only, yet unserviceable as a highway of commerce.

Cortez began the exploration of the west and northwest coast, which culminated in the discovery of Behring Strait by Behring.

The Spanish expeditions were dispatched principally by the government of New Spain, and were, as is true of nearly all the expeditions of this period (especially Spanish and English), based on the ideas of commerce and conquest.

The English expeditions of Cook, Colnet, Vancouver, and Broughton were ordered by government, but in the main the underlying impetus was commerce, except for the Jesuits and Franciscans, who went as missionaries to spread the faith.

The expeditions, then, were naval, military, civil, clerical, corporate, and individual. During these three centuries new countries were sought for, principally with the hope to find gold and spices, to found government, and aggrandize religion, while in these later days the religious zeal and love for gold have been replaced by the more peaceful ways of commerce and competition that are now making known the remaining portions of the globe available for civilization.

The "northern route to China" was a problem long cultivated, while the full discovery of America was mainly completed in modern times. In the sixteenth century explorations reached 43 degrees north latitude. From 1602 to the middle of the eighteenth century no Spanish expedition reached the cold and inhospitable northwest coast. Meanwhile the Jesuits and Franciscans "civilized" Upper and Lower California. The expeditions were substantially Spanish till the time of Drake (1579). These were quite continuous till Cabrillo (1542–'43), when little was done till Velasco (1564). The next considerable interval of quietude was from Iturbi (1615) to Ortega (1632), then Casañate (1648) to Pinadero (1664), after which, except for slight attempts ending in 1683 (Atondo), the Spanish were seen nowhere upon the coast till the expedition of Galvez (1767), about one hundred years later. For two centuries (1550–1750) nothing was done as compared with the activity from 1492 to 1550

The English expeditions (coastwise and interior) continued till 1842. Many expeditions under French auspices (1673–1750) sought for the "great river of the west" of La Hontan.

The Franciscans either accompanied exploring parties or made independent expeditions from Ruiz (1581) to Junipero Serra (1782), more than two hundred years.

The Jesuits joined expeditions as early as 1642, but commenced independent journeys under Salvatierra (1697), and continued with much activity until their expulsion (1767) from California.

The first Russian (Deschnew) explored the coast in 1648, and the last in 1841.

The French explored in the interior as early as 1639, and conducted important expeditions (1820–'42).

American explorers began with Kendrick (1788). The fur companies were active in exploration (1806–'21), as also the Russian settlements (1812–'41). Missionary travels on land were made from year to year.

Although Ulloa, in 1539, determined Lower California to be a peninsula, yet the fact was lost to view, and it was only in 1766 that Link determined and made known for all time the peninsularity.*

Cortez discovered Lower California, which Ulloa sailed around Upper California was first visited by Cabrillo (1540–'43) The interior was but imperfectly settled and explored toward the seventeenth century. It was not till the nineteenth century that this country was thoroughly explored by Americans.

From 1579 (Drake) to 1778 (Cook), (two hundred years,) except for the Russians, no one visited the northwest coast but the Spaniards.

During the thirty years closing the eighteenth century one expedition

* Lower California was first called an island by the Dutch pirates at the Bay of Tichilingue, on the southeast coast, at the beginning of the seventeenth century. Purchas, in 1625, was the first to print the above error.

after another, combining traffic and exploration, almost yearly revealed all the mysteries of the West. Even trading voyagers wrote narratives, each one bringing new facts and names.

Cabrillo's was the most remarkable in the sixteenth and Viscaìno's in the seventeenth century of all the Spanish voyages. The latter made the first reliable astronomic observations and general rude reconnaissance of the coast, while Vancouver conducted what might be termed the first continuous reconnaissance. Good observations were also made by Cook, Gali, Perouse, and Malaspina. Mackenzie was the first to reach the northwest coast from the east. Vancouver's time was the most active in the history of west coast explorations, during which a total of thirty vessels took part, with officers of ability, and accompanied by astronomers. The Franciscans succeeded the Jesuits. Most of the French came from Canada. In 1640 some Cossacks sailed down the Amoor River to the Pacific. Deschnew reached Behring Strait along the north coast of Siberia. Kamchatka was discovered at the end of the seventeenth century. The Hudson Bay Company first explored the Yukon. The missions were the basis of settlement and assisted in establishing government.

The scientific and commercial world for a long time reaped no benefits from the Spanish expeditions, the records of which were retained by the court.

Prof. George Davidson makes comparison of the nomenclature used by Ulloa, Cabrillo, Ferello, and Viscaìno, comparing it with that of to-day. (See Appendix 7, U. S. Coast and Geodetic Survey, 1886.)

The Kohl manuscript refers to this feature at great length in his hydrographic descriptions. It does not appear that the numerical latitudes and longitudes used by the several expeditions in plotting their routes have ever appeared in print. They doubtless rest principally in the old archives of "New Spain," in the City of Mexico, and at the hydrographic bureaus at Madrid and London, where nothing less than a scientific search will develop their existence and comparative value. However, as before stated, these have all been replaced by later determinations.

Want of time, delicate health, and various duties have prevented such a digest of the great mass of facts at disposal as would summarize all the leading events and results, and hence one must be content with the presentation of a chronological list, with remarks thereon, as an index, at least, to what took place during an interval of fully three centuries, trusting that the scientific as well as literary history of these endeavors will be fully treated hereafter.

CHRONOLOGICAL STATEMENT OF VOYAGES AND EXPLORATIONS TO THE WEST COAST AND INTERIOR OF NORTH AMERICA BETWEEN 1500 AND 1800.*

(Including Columbus and Corte Réal.)

NOTE.—The following abbreviations have been used in list of authorities: (1) K. for Dr. J. G. Kohl; (2) M. for de Mofras; (3) B. for Burney; (4) G. for Greenhow; (5) T. for Twiss. For nationalities: (1) I. for Italian; (2) P. for Portuguese; (3) S. for Spanish; (4) F. for French; (5) E. for English; (6) Gr. for Greek; (7) R. for Russian; (8) G. for German; (9) D. for Danish; (10) H. for Hungarian; (11) A. for American; (12) Fr. for Franciscan.

No.	Name.	Nation.	Year	Authority.	Remarks.
1	Corte Réal	P	1500	G. B.	Belief in the fictitious "Straits of Anian" grew out of a supposed voyage by the brothers Corte Réal. No authority for this. Anian appeared about 1566 in Italy. (Harrisse.)
2	Columbus	I	1502	M	During fourth voyage attempted to find a strait leading to the South Sea and land of the spices. (Did not reach the main-land. Kohl, p. 514, U. S. C. S., 1884.)
3	(H) Nuñez de Balboa	S	1513	M	Discovered and established existence of the South Sea, from heights near Panama.
4	Tello de Guzman	S	1515	Dr. S. Ruge	The first to visit Panama.
5	Pineda	S	1519	K	Discovered Mississippi River and named it "Rio de Espiritu Santo."
6	Espinosa	S	1519	Ruge	Sails from Panama as far as the Gulf of Nicoya, in 10° north latitude. Visited in canoes in 1517 by Hurtado.
7	Cortes	S	1522–'24	M	Sent several expeditions to west coast of Mexico.
8	Gonzalez de Avila	S	1522	Ruge	Discovers the west coast of Nicaragua. His pilot Niño went even as far as Chiapas.
9	Garay	S	1523	K	Discovered mouth of Rio Grande del Norte.
10	Guevara	S	1526	Bancroft	Via Straits of Magellan reached Tehuantepec and Zacatula.
11	Mendoza	S	1528	M	Continued the explorations of coast of New Spain. M. de Mofrat and his researches are unknown to me. Of Hurtado de Mendoza I only know the expedition of 1531, undertaken by orders of Cortez. Mendoza was killed by the natives on the coast of Cinaloa. Before him Nuño de Guzman had discovered Jalisco and Cinaloa in 1530. (Professor Fischer.)
12	Narvaez	S	1528	Ruge and K.	Expedition to Florida. Narvaez dies. From his army four men, Cabeza de Vaca, Dorantes, Maldonado (Kohl says "Alonzo de Castillo"), and Estebancio, went by land, across the Mississippi River, through New Mexico and Arizona, to Culiacan, 1516. Kohl says 1529.
13	Maldonado	S	1528	G	Explored 100 leagues of west coast of Mexico.
14	Guzman	S	1530	Ruge	By land to the west coast of Mexico, to Sinaloa ("Nueva Galicia").

* Copies of this list as at first compiled having been submitted to James Carson Brevoort, Rev. B. F. De Costa, D. D., Henry Harrisse, Professor Fischer, and Professor Ruge, and it has been revised in accordance with their suggestions, as found noted.

CHRONOLOGICAL STATEMENT OF VOYAGES AND EXPLORATIONS, ETC.—Continued.

No.	Name.	Nation.	Year.	Authority.	Remarks.
15	Mendoza	S	1532	G. B. M. and K. (See also Herrera and Navarrete; sailed from Acapulco.)	Reached 27° north longitude at west coast of Mexico. This expedition is lost to view. Not known how far it went. (Bernal Diaz del Castillo, Lib. XII, p. 2. R.)
16	Grijalva	S	1533	Colecc. de doc. inedit., XIV, p. 128.	Discovers St. Thomas (St. Benedito. R.).
	Bezerra	S	1533–'34	G., B., M., and K.	Sailed from Tehuantepec, Gulf of California. (See Gomara.) Ximenez, the pilot who murdered Bezerra, discovered Lower California.
17	Cortes	S	1535–'37	G., B., M., and K.	Sailed from Chiametta. Takes possession in person of southeast part of Lower California. Gomara says it is not known how far up the Gulf of California Cortez sailed.
18	Cabeza de Vaca	S	1536	K	From Mississippi River Valley, via what is now New Mexico, to northern Mexico. (Member of Narvaez expedition.)
19	De Soto	S	1538	K	Explored a part of the lower Mississippi Valley. Was followed by Moscoso, who recognized the delta and afterward went into interior of Texas. Then for one hundred years the Spaniards did not add to the knowledge of this region.
20	Ulloa	S	1539–'40	B., G., T., M., and K.	From Acapulco. Reconnoiters both shores of Gulf of California. Subsequently visits Magdalena Bay and sails around Lower California. Went as far as Isla de los Cedros (28° 10′ north), from whence he sent one ship back, proceeded farther, and not heard from again. (R.) Latitude 30° north. (K.) (See also Ramusio and Hakluyt.)
21	Niza, Marcos de	Fr	1539	K., B., G., and Whipple.	From Culiacan penetrating northward found the seven cities of Cibola, alleged to have been discovered by Cabeza de Vaca.
22	Alarcon	S	1540	B., G., M., K., and Whipple.	Sails from Mexican coast. Adjunct to Coronado's expedition. Discovered Colorado River and ascended it 85 leagues.
23	Coronado	S	1540–'42	G., B., M., K., and Whipple.	Reached the seven cities of Cibola, the province of "Quivira," and northward to 40° north latitude.
24	Cabrillo	S	1542–'43	G., T., B., M., and K.	Sails from Navidad, Mex. Examined west coast of California, reaching approximately 43° north latitude. Discovered San Clemente, Santa Catalina, and St. Bernardo Islands, Santa Barbara channel, and bays of San Diego and Monterey. After Cabrillo's death (January 3, 1543), his pilot Ferrelo sails northward, presumably to 43° north. (R.) Cabrillo was a Portuguese in Spanish service. I do not believe that he passed Cape Mendocino. (See also Navarrete and Herrera.)
25	De Soto	S	1541	G., K	Discovered the Mississippi River near the mouth of the Arkansas. Sailed from Cuba, May 18, 1539, reaching Tampa.
26	Moscoso	S	1542–'43	K	Explored about one hundred miles of lower Mississippi, recognized the delta, and explored along the coast of Texas. Succeeded De Soto.
27	Ocampo	S	1543	K	Member of Coronado expedition. Passed from Quivira, through the region now known as Texas, and came to Panuco.
28	Olnos	S	1544	K	From Panuco northward toward confines of Florida.

CHRONOLOGICAL STATEMENT OF VOYAGES AND EXPLORATIONS, ETC.—Continued.

No.	Name.	Nation.	Year.	Authority.	Remarks.
29	Bazares	S	1558	K	Coasted north from Panuco, probably as far as Matagorda Bay.
30	Velasco	S	1564	M	Made an expedition to the California coast.
31	Urdañeta	S	1568	G., B., and K	Claimed by "one Salvatierra" to have made the northwest passage. Unauthentic. (R.) Went from Phillipine Islands to Mexico. (K.)
32	Ladrillero	S	1574	G., B., and K	Pretended to have sailed through a passage near Newfoundland from Atlantic to Pacific.
33	Drake	E	1579	T., G., B., M., and K.	Sailed from England via Magellan Straits. Reached about the same latitude attained by Cabrillo. Claimed by many to have discovered San Francisco Bay. Named the California coast "New Albion." (See Fletcher: The world encompassed. An English freebooter.)
34	Ruyz (spelled "Ruiz" by Kohl.)	Fr	1581	K. and Whipple.	Travels north from the valley of San Bartolomeo, near the silver mines of Santa Barbara, at outskirts of Spanish settlements in Mexico, 160 leagues, reaching New Mexico.*
35	Gali	S	1582–'84	M., B., and K	From Acapulco. Reconnoitered coast north of 37th parallel. Made no important discoveries. (Gali: Le Grand Routier de Mer. See also Hakluyt.)
36	Espejo	S	1582–'83	K. and Whipple.	Visits Pueblos on Rio Grande, also Zuñi. A principal discoverer in New Mexico.
37	Juan de Oñate	S	1591	K. and Davis, p. 267.	Explores and colonizes New Mexico, and founds Santa Fe in 1611. The Rio Grande, believed for a long time to head in Salt Lake, was laid down as entering the Gulf of California, until corrected by Coronelli on his map of approx., 1680. Results meager.†
38	Cavendish	E	1587	G. and K	Touched at southern end of Lower California. An English freebooter.
39	De Fuca. (Unauthenticated. R.)	Gr	1592	G., T., B., M., and K.	Pretended to Michael Lock to have made the northwest passage.
40	Cermeñon	S	1595	M. and K	From Mexican coast. Wrecked either in or near San Francisco Bay.
41	Viscaino	S	1595	B	Examines the lower part of the Gulf of California. (Doubtful.) Kohl gives only 1596.
42	Viscaino	S	1596	G., T., B., M., and K.	From Acapulco. Does not pass beyond lower entrance of the Gulf of California. Mentions Island of Santa Cruz.
43	Viscaino	S	1602–'03	G., T., B., M., and K. Coleccion de doc. inedit. rel. al desc., tom. VIII, p. 539. Madrid, 1867. Navarrette in colec. d. doc. ined. p. l. hist. d'España, XV, 45. (R.)	From Acapulco. Reaches Cape Blanco or approx. 42° north latitude. (R.) (Aguilar probably saw the mouth of the Columbia River.—K.) His companion, Aguilar, went as far as 43° north and to Cape Blanco. (R.) Did not visit the Gulf of California. Mentions Sierra de St. Lucia (Coast Range of California). Discovered Point Reyes. (See also Torquemada and Navarette.)
44	Maldonado (fictitious)	S	1609	G., T., B., M., and K.	Presented *fictitious* account of voyage by the northwest passage.

* The following entradas into New Mexico were made: Rodriguez, 1581–'82; Morlette in 1591, and Bonilla about 1596. (See Bancroft, Northwest Coast, vol. 1, p. 20.) Also Francisco Cano, 1568; Chamuscado, 1581; Martin, 1583; Castaño, 1590, and Humaña, 1599. (See Narr. and Crit. Hist., vol. II, p. 504.)

† Texas was entered by Perea and Lopez, 1629, and Captain Vaca, 1634. (See Bancroft, Northwest Coast, vol. I.)

CHRONOLOGICAL STATEMENT OF VOYAGES AND EXPLORATIONS, ETC.—Continued

No.	Name.	Nation.	Year.	Authority.	Remarks.
45	Iturbi	S	1615	M. and K.	Made reconnaissance along east coast of Gulf of California to approx. 30° north latitude. Did not reach the mouth of the Colorado. History written by Father Andres Perez de Ribos, a Jesuit.
46	Ortega	S	1632	M. and K	Made three visits to the southerly parts of the Gulf of California lying between Cape St. Lucas and the Bay of La Paz, from whence pearls were brought.
47	Carboneli	S	1636	M. and K.	Made visit for pearls to Gulf of California. Did not reach the mouth of the Colorado.
48	Nicolet	F	1639	K.	Believed to have been on the waters of the Wisconsin.
49	Cañas, Cestiude	S	1642	K.	Sailed from near Bay of La Paz with soldiers and missionaries, 40 leagues to the northwest, f r pearls and information. Report written by Father Jacinto Cortes, a Jesuit.
50	Jesuits		1642	M	First voyage for founding California missions. They furnished missionaries, journalists, cosmographers, and historians to nearly all the government expeditions.
51	Deschnew	R.	1648 (R.)	K.	A Cossack, who sailed from north Siberia through the Arctic Ocean and Behring Strait. Neither understood nor published the discovery of this strait. Discovered Kamschatka. Does not mention the American continent.
52	(H) Porter y (Portél de) Casanate.	S	1648	M. and K.	To the east coast of Lower California. Did not reach the mouth of the Colorado.
53	Piñadero	S	1664–'67	K.	Sailed to coast of Lower California for pearls, as also in 1667. No important results. Colorado River not seen.
54	Lucenilla, also Lũzanilla	S	1668	K.	Made similar voyage to that of Piñadero. No important results. Colorado River not seen.
55	Allouez	F	1669	K.	Made discoveries on the Wisconsin River.
56	Marquette	F	1673	Charlevoix and Schoolcraft.	Entered the Mississippi River from the Wisconsin, passed the mouths of the Missouri and Ohio, reached the Arkansas, and returned via the Illinois.
57	Hennepin	F	1680	Warren	Named St. Peter's River and Falls of St. Anthony.
58	La Salle	F	1682 (R.)	K. and Warren	In 1678 started from Canada to find northern route to China. Discovered mouth of Mississippi River.
59	La Hontan	F.	1683	K.	Explored the Des Moines River and heard of a great western river running to the ocean (probably the Columbia), 1687, in the vicinity of the Yellowstone Park. Brought to France sketch of a map painted by natives on a buffalo skin.
60	(H) Alondo (Navarrete spells the name Atondo. R.).	S	1683	K.	Cost about 225,000 pesos. Results meager. Explorations in interior. Returned to Mexico 1685. Reached a bay on east coast of Lower California at approx. 26° 30′ north latitude. Accompanied by Father Kuhn, the cosmographer of the expedition, who wrote the report.
61	Coxton, Captain		1688	G	From north Pacific up a long river which ran out of a great lake called Thoyaga.

NOTE.—Fonte (fictitious) supposed to have been a Spaniard sailing from Peru in 1640 (G., B., M., and K). Another *pretended* voyage by northwest passage came into note in 1708. Brought before French Academy in 1750. Kohl says there was no such man and no such expedition.

CHRONOLOGICAL STATEMENT OF VOYAGES AND EXPLORATIONS, ETC.—Continued.

No.	Name.	Nation.	Year.	Authority.	Remarks.
62	Le Sueur	F	1695	Warren	Discovers Blue Earth, on St. Peter River.
63	Salvatierra	I (Jesuit).	1697	G., K., and M.	Founded the first mission in Lower California.
64	Iberville	F	1698-'99	K.	Entered Mississippi River from its mouth. Discovered Lakes Maurepas and Pontchartrain, settling at Biloxi.
65	De Fonte	F	1700	K.	Made expeditions up and down the Mississippi River.
66	Kuhn (Kino)	G (Jesuit)	1701-'03	G., M., and K.	Discovers the peninsularity of Lower California. Dies in 1710, leaving the question unsettled. (K.) Reached the mouth of the Colorado in 1702.
67	Guillen	G (R.)	1719	M	Makes overland expeditions to California.
68	Ugarte	Jesuit	1721	K.	Sailed along east coast of Lower California, reaching the mouth of the Colorado in July, 1721.
69	Charlevoix	F	1721	K.	Explored along upper Mississippi. Learned from Indians of Missouri heading in high mountains, and of a western river leading to the ocean.
70	Behring	D	1728	G., T., and K.	Reaches northeast extremity of Asia, approx. north latitude 66°. Enters straits called by his name. Stated vaguely that in 1730 Krupischeff and Gwozdef followed Behring, reaching the American coast. (Bancroft.)
71	Varennes de la Vérandrye.	Fr	1731	Ruge	Discovers Red River and Lake Winnipeg.
72	Taraval	Jesuit	1732	K.	Explored from approx. latitude 28° north, along eastern coast of Lower California, toward Pacific.
73	Du Pradt (Du Pratz. K.)	F	1735	K.	Learned from a Mississippi Valley Indian more details of the "great western river."
74	Behring (Bering, R.)	D	1741	G. and T.	Discovers Aleutian Islands, about 60° north latitude. Points to separation between Asia and America. Explores 300 miles of American coast.
75	Steller	G	1741	G. Steller, journey from Kamschatka to America.	First scientific exploration on the west coast near Cape (Island of) St. Elias. (R.)
76	Tchirikof (Tschirikow. K.)	R	1741	G., T., and K.	Discovers Prince of Wales Archipelago.
77	Sedelmayer	Fr	1744	Whipple	Followed the Gila River to the Colorado.
78	Consak	Jesuit	1746	M. and K.	Sailed from eastern coast of Lower California, (28° north latitude). Explored lower part of the Colorado River to establish missions. Nearly same route as Ugarte. Reached the mouth of the Colorado July 11, 1746.
79	Verendryce (Verenderye)	F	1755	K.	Made attempts to reach the mountains near the source of the Missouri River.
80	Glottof	R	1763-'65	Bancroft	Reached Kodiak on trading expedition. From 1745 (Nevódchikof) Siberian merchants made trips to the Aleutian Islands.
81	Synd	R	1766	K.	Follows Kamschatka coast to 66° north latitude.
82	Carver	E	1766-'67	B. and K	Started from Boston. Visited the upper Mississippi region. Returned for lack of means. Gave the name of Oregon to the "river of the west." (See Carver's map in September number of Journal of Military Service Institution, 1883. Symons: "The Army and the Exploration of the West.")

CHRONOLOGICAL STATEMENT OF VOYAGES AND EXPLORATIONS, ETC.—Continued.

No.	Name.	Nation.	Year.	Authority.	Remarks.
83	Link	Jesuit	1766	K.	Walked across great part of Lower California, establishing its peninsular form. Reached a point twenty or thirty leagues from the Colorado and turned back. Last of the Jesuit explorations.
84	Galvez	S	1767-'68	M	Travels in California, establishing missions in Monterey. Travels by land from San Diego to Monterey. (R.)
85	Krusenstern (Captain Krinitzyn and Lieutenant Lewashoff. K.)	R	1768	G. and K.	Sails to Aleutian Islands. Explores southern part of Alaskan coast.
86	Franciscans	Fr.	1769-'70	G., T., and K.	Make settlements at San Diego and Monterey.
87	D'Auteroche	F	1769	K.	Occupied Transit of Venus Station at southern extremity of Lower California. Determined its longitude with greater accuracy. Vancouver made comparisons as late as 1793.
88	Portala	S	1769	K.	Overland from Velicata, Lower California, to San Diego. Traversed from Colorado River to San Diego for the first time. Mission of San Diego established.
89	Vila	S	1769	K.	From San Blas, Mexico, to San Diego. Assisting land expeditions and rediscovering San Diego.
90	Portala	S	1769-'70	K.	Land expedition in search of Monterey, reaching 37° 45′ north latitude, in view of Bay of San Francisco.
91	Perez	S	1770	K.	Sailed from San Blas to Monterey. Reached Santa Barbara only, and returned to San Diego, thence sailed to Monterey, reaching that bay 167 years after Viscaino.
92	Portala	S	1770	K.	Overland from San Diego to Monterey, founding that mission.
93	Serra	Fr.	1770-'71	K.	Overland between Monterey and San Diego, establishing missions of San Buenaventura and San Gabriel.
94	Benyowsky	H	1771	G	Visits several Aleutian Islands. No new discoveries.
95	Hearne	E	1771	G	Explores from Hudson's Bay, discovers Great Slave Lake, and follows Coppermine River to the Arctic.
96	Perez	S	1772	K.	From San Blas, Mexico, to Monterey via San Diego.
97	Com. Don Pedro Fages (K.) and Crespi.	S	1772	K.	From Monterey northward toward San Francisco Bay.
98	Perez	S	1774	K., G., T., and M.	From Monterey Bay. From San Blas to San Diego and Monterey, and thence northward to about 54° 30′ north latitude, discovering Nootka Sound. Visited several points afterwards claimed to be discovered by the English. (See Humboldt: New Spain.)
99	Anza	S	1774	K.	Overland from Sonora to Monterey. Crossed the Colorado, establishing a new route between California and New Mexico, through Sonora, for supplying the missions.
100	Franciscans	Fr	1774	K.	Mission of San Juan Capistrano established.
101	Heceta with	S	1775	G., T., M., and K.	From San Blas. Discovered the mouth of the Columbia River, but did not enter it. From San Blas to explore northward to 65th degree. Discovered in latitude 57° 2′ north a great mountain (Mount Edgecombe). (See also Barrington; Miscellanies and Maurelle; Diary of the voyage.) Heceta and Ayala sailed together. (R.)
	Ayala and	S	1775	K.	To Monterey, thence San Francisco Bay, making its first survey.
	Bodega	S	1775	K.	Reached 58th degree north latitude.

CHRONOLOGICAL STATEMENT OF VOYAGES AND EXPLORATIONS, ETC.—Continued.

No.	Name.	Nation.	Year.	Authority.	Remarks.
102	Garces	Carmelite.	1775	K.	From New Mexico to San Diego, crossing the Colorado, and opening a new route near 35th parallel.
103	Anza	S.	1775	K.	From Presidio San Miguel in Sonora to mission San Gabriel. Crossed the Colorado River.
104	Frobisher	E.	1775	Ruge	Churchill and miss.
105	Anza	S.	1776	K.	Overland, Monterey to San Francisco Bay, making plan of bay from land side. Second land expedition to San Francisco Bay.
106	Quiros and Moraga	S.	1776	K.	Combined land and sea expedition, Monterey to San Francisco Bay. Made further examinations in and around the bay, and discovered the San Joaquin River.
107	Rivera	S.	1776	K.	Monterey to northward, founding mission Santa Clara.
108	Cook	E.	1776-'78	G. and K.	Sails for northwest passage and reaches 68° north latitude. Discovered Nootka Sound and Prince William's Sound, 60° north latitude. Believed firmly in water communication between Behring Straits and Baffin's Bay.
109	Escalante	Fr.	1776-'77	M.	From Santa Fe to border of Great Salt Lake and return.
110	Pond	E.	1778	Ruge	Discovers the Athabasca.
111	Arteaga and Bodega y Cuadra.	S.	1779	G., M., and K.	From San Blas. Searching along west coast for arctic passage. Reached Port Bucareli, 55° 17′ north. (See Maurelle's Diary.)
112	Serra	Fr.	1782	K.	Traveled near coast from Monterey via Santa Barbara, establishing San Buenaventura.
113	Hanna	E.	1785-'86	G. and K.	Visits Nootka Sound. Discovered Fitzhugh Sound. (See Forster: History of Voyages.)
114	Lowrie and Guise	E.	1786	R.	From Nootka Sound to Prince William Sound, and discovers the coast called by Dixon Queen Charlotte Island.
115	La Perouse	F.	1786	G., M., and K.	From Brest. Visits northwest coast between 52° and 54° north latitude, touching at Monterey. Had orders to find the northwest passage. Reached latitude of Mount St. Elias. (Millet Umean: Voyage de la Perouse au tour du monde.)
116	Peters	E.	1786	G. and K.	From Bombay. Visits Nootka Sound. Probably the first to circumnavigate Queen Charlotte's Island.
117	Dixon and Portlock	E.	1786-'87	G. and K.	From England. Names Queen Charlotte's Island, Cook's River, and Prince William's Sound. (George Dixon: Voyage around the world.)
118	Berkeley	E.	1787	K.	From Ostende, under the Austrian flag. Discovers and names de Fuca Straits, and thence explored southward along the coast. Discovered Cape Classet, Barclay Sound, and showed Vancouver to be an island. Reached Nootka Sound. (See Greenhow and Forster's Voyages.)
119	Duncan	E.	1788	G.	Discovered Prince of Wales Archipelago.
120	Martinez	S.	1788	K.	From San Blas by sea to Russian settlements (Unalaska) on the Aleutian Islands. Explored also de Fuca Straits. Reached Prince William's Sound. (See Navarrette: Humboldt.)

CHRONOLOGICAL STATEMENT OF VOYAGES AND EXPLORATIONS, ETC.—Continued.

No.	Name.	Nation.	Year.	Authority.	Remarks.
121	Meares and Douglas	E	1788	G. and K	From Calcutta. Fur-trading expedition. Visits Cook's River, Nootka Sound, and names Straits of Fuca. Recognized coast of New Albion to latitude 45° north. Reached Prince William's Sound. Took possession in name of Queen. (See Hugh Murray: Historical account of discoveries in North America.)
122	Kendrick	A	1788	G	From Boston. Explores east coast of Queen Charlotte's Sound. Reaches Nootka Sound.
123	Martinez	S	1789 (R.)	G., M., and K.	From San Blas. Explores de Fuca Straits. Reached Nootka. Military trip to prevent English commerce. Claimed the whole coast for the King of Spain. (See Greenhow.)
124	Colnett	E	1789	Navarrette	Sailed February 17, 1789, from San Blas, under orders of the King of England, to fortify the harbor of Nutka (Nootka). (R.)
125	Narvaez	S	1789	M	Reaches Nootka in search of Straits of Fuca.
126	De Haro	S	1789	K	Explored de Fuca Straits.
127	Fidalgo	S	1789 (K.)	M	Explores coast north from Nootka to near 61° north latitude. Reached Prince William's Sound.
128	Eliza	S	1789 (K.)	G., M., and K	Visits Nootka Sound and Cook's River. Discovered Puget's Sound. Takes possession for the King of Spain.
129	Billings	E	1790	G	From Ocsotck. Visits Aleutian Islands. No new discoveries.
130	Quimper	S	1790	G., M., and K	Explores Straits of Fuca. Discovered Neeah Harbor. Claimed for Spain. Reached Prince William's Sound.
131	Eliza	S	1791	M. and K	More complete exploration of Straits of Fuca.
132	Vancouver	E	1791	G. and K	Sails to examine Pacific coast, 35th to 60th degree north latitude.
133	Malaspina (K.)	S	1791	G., M., and K	From Acapulco. Sails to explore the fictitious "Straits of Anian." Reached 60° north latitude opposite Mount St. Elias. Did not find, and denied the existence of a northwest passage. Made few discoveries, but many exact determinations. (See Navarrete: Humboldt, New Spain.)
134	Marchand	F	1791	G. and K	From Marseilles. Visits Norfolk Sound, near 56° north latitude. Reached Sitka. Made very few observations. (See Marchand: Voyage au tour du monde.)
135	Ingraham	A	1791	G	Visits northwest coast.
136	Gray	A	1791	G	Revisits Straits of Fuca. Discovered Gray's Harbor.
137	Vancouver	E	1792	G. and K	From Falmouth. Examines west coast, Straits of Fuca, etc. Furnished the first exact map of the lower Columbia. Found high mountain ranges along the coast; recognized these from California to Alaska. Showed "Cook's River" to be a bay, and named it Cook's Inlet. Destroyed the illusions about a northwest passage.
138	Gray	A	1792	G. and K	Enters Columbia River near its mouth. This river was believed by Aguillar to have been a bay.
139	Caamaño	S	1792	G. and K	Explores coast northeast of Queen Charlotte's Island. From San Blas, Mexico, March 20, 1792.

CHRONOLOGICAL STATEMENT OF VOYAGES AND EXLORATIONS, ETC.—Continued.

No.	Name.	Nation.	Year.	Authority.	Remarks.
140	Galiano and Valdez	S	1792	G., M., and K	From Acapulco. Explores Straits of Fuca and coast between 53° and 56° north latitude. The end of the Spanish expeditions. Discovered Frazer River.
141	Mackenzie	E	1793	T., B., and K	Discovers Fraser's River and crosses "Rocky Mountains" to Pacific at the Cascades. First to traverse parts of the Columbia in a boat. A most important exploration.
142	Broughton	E	1795–'98	K	Reached Nootka in 1796 from Sandwich Islands. Sailed thence to Monterey. (K.)
143	Krusenstern and Lysiansky.	R	1803–'05	K	From Cronstadt. Explorations in northern parts of Russian America, 1804–'05. Principally commercial.
144	Chwosdoff and Davidoff	R	1806	K	Sailed from Sitka to San Francisco, making examinations of the coast, returning to Sitka.
145	Beechy	E	1827	K	Coasted from Bering's Straits as far south as Monterey. Made map of San Francisco Harbor.
146	Belcher	E	1836–'42	K	Coasted and reconnoitered from opposite Mount St. Elias to Cape St. Lucas in 1837, also in 1839. Explored and surveyed the Sacramento River.
147	Fur companies	A and E	1806–'21	K	The Northwest, Pacific, and other fur companies explored and operated in the Northwest and along the Columbia River. The Northwest Company at one time had 25,000 "voyagers" in employ.
148	Kotzebue	R	1815–'18	K	Instructed to sail through Bering's Straits eastward to Europe. Discovered Kotzebue Sound. Believed there was water communication, because of southern current through Bering's Straits.
149	Hudson Bay Company	E	1821–'41	K	All fur companies united, with headquarters at Fort Vancouver (see Franklin, Richardson, Parry, and others), occupied the waters of the great Northwest.
150	Russian explorations	R	1812–'41	K	Made settlements and stations on the California coast up to 1841, at Bodega Bay (Port Romanzoff), etc.
151	Mission expeditions	Fr	....	K	Excursions made from San Francisco inland and between Mexico, New Mexico, and the California coast, at least up to 1811.
	French explorations	Fr	1820–'40	K	Expeditions of circumnavigation, touching at the usual places in the North Pacific, making observations and reconnaisances at and about harbors, bays, and lakes.
	De Mofras	F	1844	K	Parts of interior of Pacific coast. Last of the French explorations.
	Slacum	A	1836–'37	K	Traveled through Mexico to Guayamas. Made notes and sketches at mouth of Colorado River and elsewhere. (See Senate Ex. Doc. No. 24, Twenty-fifty Congress, second session.) No latitudes or longitudes.

NOTE.—For List of the Explorers, see Bancroft, Northwest Coast, vol. I, chap. X, pp. 310–342. List on pp. 340–342.

The principal published authorities on the grand achievements in explorations and surveys on the west coast, of the sixteenth, seventeenth, and eighteenth centuries (undertakings without a parallel in the past, when all the attendant circumstances are considered, and never to be equaled in the future), are found at length in the Kohl manuscript, while some of them, together with others consulted by myself, are herewith:

Hakluyt: Vol. III. Voyages and Navigations. London, 1600.
Ramusio: Delle navagazioni et viaggi.
Navarrete: Coleccion de los viajes y descubrimientos.

Gomara: Historia general de las Indias * * * con la conquista de México y de la Nueva España. Saragoça, 1552–'53.

Venegas: Noticia de la California. Madrid, 1757.

Herrerra: Historia general, etc. Madrid, 1730.

Burney: A chronological history of voyages and discoveries in the South Sea and Pacific Ocean. 3 vols. 4°. London, 1803.

Purchas Pilgrims: Vol. III. London, 1625.

Humboldt: Essai politique sur le royaume de la Nouvelle Espagne. Paris, Schoell, 1811. 2 vols. in 4°.

Greenhow: History of Oregon and California. Boston, 1845.

Mofrat: Exploration du territoire de l'Oregon, etc. 2 vols. Paris, 1844. [Mofrat gives a chronological bibliography on p. 485, vol. 2.]

Abert: Examination of New Mexico. 1846–'47.

Whipple: Vol. IV. Pacific Railroad Reports.

Reports, U. S. Coast and Geodetic Survey. Appendix 19, 1884, and Appendix 7, 1886.

Bancroft: History of the Northwest Coast. Vol. I, 1543–1800, 8°, pp. 735. List of authorities, pp. XVII–XXVIII.

Bancroft: History of Central America. Vol. I, 1501–'30. Summary of Geographical Knowledge to the year 1540, pp. 67 *et seq.*

Narrative and Critical History of America. Discoveries on the Pacific Coast. Vol. II, pp. 431–472. Early Explorations in New Mexico, pp. 473–504.

Ternaux-Campans (Henri): Voyages, relations et mémoires originaux pour servir à l'histoire de la découverte de l'Amérique. Paris, 1837–'41. (Two series, 10 and 8 vols.)

Recueil de Voyages et de documents pour servir à l'histoire de la Geographie depuis le XIIIe jusqu' à la fin du XVIe siècle. Jean et Sébastien Cabot.

D'apres des documen's inedit, par Henry Harrisse. Paris, Ernest Leroux, ed., 28 rue Bonaparte, 1882. Bibliographie, pp. 369–375.

OLD MAPS.

A number of photolithographs from tracings of old maps are here introduced, with a legend page facing each, intended to illustrate, though rudely and irregularly, the process of geographical information as to the North American continent between 1500 and 1800, so far as the same has been shown cartographically. While these maps are not *all* standard or typical at their dates of issue, having been selected principally from the collections made by the late Dr. J. G. Kohl and atlases found in the Congressional Library,* they are, nevertheless, suggestive, and may lead to a more critical review of the progress of American discovery, exploration, and cartography from the earliest discoveries to the commencement of the nineteenth century, from an historical and scientific standpoint which exceeds the scope of the present memoir, that proposes simply an introduction to the epitome of Warren's Memoir, and the further résumé of Government explorations and surveys within the confines of the United States.

* Copies of Hondius, edition 1609, and Senex, 1710, were furnished by and through the courtesy of Assistant J. C. Lang.

THE ISLAND OF ANTILIA, BY BENINCASA, 1463.

This is of interest principally because it may be considered as one of the first maps indicating larger countries to be found to the west of Europe.

NOTES BY KOHL.—This map is a copy of a part of a map which is to be found in a portolano of Benincasa.

Benincasa was an Italian, who composed, between 1463 and 1473, different portolanos, which are mentioned in the work of the Vicomte de Santarem, "Histoire de la Cosmographie," vol. I, p. xlii.

Our map is taken from his portolano of the year 1463. It is remarkable—

(1) Because it has in the latitude of Spain *the Island of "Antilia,"* nearly as large as Portugal, and two other large islands to the west and north of it named "Rosellia" and "Salvaga," which islands appear in the same or a somewhat varying manner and shape on many other maps, and may be considered as *the first indication of larger countries to be found to the west of Europe.*

(2) Because a whole chain of islands extends on it midway between the Canarian Islands and Ireland. Also this chain of western islands is to be found in a similar manner on different other maps of the middle of the fifteenth century. (See Santarem, Hist. de la Cosmographie, I, p. xlii, and III, p. 177; also Winsor-Kohl collection of early maps. Bibliographical Contributions, Harvard College, No. 19, p. 47; No. 245.) Under No. 20, p. 8, A. D. 1455, reference is made to a sea chart by Bartolomeus de Pareto, showing "Antilia" and an island farther west named "Roillo;" also No. 21, p. 8, A. D. 1476.)

A portolano by Andreas Benincasa, given in St. Martin (Pl. VII) and Lelewel (Pl. XXXIV). It shows "Antilia" as a western island, and the "Isola de Bracill" west of Ireland.

AMERICA FROM PTOLOMAEUS, EDIT. ROMÆ, 1508.

This map at its date (1508) was the most complete and reliable compilation extant of what was then known in regard to America. It was issued five years before Balboa discovered the Pacific Ocean.

NOTES BY KOHL.—This is a copy of a part of the celebrated map of the world added to the editiòn of Ptolomaeus, Rome, 1508. Humboldt, who in his works alludes often to this map and has given most valuable critical notes upon it, says that it has been drawn and composed *by the German Johannes Ruysh.* It was revised and corrected by two Italians, Marco of Benevent and Jonnès Cotto of Verona ("Correcta a Marco Beneventano et Joanne Cotto Veronensi"). (See upon this most interesting map Humboldt in the preface to Ghillany's German work on Martin Behaim, and Walkenaer in his "Recherches géographiques sur l'intérieur de l'Afrique septentrionale," p. 186, and, also, Biographie Universelle, tome VI, p. 207).

The title of this map is "Universalior cogniti Orbis Tabula ex recentibus confecta observationibus" (a more universal table of the known world compiled from modern observations). The principal features of this map are the following:

"*Terra Nova*" (Newfoundland), in its eastern and southern coast very well represented, is given as a *peninsula of Asia.*

"Gruenlant" or "Gruentlant" (Greenland) is likewise a peninsula of Asia, of which the countries and provinces of Mangi, Ciamban, Tebet, the points "Quinsai," "Zaiton," and the islands "Java Major" (Borneo ?), "Java Minor," and "Candyn" (?) appear. *Japan* (*or Zipangu*) *is omitted* because the author, as he says in a Latin inscription, believed that this island was now found by the Spaniards in another place, and called by them "Spagnola."

This "Spagnola" (our Haiti) he puts about sixty degrees of longitude to the west from the meridian of Ferro, and north of the tropic of Cancer. To the southeast of it he adds some of the smaller Antillian Islands—"La Dominica," "Monferrato," "Matinina" (Martinique).

To the northwest of "Spagnola" appears a country which is no doubt Cuba, or Fernandina, or Isabella, though not indicated by name. That Cuba, and Cuba only, is meant, seems evident from the mass of small islands on the north coast as well as on the south coast of this land, though it reaches as high as 40° north latitude. These groups of islands appear to be those innumerable little rocks and isles which Columbus called the Garden of the King and the Garden of the Queen.

On the south coast they are all collected in a kind of bay, which we afterwards find repeated on many subsequent maps, and of which some others have erroneously supposed that the Gulf of Mexico was indicated by it.

A Latin inscription in the west says that the King of Spain's ships did not come as yet farther, and intimates that it was unknown if this country was an island or not. This question was only settled in the year 1508, on the circumnavigation of Cuba by Ocampo. Nothing more appears of North America. Of South America, which is called "*Terra Sancte Crucis*" (the Land of the Holy Cross, after Cabral), sive Mundus Novus (the New World), nothing appears but the northern coast as far west as Ojeda (1501) discovered it, and the east coast as far south as the 38th degree south latitude. On the west coast is an inscription which says that the Spaniards had not yet penetrated farther.

The Latin inscription in the interior of South America gives a description of the natural productions of the continent, and another Latin inscription at the south end of the coast says the Portuguese navigators came as far down as 50° south latitude, but did not reach yet its southernmost end.

The editor of the Ptolomaeus, to which this map is added, makes in the book itself the further remark that he was unable to find that part of the map which related to these southern regions. *

* See also Winsor: Kohl collection, No. 28, p. 9, Bulletin No. 19.

AMERICA, FROM A GLOBE IN FRANKFORT, ABOUT 1520.

This is notable, since it is believed that it is the first map upon which the name "America" appears.*

NOTES BY KOHL.—This is a copy of a part of a map which depicts America. The drawing is contained on an old globe of the world in the city library of Frankfort on the Main.

Neither the date nor the author of the map or globe are indicated, but the whole design agrees in all its principal features with the map given on the globe of I. Schöner, of the year 1520, preserved in Nuremberg (see our collection). We know that Schöner made different globes, and that of Frankfort may also be one of them

The same as on the globe of Nuremberg, so also on this, *America is divided in two great islands* and different smaller ones. These two islands have nearly the same configuration, and are represented on their western coasts as unknown and unexplored. On both maps the northern reaches as high as 50° north latitude, and the southern as far as 40° south latitude, where on both maps is a strait.

The Antilles have on both globes the same configuration, distances, and number, and the same may be said of "Zipangu" (Japan). On both maps a vessel stands near the strait which passes through the northern and southern islands.

A nearer comparison, however, shows many different variations on both globes. At first our present map is neither so rich in names nor so special in the representation of the coast. Then the imaginary southern contiment has on our map quite another shape than on that of Nuremberg, and the same may be said of that northern island which stands for Labrador and indicates the discoveries of Cortereal. Besides this, many of the inscriptions and names on our map differ from the map contained on the globe of Nuremberg. It is therefore evident that the one is not a mere copy of the other, but that they are different independent works, made, perhaps, by

* Winsor says, p. 11, Bulletin 19, etc., No. 34: "Wieser, in his Magalhães-Strasse (p. 19), where an engraving of it is given, declares it to be the globe made to accompany Schöner's Luculentissima quædam Terræ totius Descriptio, printed in 1515, and of which two copies are now known." See also Nos. 35 and 36, same page.

the same author (Schöner?) but at different times. Because on our globe everything is less perfect and complete, it is very probable that it was constructed at an earlier period, where Schöner perhaps had not yet made so many studies of his subject. It seems that we must put it at all events *before* 1520, perhaps about 1515, and this globe, therefore, may be considered *the first map on which the name "America" occurs.* The southern continent is called "*Brasilia Regio*" (the region Brasilia). On the globe of Nuremberg it is called "Brasilia inferior."

FROM MAP OF NORTH AMERICA, BY ABRAHAM ORTELIUS, 1589.*

This map was among the best of those of America extant toward the close of the sixteenth century. The Pacific coast had already been reconnoitered above the 57th parallel by Gali.

The Ortelius has been referred to as the prototype of the modern atlas. The publication was continued to at least 1612. His map of the world appears to have been fashioned after Mercator. He prefixed to his book a list of authorities from whose labors he had constructed his own maps. The titles are wholly of the sixteenth century, and not a single Spanish one appears among them.

---

* Stevens says of Ortelius: "He was a bibliographer, a cartographer, an antiquary, * * * a good mathematician and geographer, and * * * gave his authorities." In 1570 Ortelius published at Antwerp the first edition of his Theatrum Orbis Terrarum, fifty-three copper-plate maps, engraved by Hogenberg. In 1589 there was Marchetti's edition at Brescia and a Latin one at Antwerp. (Narr. and Crit. Hist. of America.) The atlas of 1570 was one of the most celebrated geographical works of the sixteenth century, of which there have been many subsequent editions in Dutch, German, French and Italian, in which the number of maps has been much increased.

In 1606 the first English edition appeared, while the latest Italian one noted is 1697, but meanwhile other cartographers had taken the field. He was the first to collect and compile from contemporary maps. His learning, integrity, and discriminating judgment has made his atlas valuable as a trustworthy record of the best geographical knowledge of his time. (See Narr. and Crit. Hist. of America, vol. III, p. 34.)

NORTH AMERICA, BY ZALTIERI, 1566.

Remarkable in that it is reputed to be the first map upon which the Straits of Anian (Stretto de Anean) appear.

NOTES BY KOHL.—This is a copy of a printed map of North America preserved in the imperial library in Paris It has an Italian inscription as follows:

"The design of what has been discovered of New France, which we have received lately from the newest navigations of the French to those places, in which are to be seen all the islands, ports, capes, and places of the land which are in the same."

"In Venize, engraved on copper by Bolognino Zaltieri, in the year 1566."

Unhappily this map has neither latitudes nor longitudes, not even the tropics, nor any indication of a measure by miles.

In *the general configuration of North America it resembles very much other maps made at the same time in Italy.* It has in the north "Grutlandia" (Greenland?), and in the west "Giapan" (Japan), and the Strait of Anian in the same manner. (See Italian maps of this time in our collection.)

It resembles, particularly in its general features, *the map of P. Furlani*, produced at the same place (Venize) and some years before (1560). The mountains on both maps are made in the same manner. The river systems of the St. Lawrence and of the rivers of the Californian Gulf are very much alike, and so is the great ever-long northeastern wing given on both maps to North America. Zaltierie (if we may consider him as the author of this map) only deviates in this from Furlani, that he separates America from Asia by the Strait of Anian, which Furlani did not.

Some further peculiarities of his map are the following: He puts *the name La "Nova Franza" (New France) in the center of North America.* He has Newfoundland still dissolved in many islands. To the west of it he has the same river system of the St. Lawrence as Furlani, but he gives no name to this river. Besides, however, he has to the southwest of it a great lake, "Lago," and coming out from it a river which he calls "R S. Lorenzo" (St. Lawrence River), and which empties into the sea on the coast of New

England. *This is a great curiosity*, and proves that the rivers and inlets of Maine (Penobscot?) were considered as branches of the St. Lawrence, or as outlets of the Canadian lakes, of which lakes already Cartier had brought home some report.

Something not less extraordinary is also the position of the name "Apalchen" (Apallachian Mountains?) in the center of the whole continent. The author had perhaps read something of De Soto's expedition.

It is not easy to say to which "newest French expedition" (novissima navigatione dei Franzesi), of which he lately (ultimamente) received his information, the author alludes in his inscription. The latest French expeditions were those of Ribaut and Laudennière to Florida (1554), but of those the author takes on his map no notice at all. The coast of Florida is given according to the old Spanish authorities.

The latest French expeditions to the regions of the St. Lawrence were those under Roberval since 1541.

NOTE.—Kohl assumes this to be the first map upon which the "Straits of Anian" appear. (See p. 51, Winsor, A. D. 1558, referring to a map by Martines, presumably of the above date, as one of the earliest to contract the water separating America from Asia to the dimensions of a strait; also p. 20, No. 94, where Winsor compares this map with one by Des Liens (North America), same year (1566). See, also, p. 17, No. 69, A. D. 1566.) A copy of this map is found reproduced on p. 451, Narr. and Crit. Hist. of America, vol. II, and a sketch, also, on p. 93 of vol. IV.

FROM "HONDIUS," ED. 1609, AMST.

Hondius was a celebrated Dutch geographer, who edited with Gerard Mercator a once famous atlas of the world and drew many maps. In 1604 he bought Mercator's plates. He issued a new edition in 1606, to which fifty maps were added, including a few American ones, and thus began the Hondius-Mercator Atlas. He died in 1611 (p. 374, vol. IV, Narr. and Crit. Hist.).

NORTH AMERICA, FROM PURCHAS, 1625.

This map was constructed after the first voyages of Hudson, Button, and Munk (1610–'19), intending to prove the possibility of a northwest passage through which fictitious accounts of pretended voyages by Maldonado, Juan de Fuca, and Fonte had been published. California is shown as an island.

NOTES BY KOHL.—This is a copy of a map contained in the third volume of Purchas's Pilgrims, London, 1625.

Purchas calls it "*the north part of America*," and adds it to a little "Treatise of the northwest passage to the South Sea, through the continent of Virginia, and by Fretum Hudson."

Neither in this treatise, nor on the map, nor in the preface of his work, nor in the index of the maps contained in his work, Purchas says by whom and how this map was composed. On the map we find only that "R. Elstracke" *engraved* it.

Nearly all other maps in Purchas are bad and reduced copies from Hondius and others. *But this has some original value.* It was made soon after the first voyages of Hudson, Button, and Munk (from 1610–'19) to Hudson's Bay, *with the intention to prove by it the possibility of a northwest passage.* The treatise and the long inscriptions on the map itself contain an explanation of it.

Purchas says that it would be easy to sail through Hudson's Bay to the Western Ocean, and particularly to the waters of California.

Where "Button wintered," he says (near Fort Nelson), "the tides were 15 feet high, and they were particularly high with a western wind, which could only be explained by a connection of Button's Bay with the Western Ocean, which could not be far distant."

Besides this there was still much hope for open water between Button's Bay in the west and the bay in which Hudson wintered in the south. On

NOTE.—Winsor, on p. 18 of Bulletin No. 19, gives: 82, A. D. 1589. "The World, by Hondius. An engraved map, on which a statement that it is intended to show the tracks of Drake and Cavendish is signed by Jodicus Hondius, 1589. * * * In an inscription referring to the Tierra del Fuego group, Hondius remarks that Cavendish and the Spaniards do not accept Drake's views making a continent the southern boundary of the Straits of Magellan, and on later maps Hondius seems to have accepted these other views. (See Uricoechea, No. 25.)" In edition of 1609, above, a wide stretching continent is shown.

his map he represents this region as unknown. That there was no water was only discovered by Captains James and Fox, who about 1630 sailed along those coasts of Hudson's Bay.

"California," so Purchas says further, has been believed until now erroneously to be a continent. "But it is now found to be an island, stretching as far as 42° north latitude, as may appear in *a map of that island which was brought to London out of Holland.*" The Californian Gulf is, consequently, after him, no gulf, but a long strait, which he represents as certainly going as far as 42° north latitude, and which *may* go still farther north and *may* be connected with Hudson's Bay.

Hudson's Bay is stretched out two degrees too far to the south. He gives to the northern part of the Pacific Ocean the name "*Oceanus Japonicus*" (the Japanese Ocean).

His map is, perhaps, the first printed map on which we find the name of "Nova Brittannia" (New Britain) for Labrador.

All the Spanish and other foreign names on the map are so very corrupted that sometimes they even can not be recognized. (See Winsor-Kohl maps, p. 21, No. 100; also p. 53, No. 284, A. D. 1625.)

FROM A MAP OF AMERICA BY F. DE WIT. FOLIO. AMST. (WITHOUT DATE—ABOUT 1670).*

Shows California as an island. The Arctic Ocean, although already entered, is not delineated.

* The first example of De Wit's imprint appeared about 1675, at Amsterdam, with a printed index calling for 102 maps. S. Wolfgang, 1680, published an atlas, with maps by Blaeu, Visscher, De Wit, and others. Other atlases have the name of F. de Wit. The Blaeu establishment was burned in 1672 and most of the plates were lost. Those saved passed into the hands of De Wit. (P. 376, vol. IV, Narr. and Crit. Hist. of America.)

FROM MAP OF NORTH AMERICA BY JOHN SENEX,* F. R. S., LONDON, 1710.

California is still shown as an island, although Father Kuhn in 1701–3 had already again demonstrated the peninsularity of Lower California.

See Winsor, Harvard College Library, Bulletin No. 19. Kohl maps, p. 22, 1710. "John Senex's map of North America, of which there is a reproduction in David Mill's *Report on the Boundaries of the Province of Ontario, Toronto,* 1873."

The above map purports to give corrections up to date, from the observations communicated to the Royal Society at London and the Royal Academy at Paris.

---

* It appears that later the above author rejected the Lahontan story of the "Long River."

FROM MAP OF NORTH AMERICA BY EDWARD WELLS, M. A., 1722.*

California is still shown as an island, and discoveries above about 45° N. lat are ignored.

---

* The full title is "A new map of the most considerable plantations of the English in America."

The Wells atlas of 41 maps, of which No. 39 is a part of North America, is entitled "A new sett of maps, Both of Antient and Present Geography, Edward Wells, M. A., and student of Christ-Church. Oxon."

FROM MAP OF NORTH AMERICA BY THOMAS JEFFERYS, 1782.*

California is shown as a peninsula. The name of New Albion is prominent. Explorations had reached as high as 68° N. lat.

The above map purports to be a true delineation of North America with the Atlantic and Pacific Oceans, and the nearest coasts of Europe and Asia, with the tracks of the latest circumnavigators and other discoveries; also the coasts of California and New Albion. The Russian discoveries between Asia and America taken from the map published at St. Petersburg in 1774, by Mr. J. Von Stablin, secretary to the Imperial Academy.†

---

* Jeffery's American Atlas being a description of the whole conlineut of America, engraved on forty-eight copper plates, folio, was published in London 1775.

† For the published authorities on maps of North America and its west coast during this period the following may be cited:

Santarem: Cosmography and Cartography of the Middle Ages. 3 vols. 8°. Paris, 1849.

Lelewel: Géographie du Moyen Âge, Bruxelles, 1852. 3 vols. 8° and atlas.

D'Avezac: History of the Projection of Geographical Maps.

Uricoechea: Mapoteca Columbiana. London, 1860. [The British Museum has the author's copy, with additional and voluminous notes in MS. compiled subsequent to 1860, and prior to his death.]

British Museum: Catalogue of Maps, etc.

Winsor: Harvard Library, No. 18. A Bibliography of Ptolemy's Geography.

Winsor: Harvard Library No. 19. The Kohl collection of early maps.

Daly: Bulletin, Am. Geog. Soc., No. 1, 1879. The Early History of Cartography.

Narrative and Critical History of America: Vol. IV, General Atlases and Charts of the 16th and 17th centuries, pp. 369–374.

ERRATUM.

On page 513, line 5, before the word Expeditions, for English read Exploring

PART II.

EPITOME OF WARREN'S MEMOIR.—1800–1857.

MEMOIR

*   *   *   *   *   *   *

GIVING

A BRIEF ACCOUNT OF EACH OF THE ENGLISH EXPEDITIONS SINCE A. D. 1800.

*   *   *   *   *   *   *

BY

LIEUT. GOUVERNEUR K. WARREN,

CORPS OF TOPOGRAPHICAL ENGINEERS, U. S. A.

1859.

LETTER TO THE SECRETARY OF WAR.

War Department, Office of Explorations and Surveys,
Washington, D. C., March 2, 1858.

Sir: I transmit herewith a report from Lieut. G. K. Warren, Topographical Engineers, exhibiting the data and authorities from which was compiled the map of United States territory between the Mississippi River and the Pacific Ocean, intended to illustrate the reports upon the Pacific railroad explorations.

It contains a brief account of all the explorations of our territory west of the Mississippi River of approved authority, which will be not only valuable to the officers of the corps, but, it is thought, interesting to the public.

The laborious task of compiling the map and preparing the report has been performed by Lieutenant Warren while occupied with other duties of an onerous character. The more carefully his work is examined the more apparent will be the industry, care, and sound judgment with which it has been executed.

Very respectfully, your obedient servant,

A. A. HUMPHEYS,
Captain Topographical Engineers, in charge.

Hon. J. B. Floyd,
Secretary of War, Washington, D. C.

LETTER TO CAPT. A. A. HUMPHREYS, TOPOGRAPHICAL ENGINEERS.

WAR DEPARTMENT, OFFICE OF EXPLORATIONS AND SURVEYS,
Washington, D. C., March 1, 1858.

SIR: * * * This memoir is a brief account of the numerous explorations made in our territory west of the Mississippi River, and I hope may prove valuable to those seeking information with a view to developing the resources of this vast region, as well as interesting to those studying the progress of geographical discovery. The work has been in progress during the past four years; but other public duties have absorbed the greater part of my time, which must be my excuse for its defects. * * *

I have the honor to be, very respectfully, your obedient servant,

G. K. WARREN,
First Lieutenant, Topographical Engineers.

Capt. A. A. HUMPHREYS,
Corps of Topographical Engineers, in charge of
Office of Explorations and Surveys.

CONTENTS.

INTRODUCTORY REMARKS.

CHAPTER I.—*Explorations from A. D.* 1800 *to A. D.* 1832.

CHAPTER II.—*Explorations from A. D.* 1832 *to A. D.* 1844.

CHAPTER III.—*Explorations from A. D.* 1843 *to A. D.* 1852.

CHAPTER IV.—*Explorations from A. D.* 1852 *to A. D.* 1857.

Gov. I. I. Stevens and Capt. G. B. McClellan, U. S. E., exploration and survey for a railroad route, 1853–'54–'55.—Lieut. R. Arnold, U. S. A., survey, 1854.—F. W. Lander, C. E., reconnaissance, 1854.—Capt. G. W. Gunnison, T. E., and Capt. E. G. Beckwith, U. S. A., exploration and survey for a railroad route, 1853.—Capt. E. G. Beckwith, U. S. A., exploration and survey for a railroad route, 1854.—Capt. A. W. Whipple, T. E., exploration and survey for a railroad route, 1853–'54.—Lieut. R. S. Williamson, T. E., survey for a railroad route, 1853–'54.—Lieut. J. G. Parke, T. E., exploration and survey for a railroad route, 1854.—Capt. J. Pope, T. E., exploration and survey for a railroad route, 1854.—Lieut. J. G. Parke, T. E., exploration and survey for a railroad route, 1854–'55.—Lieut. R. S. Williamson, T. E., and Lieut. H. L. Abbott, T. E., exploration and survey for a railroad route, 1855.—Maj. W. H. Emory, U. S. A., United States and Mexican boundary survey, 1849–'55.—Capt. J. L. Reno, U. S. A., survey, 1853.—Capt. R. B. Marcy, U. S. A., exploration, 1854.—Alexander Ross, " Fur Hunters of the Far West," 1855.—March of Colonel Steptoe's command to California, 1854–'55.—Lieut. J. Withers, U. S. A., survey of road, 1854.—Lieut. G. H. Derby, T. E., survey of roads, 1854–'55.—Lieut. G. H. Mendell, T. E., reconnaissance, 1855.—Capt. J. H. Simpson, T. E., survey of roads, 1855.—Lieut. G. K. Warren, T. E., reconnaissance, 1855.—Lieut. F. T. Bryan, T. E., reconnaissance, 1855.—Lieut. J. C. Amory, U. S. A., reconnaissance in 1855.—Major Merrill, U. S. A., reconnaissance, 1855.—Lieut. I. N. Moore, U. S. A., map of part of New Mexico, 1855.—Lieut. E. L. Hartz, U. S. A., reconnaissance, 1856.—Lieut. F. T. Bryan, T. E., survey of road, 1856.—Capt. J. H. Dickerson, U. S. A., survey of road, 1856.—Lieut. W. D. Smith, U. S. A., reconnaissance of route, 1856.—Capt. A. Sully, U. S. A., reconnaissance, 1856.—Lieut. G. K. Warren, T. E., reconnaissance of Missouri and Yellowstone, 1856.—Explorations ordered in 1857.

* * * * * * * * *

INTRODUCTORY REMARKS.

* * * * * * * * *

Before detailing the manner in which the compilation has been made, I have therefore thought it desirable to give a brief account of each of the different explorations, * * * the methods employed in observing, the maps prepared, etc., in order of date.

By this undertaking I hope to promote the consultation of the original reports and maps, by pointing out to each investigator those works which probably contain information about the region of country especially interesting to himself. As a general rule, I shall confine myself to the explorations made in the territory of the United States.

The maps of the old Spanish and French navigators and explorers who visited the Mississippi, the Gulf of Mexico, and the shores of the Pacific, and who often examined portions of the interior, have nearly all been replaced within our territory by more accurate determinations of our own. They have, therefore, little practical value in this connection, and will not be specially noticed. An almost complete account of Spanish discoveries in New Mexico prior to 1811 can be found in Baron Humboldt's New Spain. The subject is still further discussed in Lieut. James Abert's report of reconnaissances in New Mexico in 1846, Capt. A. W. Whipple's report of survey of railroad route near the 35th parallel, and elsewhere.

A valuable history of the progress of early discoveries on the western coast of North America can be seen in a French work by M. Duflot de Mofras, published in 1844, and also in Mr. Robert Greenhow's book on Oregon and California, published in 1845. This last work is accompanied by a map "of the western and middle portions of North America," compiled by Mr. Greenhow.

* * * * * * * * *

The first exploration which seems to require a detailed notice is that of Captains Lewis and Clarke, U. S. A., directed by President Jefferson in 1803

* * * * * * * * *

As the explorations are mentioned in order of date, the various examinations in the same region, or along the same route or river, are necessarily separated. To avoid the difficulty which this arrangement presents in making a prompt reference to all the sources of information of any one subject, an index has been prepared which will be found at the end of this memoir. The political and military divisions of the country are taken in the index as they appear on the first edition of the map, which was correct at the date of this report.

CHAPTER I.

EXPLORATIONS FROM A. D. 1800 TO A. D. 1832.

Captains Lewis and Clarke, U. S. A., 1804–'5–'6.—Major Pike, U. S. A., 1805–'6.—Humboldt's New Spain, 1811.—Rector, C. E., and Roberdeau, T. E., map, 1818.—Major Long, T. E., first expedition, 1819–'20.—Major Long, T. E., second expedition, 1823.—J. C. Brown, C. E., survey, 1825–'26–'27.—R. Richardson, C. E., survey, 1826.—Northwest boundary Commission, 1828.—British Admiralty charts, 1828.—Lieutenant Hardy, R. N., Explorations Gulf of California, 1825–'26–'27–'28.—Ross Cox's "Adventures on the Columbia," 1832.—Lieutenant Allen, U. S. A., reconnaissance of the source of the Mississippi, 1832.—Schoolcraft's Narrative, 1832.—Finley's Map of North America, 1826.

EXPLORATIONS OF CAPT. MERIWETHER LEWIS, U. S. A., AND CAPT. WILLIAM CLARKE, U. S. A., IN 1804–'5–'6.

The narrative I have consulted most particularly is entitled "*Travels to the Source of the Missouri River and across the American Continent to the Pacific Ocean, performed by order of the Government of the United States in the years* 1804, 1805, *and* 1806. *By Captains Lewis and Clarke; published from the official report, and illustrated by a map of the route and other maps. London: Printed for Longman, Hurst, Rees, Orme, & Brown, Paternoster Row.*—1814." This book consists of one volume quarto, illustrated by a map on a scale of seventy miles to an inch, showing the country from Lake Superior and the Mississippi to the Pacific Ocean, between the 39th and 49th parallels. The other maps are enlarged plans of certain important localities. Another and more common edition, published by the same parties in 1817, is composed of 3 volumes 8vo, with a map on a scale of about eighty miles to an inch.

An account of the expedition was also published in 1808, by Patrick Gass, a sergeant on the exploration; it contains some particulars not noticed in the official narrative.

An abridged edition, prepared by Archibald M. Vickar, was published in two volumes in Harper's Family Library Series, in 18—. The map accompanying this edition has one glaring error, in placing a high range of mountains ranging east and west between the Missouri and Yellowstone Rivers.

* * * * * * * * *

THE JEFFERSON PRODROME AND THE APOCRYPHA.*

On the 19th of February, 1806, the expedition being then still in progress, President Jefferson addressed to Congress a communication entitled as follows:

[1806.] *Message | from the | President of the United States | communicating | Discoveries | made in exploring | the Missouri, Red River and Washita, | by | Captains Lewis and Clarke, Doctor Sibley, | and Mr. Dunbar; | with | a Statistical Account | of the | Countries adjacent. | — | February* 19, 1806. | *Read, and ordered to lie on the table.* | — | *City of Washington: | A. & G. Way, printers.* | . . . | 1806.
8*vo. pp.* 1–171, 3 *l.* (*State Papers.*)

[1806.] *Message | from the | President of the United States, | communicating | Discoveries | made in exploring the | Missouri, Red River and Washita, | by | Captains Lewis and Clarke, Doctor Sibley | and Mr. Dunbar; | with | a Statistical Account | of the | Countries adjacent.* | — | *Read in Congress, February* 19, 1806. | — | *New-York: | Printed by Hopkins and Seymour, | and sold by G. F. Hopkins, No.* 118, *Pearl-street.* | — | 1806.
One vol. 8*vo, pp.* 128 +1 *folded l. not paged.*

[1807.] *Travels | in the | Interior Parts of America; | communicating | Discoveries | made in Exploring | the Missouri, Red River and Washita, | by | Captains Lewis and Clark, | Doctor Sibley, | and | Mr. Dunbar; | with | a statistical account | of the | Countries adjacent.* | — | *As laid before the Senate, | by the | President of the United States. | In February,* 1806 | *and never before published in Great Britain* | — | *London: | Printed for Richard Phillips,* 6, *Bridge street, | Blackfriars, | By J. G. Barnard,* 57, *Snow Hill.* | — | 1807.
8*vo, pp.* 1–116, *with a folding table. Forming part, separately paged, of Vol. VI of Phillip's "Collection of Modern and Contemporary Voyages," &c.*

[1809.] *"The Travels of Capts Lewis and Clarke, from St. Louis, by way of the Missouri and Columbia rivers, to the Pacific Ocean; performed in the years* 1804, 1805, *and* 1806, *by order of the government of the United States, containing delineations of the manners, customs, religion, &c. of the Indians, compiled from Various Authentic Sources, and original Documents, and a Summary of the Statistical View of the Indian Nations, from the official communication of Meriwether Lewis. Illustrated with a Map of the Country, inhabited by the Western Tribes of Indians.* 8*vo, pp. ix and* 309. *London,* 1809."

[1809.] *The | Travels | of | Capts. Lewis & Clarke, | by order of the | Government of the United States, | performed in the years* 1804, 1805, *&* 1806, | *being upwards of three thousand miles, from | St. Louis, by way of the Missouri, and | Columbia Rivers, to the | Pacific Ocean: | Containing an Account of the Indian Tribes, who inhabit | the Western part of the Continent unexplored, | and unknown before. | With copious delineations of the manners, cus- | toms, religion, &c. of the Indians. | Compiled | From various authentic sources, and Documents. | To which is subjoined, | A Summary of the Statistical View of the Indian | Nations, from the Official Communication of* | — | *Meriwether Lewis.* | — | *Embellished with a Map of the Country inhabited by | the Western Tribes of Indians, and five Engravings | of Indian Chiefs.* | — | *Philadelphia: Published by Hubbard Lester.* | . . . . | 1809. | *Price* — 1 *dollar* 62½ *cts.* |
One vol., 12*mo, pp. i–xii,* 13–300, *pll.* 5, *map, and tail-piece (scroll and pen).* (*Copywright dated April* 17, 1809.)

* The subjoined titles are extracted from the admirable résumé "of the various publications relating to the travels of Lewis and Clarke," by Dr. Elliott Coues, U. S. A. For which see Bulletin No. 6 of the United States Geological and Geographical Survey of the Territories.

[1812.] *An | Intersting Aeccount | of the | Voyages and Travels | of | Captains Lewis and Clark, | in the years* 1804, 1805, *and* 1806. | *Giving a faithful description of the river Missouri and | its source—of the various tribes of Indians through | which they passed— | manners and customs—soil—climate | —commerce—gold and silver mines—animal and vege- | table productions interspersed with very enter- | taining anecdotes, and a variety of other useful and | pleasing information remarkably calculated to de- | light and instruct the readers – to which is added a | complete dictionary of the Indian tongue. | By William Fisher, Esq. | — | Baltimore. | Printed by Anthony Miltenberger, For the purchasers.* | 1812.

One vol., 12*mo,* 2 *portraits, pp. v–xv,* 16–326.

[1813.] *An | Interesting Account | of the | Voyages and Travels | of | Captains Lewis and Clarke, | in the years* 1804–5, *&* 6. | *Giving a faithful description of the river Missouri and | its source—of the various tribes of Indians through | which they passed—manners and customs—soil | —climate—commeree—gold and silver | mines—animal and vegetable | productions. | Interspersed | With very entertaining anecdotes, and a variety of | other useful and pleasing information, re- | markably calculated to delight and | instruct the readers. | To which is added | A complete Dictionary of the Indian tongue | — | by William Fisher, Esq. | — | Baltimore: | printed and published by P. Mauro, | N°.* 10, *North Howard St.* | 1813.

One vol., 12*mo, portraits?* pp. iii–xii,* 13–262, *with* 3 *full-page wood-cuts.*

[1840.] *The | Journal | of | Lewis and Clarke, | to the Mouth of the Columbia River | beyond the Rocky Mountains. | In the years* 1804–5, *&* 6. | *Giving a faithful description of the River Missouri | and its source—of the various tribes of Indians | through which they passed—manners and cus- | toms—soil—climate—commerce—gold and | silver mines—animal and vegetable | productions, &c. | New Edition, with Notes. | Revised, corrected, and illustrated with numerous | wood cuts. | To which is added | a complete dictionary of the Indian tongue. | — | Dayton, O. |*

Published and sold by B. F. Ells, | John Wilson, Printer | . . . . | 1840.

One vol., 16*mo, pp. i–xii,* 13–240, *portraits of Lewis and of Clarke, and* 14 *other full-page wood-cuts.*

[1807.] *A Journal | of the | Voyages and Travels | of a Corps of Discovery, | under the command of Capt. Lewis and Capt. | Clarke, of the Army of the United States, | from | the mouth of the River Missouri through the | interior parts of North America | to the Pacific Ocean, | during the years* 1804, 1805, *&* 1806. | *Containing | An authentic relation of the most interesting transactions | during the expedition,—A description of the country,— | And an account of its inhabitants, soil, climate, curiosities | and vegetable and animal productions. | — | By Patrick Gass, | one of the persons employed on the expedition. | — | With geographical and explanatory notes | by the publisher. | — | [Copy-right secured according to law.] | Pittsburgh, | printed by Zadok Cramer, | for David M'Keehan, Publisher and | proprietor.* . . . . . 1807. |

One vol., 12*mo, pp. i–viii,* 9–262. (*No illustrations.*)

[1810.] *A | Journal | of the | Voyages and Travels | of a Corps of Discovery, | under the command of Capt. Lewis and Capt. | Clarke, of the Army of the United States, | from | the mouth of the River Missouri through the | interior parts of North America, | to the Pacific Ocean, | During the years* 1804, 1805. *and* 1806. | *Containing | an authentic relation of the most interesting transac- | tions during the expedition,—A description of | the country,—And an account of its inhabi- | tants, soil, climate, curiosities, and ve- | getable and animal productions. | — | By Patrick Gass, | one of the persons employed in the expedition. | — | With | geographical and explanatory notes. | — | [Copy-right secured according to Law.] | — | Philadelphia: | Printed for Mathew Carey, | No.* 122, *Market-street.* | — | 1810.

One vol., 12*mo, pp. i–viii,* 9–262, *with* 6 *full-page wood-cuts.*

[1810.] "*Voyages des capitaines Lewis et Clarke, depuis l'embouchure du Missouri jusqu'à l'entrée de la Colombia, dans l'Océan Pacifique, fait dans les années* 1805–06, *par ordre du gouvernement des États-Unis, contenant le Journal des événements les plus remarquables du voyage, la description des habitants, du sol, les productions animales et végétables, etc.; trad. en français par A.-J.-N. L.* (*Lallemant*). *Paris, A. Bertrand,* 1810, *in-*8, *avec carte,* 6 *fr.*"

[1814.] *History | of | The Expedition | under the command of | Captains Lewis and Clark, | to | the sources of the Missouri, | thence | across the Rocky Mountains | and down the | River Columbia to the Pacific Ocean. | Performed during the years* 1804–5–6. | *By order of the | Government of the United States. | Prepared for the press | by Paul Allen, Esquire. | In two volumes. | Vol. I[II]. | Philadelphia: | Published by Bradford and Inskeep; and | Abm. H. Inskeep, Newyork. | J. Maxwell, Printer.* | 1814.

Two vols., 8vo. *Vol. I, pp. i–xxviii,* 1–470, *maps. Vol. II, pp. i–ix,* 1–522, *maps.* (> *Vol. II, Chap. VII, "A general description of the beasts, birds, and plants, &c., found by the party in this expedition," pp.* 148–201.)

[1815.] *Travels | to the source of | the Missouri River | and across the | American Continent | to | the Pacific Ocean. | Performed by order of | the Government of the United States, | in the years* 1804, 1805, *and* 1806. | — | *By Captains Lewis and Clarke.* | — | *Published from the Official Report, | and illustrated by a map of the route, | and other maps.* | — | *A new edition, in three volumes. | Vol. I, [II, III.]* | — | *London: | Printed for Longman, Hurst, Rees, Orme, and Brown. | Pater-noster-Row.* | 1815.

Three vols., 8vo. *Vol. I, pp. i–xxvi,* 1 *l. not paged,* 1–411, *maps* 3. *Vol. II, pp. i–xii,* 1–434, *maps* 3. *Vol. III, pp. i–xii,* 1–394. (> *Vol. III, Chap. XXIV, "A general description of the beasts, birds, plants, &c., found by the party in this expedition," pp.* 1–73.)

[1815.] "(*Lewis und Clarke.*) *Tagebuch e. Entdeckungsreise durch Nord.-Amerika in d. Jahren* 1804–6. *Aus d. Engl. v. Weyland. Mit* 1 *Karte.*" <*Neue Bibliothek der wichtigsten Beschreibungen, u. s. w.* (*Weimar, gr.* 8vo.) *Bd. I,* 1815.

[1816–'18.] *Reize | naar | de Bronnen van den Missouri, | en door het vaste land van America | naar de Zuidzee. | Gedaan op last van de Regering der Vereenigde Staten van America, | in de jaren* 1804, 1805 *en* 1806. | *Door de Kapiteins | Lewis en Clarke. | Met eene Kaart.* | — | *Uit het Engelsch vertaald door | N. G. Van Kampen.* | — | *Eerste [tweede, derde en Laatste] Deel.* | * | *Te Dordrecht, | Bij A. Blussé & Zoon* | 1816. [1817, 1818].

Three vols. 8vo. *Vol. I,* 1816, *pp. i–xxxii,* 1–398, *map. Vol. II,* 1817, *pp. i–viii,* 1–390. *Vol. III,* 1818, *pp. i–xii,* 1–335.

[1842–'75.] *History | of | the Expedition | under the command of | Captains Lewis and Clarke, | to | the sources of the Missouri, thence across the Rocky | Mountains, and down the River Columbia to the | Pacific ocean; performed during the | years* 1804, 1805, 1806, | *by order of the | Government of the United States. | Prepared for the press | by Paul Allen, Esq. | Revised and abridged by the omission of unimportant de- | tails, with an introduction and notes, | by Archibald M'Vickar. | In two volumes. | Vol. I. [II.] | New York: | Harper & Brothers, Publishers, | Franklin Square.* | 1868.

Two vols. 18mo, *some of the issues forming part of Harpers' series, "The Family Library," Vol. I, pp. i–vi, i*–v*, vii–li,* 53–371, 3 *maps. Vol. II, pp. i–x,* 11–395, 3 *maps.* (>*Vol. II, Appendix, "Further enumeration and description of the Quadrupeds, Birds, Fishes, and Plants noticed during the Expedition," pp.* 339–378.)

* * * * * * * * *

These explorers began to ascend the Missouri River in keel boats, cordeled by hand, in 1804. They were provided with compasses for determining their courses, and with chronometers, sextants, and artificial horizons for obtaining latitudes and longitudes. They spent the winter of 1804 and 1805 at Fort Mandan, opposite the existing Ree village, or Fort Clarke. The next season, having ascended the Missouri to the Three Forks, and named them Jefferson, Madison, and Gallatin, and believing the first to be the main stream, they followed it to its source.

* * * * * * * * *

It does not appear from the journal I have read that the explorers relied much upon determinations for longitudes. That of the mouth of the Platte was taken by them half a degree too far west; that of the mouth of the Yellowstone accords well with the best recent determinations; that of the mouth of the Columbia was taken one degree too far west. The place which they mention as the extreme navigable point of the Missouri is placed by their observations on latitude 43° 30′, while the most southern point on Jefferson Fork is, according to Governor Stevens's map, in about latitude 44° 30′; thus showing a considerable discrepancy. Most of the routes and rivers they examined have been re-explored, the only exceptions being the sources of Salmon River, the Missouri River from the Gate of the Mountains to its source, and the Yellowstone from the point where Captain Clarke struck it to the mouth of Powder River. The tests to which the maps of this exploration have been subjected prove them to have been carefully made and with great accuracy, considering the means and circumstances of the party.

The original map represents the different ridges of the Rocky Mountains with a general northwest trend from the Black Hills westward, and it is neither responsible for the error of representing those north of the Platte with a northeast trend nor for the false indication of a range of mountains running east and west between the Yellowstone and Missouri. Deceived by the size of the Wallamath at its mouth, these explorers supposed it to be a stream of great length, and represented it on their map as heading to the southwest in the vicinity of what is now known to be the Great Salt Lake. The names they gave to the rivers have been generally adopted, although a little confusion exists about some of the smaller ones. Captain Lewis's melancholy death occurred before the completion of the narrative, thus devolving the whole labor of the report upon his able associate, Captain Clarke. Several editions of the work have appeared, differing somewhat from each other; and thus, no doubt, has arisen the misunderstanding now existing concerning the names of places.

EXPLORATIONS OF MAJOR Z. M. PIKE, U. S. A., 1805-'6-'7.

The narrative I have consulted is entitled "*An Account of Expeditions to the Sources of the Mississippi, and through the western parts of Louisiana, to the Sources of the Arkansas and Pierrejaun Rivers, performed by order of the Government of the United States, during the years* 1805, '6, *and* '7*; and a Tour through the interior parts of New Spain, when conducted through these provinces by order of the Captain General, in* 1807. *By Major Z. M. Pike; illustrated by maps and charts. Published by C. & A. Conrad & Co., Philadelphia. John Binus, printer.*—1810." Accompanying it is a map of the Mississippi River from the mouth of the Missouri River to Leech Lake, on a scale of about 25 miles to one inch; a map, in two sheets, on a scale of about 40 miles to one inch, showing the supposed positions of the Platte, Arkansas, and Red Rivers, from their mouths to their sources; and a map of New Spain, in two sheets, on a scale of about 75 miles to an inch.

In 1805 and 1806 Lieutenant Pike,* in his expedition to the sources of the Mississippi, ascended the stream from the mouth of the Missouri to what is called Upper Red Cedar Lake (since named Cass Lake), and examined Turtle River, an affluent of this to its sources. He also examined Leech Lake and Leech River to its junction with the Mississippi. His map of the river gives its general direction with considerable accuracy, and is the more creditable to him, since, in his own language, "in the execution of this voyage I had no gentlemen to aid me, and I literally performed the duties (as far as my limited abilities permitted) of astronomer, commanding officer, clerk, spy, guide, and hunter."

Lieutenant Pike's second expedition was to the sources of the Arkansas, with the intention of passing thence south to those of Red River of Louisiana, and descending this stream to Natchitoches. He was accompanied by Lieut. James B. Wilkinson, U. S. A., and Dr. J. H. Robinson, M. D., and was provided with a sextant, chronometer, and compasses.

* * * * * * * * *

Nearly every part of the country traversed by Lieutenant Pike has since been explored by parties better provided with instruments, and his determinations are now replaced by others more accurate.

---

* Major Pike was a lieutenant while making both of the explorations noticed here, and was promoted after his return.

Red River, the discovery of whose sources was one of the main objects of Major Pike's expedition, was examined in 1806 by a party under Captain Sparks from the mouth as far up as the Spanish border. Here he was met by a Spanish force very much superior to his in numbers, and prevented from going further.

At this time the boundary between Louisiana and New Spain was not definitely agreed upon, and the Americans and Spaniards each maintained troops near the border to prevent the incursions of the opposite party. Burr's schemes were also agitating the public mind, and probably increased the suspicions of the governments of both nations.

* * * * * * * * *

HUMBOLDT'S NEW SPAIN, 1811.

The edition of this work, which I have consulted, is entitled "*Political Essay on the Kingdom of New Spain, containing researches relative to the geography of Mexico; the extent of its surface, and its political division into intendancies; the physical aspect of the country; the population; the state of agriculture and manufacturing and commercial industry; the canals projected between the South Sea and Atlantic Ocean; the Crown revenues; the quantity of the precious metals which have flowed from Mexico into Europe and Asia since the discovery of the New Continent; and the military defence of New Spain. By Alexander de Humboldt; with physical sections and maps, founded on astronomical observations and trigonometrical and barometrical measurements. Translated from the original French by John Black. Second edition. London: Printed for Longman, Hurst, Rees, Orme, & Brown, and H. Colburn.*—1814." It is accompanied by an original map, on a scale of 120 miles to an inch, "*of New Spain, from* 16° *to* 38° *north latitude*," between the 94th and 114th meridian; "*reduced from the large map drawn from astronomical observations at Mexico, in the year* 1804, *by Alexander de Humboldt; and comprehends the whole of the information contained in the original map, except the heights of the mountains.*"

This work, completed by the Baron Humboldt for the Spanish Government in 1808, is almost a complete summary of all the explorations made by the Spaniards down to the date of its preparation, and is therefore of much value in showing the extent of their knowledge at that day. It shows that Father Escalante, in 1777, visited or gained information about Lake

Timpanogos (doubtless Utah Lake, which has an affluent now called by that name, and which is fresh, like the one described by him), and also Lake Salado (probably Sevier Lake), which, he says, receives the waters of the Rio de San Buenaventura, its western limits being unknown. Baron Humboldt did not entertain the idea that any large river flowed into the Pacific Ocean from the region which now composes the Territory of Utah, as was generally represented on all the English maps. His work does not, however, give any positive information about the topography and hydrography of any portion of our present territory which the explorations of our Government have not replaced by more accurate results. Still, as it has formed the basis of many classifications of the great mountain system and abounds in valuable enunciations of the true principles of hydrography and topography, no one should neglect to consult it whose scientific investigations extend to the country west of the Mississippi.

RECTOR'S AND ROBERDEAU'S COMPILED MAP, 1818.

This map is titled, "*Sketch of the western part of the continent of North America, between latitude* 35° *and* 52° *N.*," from the 87th meridian to the Pacific Ocean, on a scale of about 47 miles to an inch. "*This map, of an extent of country including more than* 20° *of latitude and* 50° *of longitude, was originally drawn under the inspection of William Rector, esquire, surveyor of the United States for the Territories of Missouri and Illinois, and was by him presented to the General Land Office, January* 21, 1818. *It is probably the most correct map of the country now extant. Signed, Josiah Meigs, General Land Office, January* 21, 1818; *Roberdeau, U. S. T. Engineers, del.*"

From the year 1807 to 1819 our country was much of the time involved in foreign difficulties, and little was done, so far as I have been able to learn, in exploring our western possessions. This map of Rector and Roberdeau has, I believe, never been published.

* * * * * * * * *

MAJOR S. H. LONG'S FIRST EXPEDITION, 1819 AND 1820.

"*Account of an Expedition from Pittsburg to the Rocky Mountains, performed in the years* 1819 *and* 1820, *by order of the Hon. J. C. Calhoun, Secretary of War, under the command of Major Stephen H. Long, from the notes of Major*

Long, Mr. T. Say, and other gentlemen of the exploring party: compiled by Edwin James, botanist and geologist for the expedition. In two volumes, with an atlas. Philadelphia: H. C. Carey and I. Lea, Chestnut street.—1823." This book also contains Major Long's official report. Accompanying the publication is a map, in two sheets, on a scale of 75 miles to an inch, embracing the country from the meridian of Washington to the Rocky Mountains, between the 33d and 47th parallels. The original map in the Topographical Bureau is in one sheet, on a scale of 36 miles to an inch. The same work was republished "*in three volumes in London: printed for Longman, Hurst, Rees, Orme, & Brown, Paternoster Row.*—1823."

This expedition started from Pittsburgh, Pa., early in April, 1819, on board the small steam-boat *Western Engineer*, under command of Major Long. He was assisted by Major Biddle, Lieut. J. D. Graham, U. S. A., Cadet W. H. Swift, Dr. Baldwin, Dr. Thomas Say, Mr. Jessup, Mr. T. R. Peale, and Mr. Samuel Seymour. They were provided with chronometers, sextants, telescope for observing occultations and eclipses, and with compasses. They descended the Ohio River to its mouth, ascended the Mississippi to the mouth of the Missouri, and up this river to Old Council Bluff, which was the end of their travels that season, the main body wintering there at Engineer Cantonment.

* * * * * * * * *

Major Long returned to the seat of General Government during the winter, and was accompanied the next spring by Capt. John R. Bell, U. S. A., who took the place of Major Biddle, and by Dr. E. James, as botanist and geologist, in the place of Dr. Baldwin and Mr. Jessup, the former having died while ascending the Missouri River. Lieutenant Graham returned from Engineer Cantonment with the steam-boat.

* * * * * * * * *

This was the third attempt by exploring parties, under the United States Government, to discover the sources of Red River. The explorations of Major Long's expedition, made in Arkansas and Missouri on their return, have been replaced by the surveys of the United States Land Office. The only portions of the route of this exploration which have not been reexamined are the trails from the Arkansas to the Canadian, and from the Great Bend of the Arkansas to Fort Gibson.

The astronomical observations by Major Long, Lieutenant Graham, and Lieutenant Swift consisted of altitudes and lunar distances by the sextant and eclipses of Jupiter's satellites, observed with a four-foot telescope. The relation of their determinations to those of subsequent parties will be discussed hereafter. Their barometers were all broken before they reached the forks of the Platte. On the map which was made by Major Long we see the Black Hills of Nebraska represented as a north and south range, differing from Lewis and Clarke's map, which gave them a northwest trend. This is the first original map which represents this range as running north.

MAJOR LONG'S EXPEDITION TO THE SOURCE OF THE ST. PETER'S RIVER.

The work I have consulted is entitled "*Travels in the Interior of North America, with the particulars of an Expedition to the Lakes, and the source of the St. Peter's river. By Messrs. Long, Keating, and Colhoun; in two volumes. London: Printed for G. B. Whittaker, Ave Maria lane.*—1828." It is accompanied by a map, on a scale of 35 miles to an inch, exhibiting the route of the expedition. It includes the area limited on the northeast by a line drawn from Lake Winnipeg to the east end of Lake Ontario; on the southeast by a line from Lake Ontario to Pittsburgh; on the southwest by one from Cincinnati to Rock Island, in the Mississippi; and on the northwest by one from the Mandan villages to Lake Winnipeg.

This expedition was commanded by Maj. S. H. Long, topographical engineer, who was assisted by Thomas Say, zoologist, antiquarian, and botanist; William H. Keating, mineralogist and geologist; and James C. Colhoun, astronomer, who was supplied with a sextant and pocket chronometer. Distances were estimated and courses taken by compasses. Mr. Say and Mr. Keating, by the latter of whom the published narrative was written, acted as joint literary journalists. They started from Philadelphia in April, 1823; traveled to Wheeling; thence to Columbus; thence to Fort Wayne, on the Miami River, where they obtained a few soldiers to accompany them, and thence to the southern extremity of Lake Michigan. The journey between these last two places was through a wilderness, and on reaching Chicago they found it to consist "of a few miserable huts, inhabited by a miserable race of men," though it was, "perhaps, one of the oldest settled places in the Indian country." From this point they proceeded through the unknown wilderness to Fort Crawford, or Prairie du Chien, at the junction of the Wisconsin and Mississippi Rivers. From this point one portion proceeded rapidly by land up the right bank of the Mississippi to Fort Snelling. The other part arrived there soon after by water. This place had been visited by Major Long in 1817, and its site recommended for a permanent military post, which was established in 1819.

* * * * * * * * *

The astronomer, Mr. Colhoun, made numerous observations, which embraced every kind of which a sextant is capable. Our knowledge of the route has been improved by other explorers from the mouth of the St. Peter's River to the 49th parallel, but from that point to the mouth of Dog River this map is our only authority along the route explored. The Shayenne River, which Major Long supposed to be only 50 miles long, has since been shown to have a valley about 300 miles in length.

J. C. BROWN'S SURVEY OF ROAD FROM FORT OSAGE TO TAOS, 1825 1826, AND 1827.

In the Topographical Bureau there is one map, in two sheets, of this survey, on a scale of 4 miles to an inch; another on a scale of 12 miles to an inch, and a third on a scale of 4 miles to an inch, in thirty-one sections, "of the road surveyed and marked out from the western frontier of Missouri, near Fort Osage, to San Fernando de Taos, near Santa Fé, in New Mexico, by order of the Government of the United States, in the years 1825, 1826, and 1827, with accurate and minute notes and directions for the use of travelers," which begins thus: "The following pages contain a map of the road, as surveyed and marked out from the frontier of Missouri to Taos, the first settlement in the direction to Santa Fé, under the direction of Benjamin Reeves, George C. Sibley, and Thomas Mather, commissioners appointed by the President of the United States for that purpose."

This survey was made with a chain and compass, corrected by observations for latitude with a good sextant. The longitudes were referred to the meridian of Fort Osage, which was taken at 93° 51′ 03″. This road is that of the Santa Fé trail, along the divide between the Kansas and Arkansas Rivers.

* * * * * * * * *

These maps, though not displaying great skill in topographical representation, were constructed from a survey more elaborate than any subsequent one over the same route. They are therefore of much value at the present time. The names now in use along the line were many of them given by this party. I am not aware that the original map and notes have ever been published.

R. RICHARDSON'S SURVEY OF ROAD FROM LITTLE ROCK TO FORT GIBSON, 1826.

The map of this road, in the Topographical Bureau, is constructed on a scale of four miles to an inch. The survey was made, I believe, with a chain and compass, and is valuable as showing the relative longitudes of Fort Smith and Fort Gibson. It does not seem to have been used on late compilations.

NORTHWEST BOUNDARY COMMISSION, 1828.

The commissioners appointed under the treaty of Ghent for ascertaining and establishing the north and northwestern boundary between the United States and Great Britain made a decision (June 18, 1822) at Utica, N. Y., which was published by a resolution of the United States House of Representatives in 1828. As this publication extends their labors no further west than the outlet to Lake Superior, the information and maps do not relate to the region under consideration. I believe that the surveys made under the commission were extended as far west as the Lake of the Woods, and according to these the boundary line was fixed in the second article of the Ashburton treaty. In the State Department there is a map, in five sheets, on a scale of an inch to two miles, a reduction of which was published on Nicollet's map of the hydrographical basin of the Upper Mississippi. The original maps have the following title:

"Map of a part of certain surveys along the water communications northward of Lake Superior, commencing at the mouth of the Pigeon River and extending westward to Lake Namekan; made by order of the honorable the commissioners under the sixth and seventh articles of the treaty of Ghent.

"Signed:

"PETER B. PORTER, } *Commissioners.*
"ANTH. BARCLAY, }
"I. FERGUSON, *Surveyor.*
"GEORGE W. WHISTLER, *U. S. Artillery,*
"*Draughtsman and Assistant Surveyor.*"

BRITISH ADMIRALTY CHART OF LAKE SUPERIOR, 1828.

This chart, published from reconnaissances made by Lieut. H. W. Bayfield, R. N., are, to this day, the best we have of the northern shore of Lake Superior.

LIEUTENANT HARDY, R. N.—EXAMINATION OF GULF OF CALIFORNIA, 1825, 1826, 1827, AND 1828.

Lieutenant Hardy visited the whole coast of the Gulf from Mazatlan around by the mouth of the Colorado to Loredo, in search of pearl fisheries. He did not determine any positions by astronomical observations, and his map has not been used by me.

ROSS COX.—ADVENTURES ON THE COLUMBIA RIVER.

This book is entitled "*Adventures on the Columbia Rirer, including a Narratire of six years on the Western side of the Rocky Mountains among various tribes of Indians hitherto unknown, together with a Journey across the American Continent: By Ross Cox. Published by J. J. Harper, New York.*—1832."

The journey across the continent was made up the Columbia to one of its northern sources, crossing the Rocky Mountains at the head of the Athabasca River, near Mount Hooker, in about latitude 52° 10′ north. The book is very interesting and instructive in regard to the early operations of the fur companies.

RECONNAISSANCE OF THE SOURCES OF THE MISSISSIPPI RIVER, BY LIEUT. J. ALLEN, U. S. A., 1832.

The report of Lieutenant Allen, with map, on a scale of 5.75 miles to an inch, exhibiting the Mississippi River from Lake Pepin to its source, together with the country adjacent to his routes, is printed in Ex. Doc. No. 323, 1st session Twenty-third Congress.

* * * * * * * * *

"I was not furnished with, nor could I procure at Fort Brady, any instruments by which to fix, from astronomical observations, the true geographical positions of points necessary to be known for the construction of an accurate map; and to obviate this inconvenience I had recourse to a method of tracing the whole route between the few points fixed and given by the observations of former travelers. For this purpose a compass, the only instrument I had, was placed in my canoe, where it was constantly under my eye; and as the canoe proceeded in the line of a river I carried my observations from the compass to a field-book at every bend or change of direction, thus delineating in my field-book all the bends of the river precisely as they occurred; and by establishing a scale of proportions in the lengths of the reaches I was also in this way enabled to lay down and preserve the general curve of a river with surprising accuracy, as was tested afterwards in constructing on my map the routes of rivers between known points. The distances were estimated with great pains and care, and from the combined judgment of all the gentlemen of the party. * * *

"On the portion of the Mississippi above Cass Lake, which was the least known of any part of the river and route, I bestowed on the tracing and computing of distances the most unremitted attention."

To Lieutenant Allen we are indebted for the first topographical and hydrographical delineation of the source of the Mississippi; and this, somewhat improved by Mr. Nicollet, is our authority at the present day for the Mississippi above the mouth of Swan River. Lieutenant Allen was a companion of Mr. H. R. Schoolcraft, whose labors and writings are so well known.

SCHOOLCRAFT'S NARRATIVE OF THE EXPEDITION TO THE SOURCE OF THE MISSISSIPPI IN 1832.

The title of this work is as follows: "*Narrative of an Expedition through the Upper Mississippi to Itasca Lake, the actual source of this river, embracing an exploration through the St. Croix and Burntwood (or Brule) rivers, in* 1832, *under the direction of Henry R. Schoolcraft New York: Published by Harper & Brother, No.* 82 *Cliff street.*—1834." This book is embellished by "A sketch of the sources of the Mississippi River, drawn from Lieutenant Allen's observations in 1832, to illustrate Schoolcraft's inland journey to Itasca Lake, in two sheets, on a scale of about 11 miles to an inch."

Mr. Schoolcraft's object on the expedition in 1832 was to attempt a reconciliation of the difficulties between the Chippeway and Sioux Indians. The routes he pursued were nearly those mapped by Lieutenant Allen, as already described.

In the same book is a brief account of Mr. Schoolcraft's examinations in 1831 (in connection with his duties in relation to Indian affairs) of the country between Lake Superior and the Mississippi. His route lay up the Mauvaise or Bad River to its source, and thence down the Chippeway to its mouth.

Mr. Schoolcraft had also accompanied Gen. Lewis Cass in his expedition to the sources of the Mississippi in 1820, at which time the highest point reached was the lake called Red Cedar by Pike, but since generally known as Cass Lake.

Mr. Schoolcraft published a beautiful description of this expedition, called, "*Narrative Journal of Travels from Detroit, northwest through the great chain of American Lakes, to the sources of the Mississippi river, in the year* 1820. *By Henry R. Schoolcraft. Albany: Published by E. & E. Hosford.*—1821." It is accompanied by a map on a scale of 65 miles to an inch, exhibiting the region bounded by the 1st and 21st meridians west from Washington and the 41st and 51st parallels.

The Mississippi River, whose extreme sources Messrs. Allen and Schoolcraft have the honor of first exploring, was discovered by Hernando de Soto, who reached its banks probably near Memphis in 1541. Father Marquette and Sieur Joilet first saw it in 1673. Father Hennepin visited it in 1680, and named the St. Peter's River and the Falls of St. Anthony. The mouth was discovered in 1683 by the Sieur La Salle, who sailed down the Illinois River to the Mississippi, and navigated it to the Gulf of Mexico. M. Le Sueur visited it probably as early as 1695, at which time he discovered the blue earth on the St. Peter's. In 1702 he floated two thousand pounds of this material to the mouth of the Mississippi. These statements in regard to the discovery of the Mississippi I have taken principally from Mr. Keating's narrative of Major Long's expedition to the sources of the St. Peter's River.

We are indebted to Capt. Jonathan Carver, who visited the Upper Mississippi in 1766–'68, for much of our early knowledge of the Upper Mississippi valley, although some of his statements must be received with caution. He claims to have first conceived the idea of passing from the sources of the Missouri to the Pacific Ocean. An expedition to this effect was actually fitted out by the aid of Mr. Whitworth, when the growing troubles of the colonies with the mother country led to its abandonment.

* * * * * * * * *

CHAPTER II.

EXPLORATIONS FROM A. D. 1832 TO A. D. 1844.

Captain Bonneville, U. S. A., expedition, 1832 to 1836.—Discovery of Great Salt Lake and Humboldt River.—Irving's Astoria.—Lieut. E. Steen, U. S. A., map, 1835.—Topographical Bureau, map of Western Frontier, 1837.—C. Dimmock, C. E., survey, 1838.—Capt. W. Hood, T. E., memoir and map, 1839.—Topographical Bureau, map of Oregon, 1838.—Survey boundary Louisiana and Texas, 1840.—Commander Wilkes, U. S. N., map of Oregon, 1841.—Kendall's Santa Fé Expedition, 1841.—Professor Nicollet's exploration and map, 1835–'40.—Lieut. J. C. Fremont, T. E., exploration, 1842.—Capt. N. Boone, U. S. A., expedition, 1843.—Capt. J. Allen, U. S. A., expedition, 1843.—Topographical Bureau, map of Texas, 1844.—Gregg's Commerce of the Prairies, 1844.

BONNEVILLE'S EXPEDITION TO ROCKY MOUNTAINS, 1832 TO 1836.

The narrative I have perused is entitled "*The Rocky Mountains; or, Scenes, Incidents, and Adventures in the Far West; digested from the Journal of Captain B. L. E. Bonneville, of the Army of the United States, and illustrated from various other sources. By Washington Irving. In two volumes. Philadelphia: Carey, Lea & Blanchard.*—1837." This is accompanied by two maps; one on a scale of 23 miles to an inch, showing the sources of the Missouri, Yellowstone, Platte, Green, Bear, Snake, and Salmon Rivers, and a portion of Lake Bonneville (Great Salt Lake); the other, on a scale of 50 miles to an inch, giving the country from the Rocky Mountains to the Pacific, between the parallels of 38° and 49° north latitude.

Captain Bonneville's explorations were made in prosecution of the fur trade, which was his principal object, and very great accuracy in the map is not therefore to be expected. His letter of instructions, from Major-General Macomb, dated Washington, August 3, 1831, contains the following directions: "The leave of absence which you have asked, for the purpose of enabling you to carry into execution your design of exploring the country to the Rocky Mountains and beyond, * * * has been duly considered and submitted to the War Department for approval, and has been sanctioned. You are therefore authorized to be absent from the Army till October, 1833. It is understood that the Government is to be at no expense in reference to your proposed expedition, it having originated with yourself. * * * You will naturally, in preparing yourself for the expedition, provide suitable instruments."

* * * * * * * * *

Having made his arrangements for the year he visited the Great Salt Lake and saw its northern portions. "To have this lake properly explored and all its secrets revealed was the grand scheme of the captain for the present year. * * * This momentous undertaking he confided to Mr. Walker, in whose experience and ability he had great confidence." "He instructed him to keep along the shores of the lake, and trap in all the streams on his route. He was also to keep a journal and minutely to record the events of his journey and everything curious or interesting, and make maps or charts of his route and of the surrounding country." No pains nor expense were spared in fitting out this party, which was composed of forty men. They had complete supplies for a year, and were to meet Captain Bonneville in the ensuing summer in the valley of Bear River, the largest tributary of Salt Lake.

This party endeavored to proceed south over the great barren salt plain lying to the west of the lake, but their sufferings became so great, and the danger of perishing so imminent, that they abandoned the proposed route and struck to the northwest for some snowy mountains in the distance. Thus they came upon Ogden's (Humboldt) River, and followed down it to the "sinks," or place where it loses itself in the sand. Continuing on they crossed the Sierra Nevada, in which they were entangled for twenty-three days, suffering very much from hunger, and finally reached the waters of the Sacramento; thence turning south they stopped at the Mission of Monterey. After a considerable sojourn the party started to return. Instead of retracing their steps through the Sierra Nevada they passed round its southern extremity, and crossing a range of low hills, found themselves in the sandy plains south of Ogden's River, where they again suffered grievously from want of water. On this journey they encountered some Mexicans, two of whom accompanied them to the rendezvous appointed by Captain Bonneville. The return route of this party probably was nearly that taken by Captain Fremont in 1842, and known as the Santa Fé trail to California. They thus traveled quite around the Great Basin system.

While this expedition was in progress Captain Bonneville made an excursion to the headwaters of the Yellowstone. Leaving Green River he moved east to the sources of the Sweetwater, so as to turn the Wind River Mountains at their southeast extremity; thence striking the head of the Popo Agie, he passed down it to Wind River, which he followed through the gap of the Little Horn Mountains, and through the Big Horn range. Below these mountains the river becomes navigable for canoes, and takes the name of the Big Horn River From this point he returned to Wind River and attempted to cross the Wind River Mountains direct to his caches on Green River. In this he was foiled by the chasms and precipices and compelled to take his former route around their southeastern extremity. From the depot he went up to the sources of Green River, crossed the mountains between its source and that of Wind River, and again returned to Green River by the Sweetwater. He then passed over the mountains to the Bear River Valley, and thence to the Port Neuf River, where he established his winter quarters.

During the winter he started to visit the Columbia, passing down the Snake River Valley, through the Grand Ronde and over the Blue Mountains to Walla-Walla. He returned to Bear River in the succeeding June. On the 3d of July, 1834, he made a second visit to the Columbia, and returned to spend the winter on Bear River. In 1835 he returned home* by way of the Platte River.

Captain Bonneville's maps, which accompany the edition of Irving's work, published by Carey, Lea & Blanchard in 1837 (the later editions generally do not give the original maps), are the first to correctly represent the hydrography of this region west of the Rocky Mountains. Although the geographical positions are not accurate, yet the existence of the great interior

* Captain Bonneville's long-continued absence after the expiration of his leave, during which time no news was received from him at the War Department, led to his name being dropped from the Army Register. He was, however, restored, and now holds the commission of colonel of the Third infantry.

basins (without outlets to the ocean) of Great Salt Lake, of Mary's or Ogden's River (named afterwards Humboldt by Captain Fremont), of the Mud Lakes, and of Sevier River and Lake, *was determined* by Captain Bonneville's maps, and they proved the non-existence of the Rio Buenaventura and of other hypothetical rivers. They reduced the Wallamuth or Multonomah (Willamette) River to its proper length, and fixed approximately its source, and determined the general extent and direction of the Sacramento and San Joaquin Rivers. The map of the sources of the Yellowstone is still the best original one of that region.

* * * * * * * * *

Colonel Benton, in his "Thirty Years' View," page 580, says of Fremont's second expedition: "He was at Fort Vancouver, guest of the hospitable Dr. McLaughlin, governor of the British Hudson Bay Fur Company, and obtained from him all possible information upon his intended line of return, faithfully given, but which proved to be disastrously erroneous in its leading and governing feature." * * * "All maps up to that time had shown this region traversed from east to west, from the base of the Rocky Mountains to the bay of San Francisco, by a great river called the *Buenaventura*, which may be translated the *good chance.* Fremont believed in it, and his plan was to reach it before the dead of winter, and then hibernate upon it."

It is evident that Colonel Benton had never seen Captain Bonneville's map, or he would not have written this paragraph.

EARLY DISCOVERIES IN THE GREAT BASIN.

The exploration of the Great Salt Lake was a favorite object with Captain Bonneville; though called Lake Bonneville by Mr. Irving, its existence was well known to the traders and trappers on his arrival in that country, as was also that of the Ogden's or Mary's River. A short account of the first discoveries in this region may not be inappropriate in this place.

In Captain Stansbury's report, page 151, he says: "The existence of a large lake of salt water, somewhere amid the wilds west of the Rocky Mountains, seems to have been known, vaguely, as long as 150 years since. As early as 1689 the Baron la Hontan * * * wrote an account of discoveries in this region, which was published in the English language in 1735." This narrative of La Hontan of his journey up "La Rivière Longue," flowing into the Mississippi from the west, has for more than a century been considered fabulous. It is spoken of even by Captain Stansbury as an "imaginative voyage up this most imaginary river," up which La Hontan claims to have sailed for six weeks without reaching the source. During this voyage he learned from four Mozeemlek slaves belonging to the Indians living on the river "that, at the distance of 150 leagues from the place he then was, their principal river empties itself into a salt lake of 300 leagues in circumference, the mouth of which is two leagues broad; that the lower part of that river is adorned with six noble cities, surrounded with stone cemented with fat earth; that the houses of these cities have no roofs, but are open above, like a platform, as you see them drawn on the map; that, besides the above-mentioned cities, there are above a hundred towns, great and small, round that sort of sea, upon which they navigate with such boats as you see drawn on the map," etc.

Now, this description does not, in any particular, correspond with the Great Salt Lake; and if it was told by the savages to the baron might, with as much if not far greater propriety, be considered as referring to the Pacific Ocean, with the Columbia flowing into it.

The story of La Hontan excited much speculation and received various additions in his day; and the lake finally became represented on the published English maps of as late date as 1826 (see Plate III) as being the source of two great navigable rivers flowing into the South Sea. Here it was that historians supposed the Aztecs were located before their migration to Mexico.

Father Escalante, in 1776, traveled from near Santa Fé, New Mexico, in a northwesterly direction, to the Great Colorado. After crossing it and passing to the southwest through the country near its western bank, he turned again to the southeast, recrossed the stream, and proceeded to the Gila. During his journey he probably was in the vicinity of Utah Lake. He there met with Indians who told him of a lake to the north whose waters produced a burning sensation when they touched the skin. This lake was perhaps the Great Salt Lake; and its property of making a burning sensation when applied to the skin was probably the effect of the strong solution of salt which it contains. This lake was *not* visited by Father Escalante; and that which he represents on his map, and which is copied on Humboldt's New Spain as Lake Timpanogos, was probably what is now called Lake Utah, into which a stream flows called by the Indians Timpanogos River.

* * * * * * * * *

A portion of the Great Basin system was visited by Father Font as early as 1777, near the Mojave River (which he called Rio de los Mortires). He followed its course to the place where it sinks, and then traveled east, crossing the Colorado at the Mojave valleys, and kept on as far as the Moquis villages. A copy of his map was procured in California by Captain Ord, U. S. A., and is now on file in the Topographical Bureau.

IRVING'S ASTORIA.

"*Astoria, or Anecdotes of an Enterprise beyond the Rocky Mountains. By Washington Irving. Author's revised edition, complete in one volume. New York: G. P. Putnam*—1849." It contains a reduced copy of Wilkes's map of Oregon, and is the only edition at my command.

This beautifully written book, published first, I believe, in 1836, contains an account of the voyages and journey performed by Mr. Astor's parties. One of these, under Messrs Hunt and Crook, went, in 1811 and 1812, from the Arikaree village, on the Missouri, at the mouth of Grand or "Big River," westward through the Black Hills and Big Horn Mountains to Wind River, and thence to the sources of the Snake or Lewis River, and down that stream to the Columbia.

* * * * * * * * *

MAP OF LIEUT. E. STEEN, U. S. DRAGOONS, 1835.

This map exhibits the country from the west boundary of Arkansas and Missouri to the Rocky Mountains, between the 31st and 45th parallels, on a scale of 20 miles to an inch, it shows the route of the rangers under Colonel Manny, in 1833, who made an excursion from Fort Gibson westward as far as the head of the Little River, and back, and of the routes of the dragoons under Colonel Dodge, in 1834 and 1835.

* * * * * * * * *

Capt. R. B. Marcy, U. S. A., has since explored all this section, and information concerning it can be found in his reports.

The expedition under Colonel Dodge in 1835 started from Fort Leavenworth, proceeded up the Platte and South Fork to its source, then traveled south to the Arkansas, and returned by it and the Santa Fé road to Fort Leavenworth.

* * * * * * * * *

TOPOGRAPHICAL BUREAU MAP OF THE WESTERN FRONTIER, 1837.

This is "*A map illustrating the plan of the defenses of the western and north western frontier, as proposed by Charles Gratiot, in his report of October* 31, 1837, *compiled in the United States Topographical Bureau, under the direction of Col J. J. Abert, United States Topographical Engineers, by W. Hood.*"

This map was published (Senate document No 65, second session Twenty-fifth Congress) on a scale of 50 miles to an inch. It embraces the territory of the United States from the Gulf of Mexico to the 45th parallel of north latitude, and from the Mississippi River west to near the 103d meridian.

New Orleans and St. Louis are both represented as being in longitude 90° 25′.

SURVEY OF C. DIMMOCK IN 1838.

This survey, made with chain and compass for a military road along the western borders of Arkansas and Missouri, between Fort Smith and Fort Leavenworth, is still valuable between Old Fort Scott and Fort Smith, as it has not here been replaced by the United States Land Office surveys.

TOPOGRAPHICAL BUREAU MAP OF OREGON, 1838.

The title of this is "*A map of the United States territory of Oregon west of the Rocky Mountains, exhibiting the various trading depots or forts occupied by the British Hudson Bay Company connected with the western and northwestern fur trade, compiled in the Bureau of Topographical Engineers, from the latest authorities, under the direction of Col. J. J. Abert, by Washington Hood,* 1838. *M. H. Stansbury, del.*"

This map accompanies the report of Mr. Linn, from "the select committee to which was referred a bill to authorize the President of the United

States to occupy the Oregon Territory, submitted to the Senate," which report forms Senate document 470, second session Twenty-fifth Congress.

The map is published on a scale of 25 miles to an inch, and embraces the territory of North America from the 38th to the 55th parallel west of the 102d meridian.

All of this map, between the 40th and 50th parallels, with some trifling changes, was published in Wyndham Robertson's work, entitled "Oregon, our Right and Title," etc., published in Washington, 1846.

* * * * * * * * *

MEMOIR AND MAP BY CAPTAIN HOOD, 1839.

Capt. Washington Hood, Topographical Engineers, while stationed on the Missouri frontier, compiled in 1839 a map, on a scale of 42 miles to an inch, of the country adjacent to the headwaters of the Missouri, the Yellowstone, the Salmon, the Lewis, and the Colorado, with various observations on the subject of the practicable passes or routes through the Rocky Mountains to the Pacific, "from information obtained in frequent conversations with two highly intelligent trappers, William A. Walker, of Virginia, and Mr. Coates, of Missouri, who belonged originally to Captain Bonneville's party, but subsequently continued to roam the mountains as free trappers during six consecutive years; as also that derived from others, who were connected with surveys and expeditions as far to the westward as Santa Fé and Taos."

This map is correct in its main features, but neither it nor the notes were ever published.

* * * * * * * * *

SURVEY OF THE BOUNDARY BETWEEN LOUISIANA AND TEXAS IN 1840.

The journal of the commission will be found in Senate document No. 199, second session, Twenty-seventh Congress, and is accompanied by two maps. One, on a scale of 1½ miles to an inch, gives the Sabine River; and the other, on a scale of 4 miles to an inch, represents the meridian boundary line between the Sabine and Red Rivers, the initial point being the place where the Sabine is crossed by the parallel of 32° north latitude.

The surveys on the part of the United States of the portion north of the Sabine River were made by Lieut. Col. James Kearney, Lieut. J. Edm.

Blake, and Lieut. L. Sitgreaves, Topographical Engineers; and along the Sabine River by Maj. J. D. Graham, Lieut. T. J. Lee, and Lieut. G. G. Meade, Topographical Engineers. The surveys on the part of Texas were by Messrs. P. J. Pellows, D. C. Webber, and A. B. Gray.

UNITED STATES EXPLORING EXPEDITION UNDER COMMANDER CHARLES WILKES, U. S. N.

"*Narrative of the United States Exploring Expedition during the years* 1838, 1839, 1840, 1841, *and* 1842, *by Charles Wilkes, U. S. N., commander of the expedition, member of the American Philosophical Society, etc., in five volumes, and an atlas. Philadelphia: Lea & Blanchard.*—1845." The map extends from the 40th to the 53d parallel, and from the 106th meridian to the Pacific, on a scale of about 48 miles to an inch.

This naval exploring expedition arrived in Oregon in 1841.

A party under Lieutenant Johnson started from Nisqually, crossed the Cascades near Mount Rainier, and reached the Columbia near the mouth of the Pisquose River. Crossing the Columbia they proceeded to Fort Okinikaine, thence to the mouth of the Spokane, and thence north to Fort Colville. They then turned south, visited the Mission, and continuing on struck the Kooskoosky, about forty miles below where Lewis and Clark struck it; thence they traveled to Fort Walla-Walla. From this point they returned to Nisqually by the valley of the Yakima River, crossing the Cascade Mountains at its source.

The Columbia River was surveyed as far up as Walla-Walla, and a party was dispatched up the valley of the Willamette, and thence to the sources of the Sacramento, down which they traveled to the bay of San Francisco.

KENDALL'S NARRATIVE—SANTA FÉ EXPEDITION, 1841.

"*Narrative of the Texan Santa Fé Expedition, comprising a description of a tour through Texas, and across the great southwestern prairies, the Comanche and Caygua hunting grounds, with an account of the sufferings from want of food, losses from hostile Indians, and final capture of the Texans, and their march as prisoners to the city of Mexico, with illustrations and a map. By George Wilkins Kendall; in two volumes. New York: Harper & Brother, 82 Cliff street.*—1844." The map is on a scale of 45 miles to an inch, bounded on the north by the 38th parallel, on the east by the 91st meridian, on the south by the 19th parallel, and on the west by the 103d meridian.

This expedition left Austin, the capital of Texas, on the 21st of June, 1841. Mr. Kendall, the author of the narrative, accompanied the expedition from motives of mere curiosity and a desire of travel, being fully impressed with the idea that it was entirely a commercial expedition, and not one that would render null his passport received from the Mexican consul at New Orleans. The entire military force consisted of six companies, averaging forty men each. There was a large train of wagons containing the property of merchants who accompanied the expedition to trade at Santa Fé. The whole party was under the command of General McLeod. * * * This expedition, it is thought, may have been the first to visit the sources of Red River, but it furnished no topographical information which could be accurately represented upon a map.

I. N. NICOLLET'S EXPLORATIONS, 1836 TO 1840.

This report and map was printed by the Senate, document No 237, Twenty-sixth Congress, second session; the title being "*Report intended to illustrate a map of the Hydrographical Basin of the Upper Mississippi River, made by I. N. Nicollet while in employ under the Bureau of the Corps of Topographical Engineers. February* 16, 1841.—*Ordered to be printed, and* 200 *additional copies for the use of the Senate. Washington: Blair & Rives, printers.*— 1843." The map accompanying this document is on a scale of 1 to 1,200,000. "Reduced and compiled, under the direction of Col. J. J. Abert, in the Bureau of Topographical Engineers, by Lieut. W. H. Emory, from the map published in 1842, and from other authorities in 1843."

The map published in 1842 was on a scale of 1 to 600,000, and bore the title of "Map of the Hydrographical Basin of the Upper Mississippi River, from astronomical and barometrical observations, surveys, and information, by I. N. Nicollet, made in the years 1836, 1837, 1838, 1839, and 1840; assisted in 1838, 1839, and 1840, by Lieut. J. C. Fremont, of the Corps of Topographical Engineers, and authorized by the War Department." Both of these maps comprised the valley of the Mississippi and country adjacent, from the parallel of 38° to 48° 30′ north, between the

89th and 101st meridians west from Greenwich, and contained, in addition to the results of Mr. Nicollet's own observations and determinations, a compilation of nearly all previous authentic explorations within these limits.

Mr. Nicollet says in his introduction that "having come to this country for the purpose of making a scientific tour, and with a view of contributing to the progressive increase of knowledge in the physical geography of North America, I determined, after having explored the Alleghany range in its various extension through the Southern States, and having ascended the Red River, Arkansas River, and to a long distance the Missouri River, to undertake the full exploration of the Mississippi River from its mouth to its very sources. During the five years that I was engaged in these excursions I took occasion to make numerous observations calculated to lay the foundation of the astronomical and physical geography of a large extent of country, and more especially of the great and interesting region between the Falls of St. Anthony and the sources of the Mississippi. With these labors I connected, also, the study of the customs, habits, manners, and languages of the several Indian nations that occupy this vast region of country. At the expiration of this long (and I found it an arduous) journey, I returned to Baltimore among my good friends of St. Mary's College, where I soon received a flattering invitation from the War Department and Topographical Bureau to repair to Washington. The result of my travels was made known to these departments, upon which they thought proper to intrust me with the command of an expedition to enable me to complete to the greatest advantage a scheme which I had already projected on my visit to the far west, namely, the construction of a geographical and topographical map of the country explored." This was in the spring of 1838.

The years 1838 and 1839 were spent in explorations in Minnesota, assisted by Lieutenant Fremont. Mr. Nicollet had nearly completed the map, and written a portion of his report, when death put an end to his labors before he was enabled to finish it, or to revise what had been previously written. The report does not, therefore, do justice to the surveys, and it is impossible to specify the routes he pursued except for the years of 1836, 1838, and 1839, and somewhat imperfectly for these, even though I have consulted his original notes in the Topographical Bureau. The reconnaissances of these years are the ones which, topographically, have at present the greatest value, as nearly all the others made by him have since been replaced by more accurate surveys under the General Land Office. Wherever Mr. Nicollet went he was indefatigable in the use of the telescope for observing occultations and eclipses, and of the sextant, with which he was very skillful; with these, a pocket chronometer, artificial horizon of mercury, and barometer, he obtained results possessing remarkable accuracy for the means employed.

* * * * * * * * *

Mr. Nicollet was the first explorer who made much use of the barometer for obtaining the elevation of our great interior country above the sea. An abstract of the methods and principles by which he was governed in his explorations is given in his report, and have served as a guide to many subsequent explorers. His map was one of the greatest contributions ever made to American geography.

EXPLORATION OF LIEUT. J. C. FREMONT, TOPOGRAPHICAL ENGINEERS IN 1842.

The report of this expedition is S. Doc. No. 243, Twenty-seventh Congress, third session, and is entitled "*An Exploration of the Country lying between the Missouri River and the Rocky Mountains, on the line of the Kansas and Great Platte Rivers.*" It is illustrated by a map on a scale of 1 to 1,000,000 (nearly 16 miles to an inch), embracing the country from the forks of the Platte to the South Pass, between the forty-third and forty-fifth parallels.

Lieutenant Fremont's party consisted of about twenty-five persons, all mounted except eight who drove the carts carrying their stores. He was assisted by the since well-known topographer, Mr. Charles Preuss, and provided with chronometers, sextant, artificial horizon, telescope for observing occultations, and a barometer.

* * * * * * * * *

Lieutenant Fremont made, throughout this journey, astronomical observations whenever circumstances permitted. His barometer was broken among the Wind River Mountains.

EXPLORATION BY CAPT. N. BOONE, UNITED STATES DRAGOONS, 1843.

The manuscript copy of this map, report, and journal I obtained from the files of the Adjutant-General's Office, and it is exceedingly interesting as containing an account of a country almost unknown. The map is on a scale of 20 miles to an inch. It exhibits the country between the Arkansas and Canadian Rivers as far west as the 100th meridian. It contains no meridians or parallels, as no astronomical observations were made. Captain Boone says: "It is a map or rough sketch of the country, with the water courses running through it. The courses and distances are all estimated from point to point direct, and not according to the distance actually traveled during each day, as it was found impossible to note the courses and distances of the windings made during each day's march." This report is accompanied by a minute journal, covering fifty-five pages of letter paper, closely written, and is referred to by General Taylor, in transmitting it, as containing "much valuable and curious information, particularly in relation to the salt region on the Red Fork of the Arkansas." The map and report have never been printed.*

* * * * * * * * *

EXPEDITION OF CAPT. J. ALLEN TO SOURCE OF DES MOINES RIVER, ETC., 1843.

The report and journal of this expedition form printed House Doc. No. 168, 1st session 29th Congress. No map was printed with this report. Captain Allen submitted a map of his route with it, concerning which he makes the following remarks: "For the actual route passed over I must refer to the accompanying map, which will show it more fully and completely than it could be made by any other description. The map was constructed by Lieutenant Potter, under my immediate direction, and the care of taking minute notes on the way and the pains taken during its projection by that officer to secure all the information within its reach, will warrant me in saying that it gives a very correct delineation of the country passed over, as also the topography of other parts of this territory, perhaps the most accurate on record." The Adjutant-General (R. Jones), in his letter

* Though I am not aware that this map was ever published by the Government, the principal topographical information which it contained was embraced in a map published by the Messrs. Harper, in 1847, entitled "Harper's Cereographic Map of the United States. By Samuel Breese, A. M."

transmitting this report to Secretary Marcy, says: "Instead of the map of the route accompanying the report, I submit the more perfect map of the Upper Mississippi by Nicollet (from which Captain Allen's sketch no doubt was taken), upon which the route of the troops under his command has been carefully traced in the Topographical Bureau. Should it be determined to publish Captain Allen's route, Colonel Abert is of opinion it would be best to use the plate prepared for Nicollet's map. This would be not only much less expensive, but would probably improve the original map, which is one of much value."

* * * * * * * * *

The expedition under Captain Allen consisted of J. S. Griffin, assistant surveyor; First Lieut. P. Calhoun, 2d dragoons; Second Lieut. P. Noble, 1st dragoons; Second Lieutenant Potter, 1st infantry, and 52 soldiers. Captain Allen was supplied "with a small imperfect sextant," and no chronometer.

* * * * * * * * *

A portion of this route along the Big Sioux has not been reconnoitered since.

TOPOGRAPHICAL BUREAU MAP OF TEXAS, 1844.

The title of this is "*Map of Texas and the countries adjacent, compiled in the Bureau of the Corps of Topographical Engineers, from the best authorities, for the State Department, under the direction of Col. J. J. Abert, chief of the corps, by W. H. Emory, 1st lieutenant Topographical Engineers, War Department*, 1844," on a scale of about 70 miles to an inch.

This gave most of the information extant, at the date of compilation, respecting the country comprised between the Gulf of Mexico and the Mississippi River on the east to the Pacific Ocean on the west, between the twenty-second and forty-second parallels of north latitude. No mountains are indicated, except those inclosing the Rio Grande Valley. A lake, in the approximate position of the Great Salt Lake, is represented, and another one receiving the waters of Ogden's or Mary's River. There are no names on the lakes and rivers represented in these interior basins; but this compilation shows that the existence of these basins and lakes was, at that time, admitted as an established fact in the Topographical Bureau.

GREGG'S COMMERCE OF THE PRAIRIES, 1844.

The title page of this book is "*Commerce of the Prairies, or the Journal of a Santa Fé Trader, during eight expeditions across the Great Western Prairies, and a residence of nearly nine years in Northern Mexico, illustrated with maps and engravings. By Josiah Gregg, in two volumes. New York: Henry G. Langley*, 8 *Astor House.*—1844."

The map which accompanies the book is on a scale of 57 miles to an inch, and embraces the country from the west boundary of Missouri, Arkansas, and Louisiana, to the 108th meridian. It is based on the map of Humboldt's New Spain, that of Major Long's first expedition, and that of the road survey of J. C. Brown along the Santa Fé trail, with such corrections and additions as Mr. Gregg's own observations suggested. It was one of the most useful maps of this region at that day. The book is an interesting and valuable description of all the then known portions of New Mexico, and of the country along the routes between Fort Leavenworth and Santa Fé, and between Santa Fé and Fort Smith.

CHAPTER III.

EXPLORATIONS FROM A. D. 1843 TO A. D. 1852.

Capt. J. C. Fremont, T. E., exploration, 1843–'44.—Capt. J. C. Fremont, exploration in 1845–'46.—Lieut. J. W. Abert, T. E., reconnaissance, 1845.—Lieut. W. B. Franklin, T. E., reconnaissance, 1845.—Bvt. Maj. W. H. Emory, T. E., reconnaissance, 1846–'47.—Lieut. J. W. Abert, T. E., reconnaissance, 1846–'47.—Lieut. Col. P. St. George Cooke, U. S. A., expedition, 1846–'47.—A. Wislizenus, M. D., examination, 1846–'47.—Bvt. Capt. W. H. Warner, T. E., reconnaissance, 1847 to 1849.—Lieut. G. H. Derby, T. E., reconnaissance, 1849.—Lieut. J. D. Webster, T. E., survey mouth of Rio Grande, 1847.—Lieut. J. H. Simpson, T. E., reconnaissance along the Canadian River, 1849.—Lieut. J. H. Simpson, T. E., reconnaissance Navajo country, 1849.—Capt. R. B. Marcy, U. S. A., expedition, 1849.—Capt. H. Stansbury, T. E., expedition to Great Salt Lake, 1849–'50.—March of Rifle Regiment to Oregon, 1849.—Major Wood, U. S. Infantry, and Captain Pope T. E., expedition to Red River, 1849.—Brevet Lieutenant-Colonel Johnson, T. E., reconnaissances in Texas, 1849 to 1851.—Togographical Bureau map of territory of the United States west of the Mississippi, 1850.—R. H. Kern, C. E., reconnaissance on the Pecos River, 1850.—Lieut. J. G. Parke, T. E.. Map of New Mexico, 1851.—Captain Sitgreaves, T. E., and Lieutenant Woodruff, T. E., boundary of Creek country, 1850–'51.—Captain Sitgreaves, T. E., expedition to Zuñi and Colorado Rivers, 1851.—Lieut. G. H. Derby, T. E., reconnaissance mouth of Colorado River, 1851.—Lieut. I. C. Woodruff, T. E., reconnaissance, 1852.—Capt. R. B. Marcy, U. S. A., expedition to sources of Red River.

CAPT. J. C. FREMONT'S SECOND EXPLORATION, 1843 AND 1844.

The title of the printed report is, "*Report of the Exploring Expedition to the Rocky Mountains in the year* 1842, *and to Oregon and North California in the years* 1843–'44. *By Brevet Captain J. C. Fremont, of the Topographical Engineers, under the orders of Colonel J. J. Abert, chief of the Topographical Bureau; printed by order of the Senate of the United States. Washington: Gales & Seaton, printers.*—1845." Senate Doc. No. 174, Twenty-eighth Congress, second session.

This book contains a reprint of the report of the exploration in 1842, and the accompanying map exhibits the routes followed during that expedition, as well as during the years 1843 and 1844. The longitudes given on this map and in this report (pp. 100 and 101) differ materially from those of the first report and map; the reason for the change being explained on page

321. The new map is on a scale of 32 miles to an inch, and is "strictly confined to what was seen and to what was necessary to show the face and character of the country." It was drawn by Charles Preuss, whose skill in sketching topography in the field and in representing it on the map has probably never been surpassed in this country. The map, which in most respects may serve for a model, exhibits also a profile, made from barometrical observations, drawn with a horizontal scale of 1 to 3,000,000, or 47.35 miles to an inch, and a vertical scale about thirty times greater, or 8,500 feet to the inch.

A "topographical map of the road from Missouri to Oregon, commencing at the mouth of the Kansas, in the Missouri River, and ending at the mouth of the Walla-Walla, in the Columbia, in seven sections, from the field notes and journal of Capt. J. C. Fremont,* and from sketches and notes made on the ground by his assistant, Charles Preuss, compiled by Charles Preuss in 1846, by order of the Senate of the United States," forms a part of House Committee Report No. 145, second session Thirtieth Congress. Its scale is 10 miles to the inch. It contains detailed topog raphy and full notes of the route pursued by Captain Fremont (between the points named) in 1843, and is an excellent map for travelers. It is not, however, accurately constructed, according to the list of geographical positions given in Captain Fremont's report, and this should be borne in mind by compilers.

Throughout this lengthened exploration in the mountains and across the plains Lieutenant Fremont made many astronomical observations, determining longitude by observing occultations and eclipses with a telescope and by chronometric differences, and latitudes by observing with sextants and artificial horizons. After the investigations necessary in compiling the map which accompanies this memoir, I may be permitted to add my testimony to the truth of Captain Fremont's assertion in his notice to the reader at the beginning of his report, "that the correctness of the longitudes and latitudes may well be relied upon." They contain only such errors of longitude as are inherent to results obtained from observations made with the

* Fremont did not receive his promotion to the rank of brevet captain until the termination of his second expedition.

instruments employed. A mercurial barometer was carried across the continent on the road to Oregon as far as the Blue Mountains, where it was broken. The subsequent elevations on the route were determined by the temperature of boiling water.

The second expedition under Lieutenant Fremont left the town of Kansas on the 29th of May, 1843. The party consisted of twenty-nine men, all mounted, their stores, etc., being carried in twelve carts. He was assisted by Mr. Charles Preuss as topographer, Mr. Thomas Fitzpatrick as guide, and Mr. Theodore Talbot.

* * * * * * * * *

EXPLORATIONS OF CAPT. J. C. FREMONT, 1845-'46.

A portion of the results of this was published by the United States Senate, first session Thirtieth Congress, Mis. Doc. No. 148, entitled: "*Geographical Memoir upon Upper California, in illustration of his Map of Oregon and California, by John C. Fremont, addressed to the Senate of the United States. Washington: Wendell & Van Benthuysen, printers.*" This is accompanied by a map, drawn by Charles Preuss, on a scale of 1 to 3,000,000, embracing all the country between the 104th meridian and the Pacific Ocean, and between the 32d and 50th parallels of north latitude. It was compiled from the surveys of Captain Fremont and "other authorities," and was at the time of its publication (1848) the most accurate map of that region extant.

A great deal of information in regard to this expedition, not contained in the memoir, has been published in the newspapers and in various pamphlets.

There are probably many reasons why a complete account of this third expedition, as well as Colonel Fremont's subsequent ones, has never been published; but this desideratum will probably be soon supplied.*

Captain Fremont started upon this exploration better provided than on his previous ones. He had under his command Lieuts. J. W. Abert and William G. Peck, Topographical Engineers, and was aided by Mr. Charles Preuss and Mr. E. M. Kern, as topographers and artists. He was provided with a portable astronomical transit instrument, sextants, chronometers, and

* In press, Col. J. C. Fremont's Explorations, prepared by the author, and embracing all his expeditions. Childs & Peterson, publishers, No. 602, Arch street, Philadelphia.

barometers. No map or account has been published of his route east of Bent's Fort, but I believe it is nearly that by which he returned in 1844 He left the frontier of Missouri in May, and on arriving at Bent's Fort detached Lieutenants Abert and Peck to explore the sources of the Canadian River, and then to return to the States.

* * * * * * * * *

It is probable that the war with Mexico and the troubles between Americans and Mexicans in California, which began prior thereto, put a stop to his explorations beyond what could be obtained by ordinary observations in traveling from point to point during a period of violent hostilities.

During this expedition Captain Fremont obtained the longitude of the mouth of Fontaine qui Bouit; of the camp at Great Salt Lake; of Lassen's farm, on Deer Creek; and of the Three Buttes, in Sacramento Valley. The first two results have never been tested by any other observer with a good instrument, but are generally received as correct. The other two have been tested by land-office surveys, and by Lieutenant Williamson's second Pacific railroad survey, connecting with the Coast Survey longitude of San Francisco. Both tests indicate that his results were close approximations to accuracy. These four determinations of Captain Fremont detected some errors in his previous map, amounting in one instance to 15′ in longitude, and which furnished the means for correcting them.

A note on Captain Fremont's map of routes of 1843–'44 gives the following descriptive information: "The Great Basin: Diameter 11° of latitude, 10° of longitude; elevation above the sea between 4,000 and 5,000 feet; surrounded by lofty mountains; contents almost unknown, but believed to be filled with rivers and lakes which have no communication with the sea, deserts and oases which have never been explored, and savage tribes which no traveler has seen or described." This note, with the map and accompanying report, have conveyed the idea that this basin is encircled by a ridge of mountains forming a *rim*. This was so represented on the map compiled by Mr. Preuss in 1848, and gave rise to the belief in the existence of two long ridges running east and west, lying on the north and south of the basin, which, however, by that time had been much reduced in extent

MARCH OF AN ARMY DIVISION FROM SAN ANTONIO DE BEXAR, TEXAS, TO SALTILLO, MEXICO, 1846.

An account of this march, from a topographical stand-point (accompanied by astronomical determinations of latitude and longitude), by Capt. George W. Hughes, Corps of Topographical Engineers, forms Senate Mis. Doc. No. 32, Thirty-first Congress, first session.

The division was under the command of Brig. Gen. John E. Wool. The topographical party preceded the troops, leaving San Antonio on September 23, 1846, and consisted of the following persons, viz: George W. Hughes, captain, Topographical Engineers; L. Sitgreaves, first lieutenant, Topographical Engineers; W. B. Franklin, second lieutenant, Topographical Engineers; F. T. Bryan, brevet second lieutenant, Topographical Engineers; Dan Drake Henrie, interpreter; James Dunn, hunter and guide; two wagoners, four laborers, and two private servants.

The distance from San Antonio to the west bank of the Rio Grande over the route traversed was 164 miles; that from the Rio Grande to Santa Rosa, 209 miles; from Santa Rosa to Monclova, 72 miles; and from Monclova to Parras, 181 miles. From Monclova reconnaissances were made to Quatro Cienegas and to Saltillo and beyond in several directions via Monterey.

During a long halt at Monclova the topographical engineers were engaged in making surveys of the surrounding country and astronomical observations, reconnaissances for long distances from the camp in different directions, making computations, plotting field-notes, and reducing observations. Immediately prior to the above march, Lieutenant Franklin had made a reconnaissance of the country from La Vaca to San Antonio, Texas. The topographical party was provided with the necessary instruments for the determination of geographical positions by latitude and longitude. The computed latitudes of forty-one stations, determined by observations with the sextant on Polaris, are given, and also eight longitudes. The latter were determined (with the exception of that of one point by lunar distances) by observations on the eclipses of Jupiter and satellites. A general topographical map (scale 5 inches to 1 mile) embracing all the routes reconnoitered accompanies the above Executive document, which shows also the trace of a route from Matamoras on the Rio Grande northward to San Antonio.

RECONNAISSANCE BY LIEUT. JAMES W. ABERT, TOPOGRAPHICAL ENGINEERS, 1845.

This report forms Senate Doc. No. 438, Twenty-ninth Congress, first session, and is accompanied by a map on a scale of about 32 miles to an inch, embracing the country from the 94th meridian to the Rocky Mountains, and between the Platte River and the 35th parallel.

Lieut. J. W. Abert, assisted by Lieut. William G. Peck, Topographical Engineers, having been detached at Bent's Fort by Captain Fremont, in 1845, with instructions from him to explore the Purgatory Creek, the Canadian and False Washita Rivers, left that fort on the Arkansas on the 15th of August, 1845, with a party of thirty men, four wagons, and sixty-three horses and mules. They were supplied with a chronometer and sextant.

* * * * * * * * *

RECONNAISSANCE BY LIEUT. W. B. FRANKLIN, TOPOGRAPHICAL ENGINEERS, 1845.

An abstract of Lieutenant Franklin's journal, and a reduced copy of his map, on a scale of 75 miles to an inch, were published in House Ex. Doc. No. 2, first session Twenty-ninth Congress. The title of the map is: "Map of the Route pursued by the late Expedition under the command of Col. S. W. Kearney, United States 1st Dragoons, by W. B. Franklin, Lieutenant Topographical Engineers, attached to the expedition, 1845."

The original map is on a scale of 32 miles to an inch. The new information which it contained was published with Lieutenant Abert's map of his exploration, made in 1845, wherein credit is given to Lieutenant Franklin for the material taken from his map.

The expedition was under command of Col. S. W. Kearney, United States 1st Dragoons.

* * * * * * * * *

An account of the expedition is given in Lieut. Col. P. St. G. Cooke's late book of "Scenes and Adventures in the Army."

RECONNAISSANCE OF MAJOR WM. H. EMORY, TOPOGRAPHICAL ENGINEERS, 1846-'47.

The report forms a part of Senate Ex. Doc. No. 7, first session of Thirtieth Congress, and is entitled: "*Notes of a Military Reconnaissance from Fort Leavenworth, in Missouri, to San Diego, in California, including parts of the Arkansas, Del Norte, and Gila Rivers. By Wm. H. Emory, Brevet Major*

Topographical Engineers, made in 1846–'47, *with the advanced guard of the 'Army of the West.' Washington: Wendell and Van Benthuysen, printers.*— 1848."*

It is accompanied by a map, on a scale of about 24 miles to an inch, exhibiting only that portion of the country and the routes that came under the observation of the parties. The map contains also a barometrical profile of the route across the continent, on a horizontal scale of about 24 miles to an inch, and a vertical scale of about 8,200 feet to an inch, the vertical scale being about 15 times the horizontal. A report by Lieutenant Abert of the portions of the route between Fort Leavenworth and Bent's Fort is also appended Major Emory (then a first lieutenant of Topographical Engineers) was assisted by Lieut. W. H. Warner, Topographical Engineers, Lieut. James W. Abert, Topographical Engineers, Lieut. Wm. G. Peck, Topographical Engineers, Mr. J. M. Stanley, and Mr. Norman Bestor. His instruments were two box chronometers, two 8½-inch sextants, and one syphon barometer, which was the first mercurial barometer ever carried overland to the Pacific unbroken.

* * * * * * * * *

Lieutenants Abert and Peck did not accompany Lieutenant Emory beyond Santa Fé, instructions being given them to make certain explorations in the neighboring region.

* * * * * * * * *

RECONNAISSANCE BY LIEUTENANTS ABERT AND PECK, 1846-'47.

The results of these explorations are given by Lieutenant Abert's report, which forms a part of House Ex. Doc. No. 41, first session Thirtieth Congress. It is accompanied by a map, on a scale of 10 miles to an inch, exhibiting the portion of New Mexico between latitude 33° 30′ and 37°, and from the meridian of 104° 30′ to 108°. This map was also reduced and republished on Lieutenant Emory's map already described.

Lieutenants Abert and Peck commenced, on the 8th of October, the examination intrusted to them by Lieutenant Emory, after having previously visited certain mines. It does not appear that they were provided

*It was also published by the House of Representatives, House Ex. Doc. No. 41, first session, Thirtieth Congress.

with any instruments for making astronomical observations, and the latitudes and longitudes used were those determined by Lieutenant Emory.

* * * * * * * * *

ROUTE OF COL. P. ST. G. COOKE, 1846-'47.

This officer's report forms a part of House Executive Document No. 41, first session Thirtieth Congress, and is accompanied by a map of his route, on a scale of 12 miles to an inch; his route is also represented on Emory's map.

Colonel Cooke was sent by General Kearny from La Joya to Santa Fé, to take command of the "Mormon battalion," en route for California. Proceeding to that place, he assumed command, and on the 19th October, 1846, led the battalion, consisting of about four hundred men, each company having three mule wagons, down the Rio Grande to a point about three or four miles above San Diego, on that river.

* * * * * * * * *

EXAMINATIONS BY A. WISLIZENUS, M. D., 1846-'47.

The account and results of this form Senate Mis. Doc. No. 26, first session Thirtieth Congress, and are entitled: "*Memoir of a tour to Northern Mexico, connected with Colonel Doniphan's Expedition, in* 1846 *and* 1847. *By A. Wislizenus, M. D., with a scientific appendix and three maps. Washington: Tippin & Streeper, printers.*—1848." These maps are, 1st, a map of the country from the 25th to the 39th parallel, between the 94th and 107th meridians, on a scale of 50 miles to an inch, exhibiting the topography of the route traveled over; 2d, a map or geological sketch of the same country, on a scale of 80 miles to an inch; and 3d, a barometrical profile of the route, on a horizontal scale of 36 miles to an inch and a vertical scale of 2,000 feet to the inch, the vertical scale being 95 times the horizontal.

Dr. Wislizenus undertook this scientific tour at his private expense. Leaving St. Louis in the spring of 1846, he followed the Santa Fé road, by the Cimarron route, to Santa Fé. Thence he went down the Rio Grande Valley to El Paso and Chihuahua. Here the derangement which the Mexican war produced kept him for six months "in a very passive condition." On Colonel Doniphan's arrival in that neighborhood he accepted a situation in the medical department of the Army, and returned with the troops, by way of Monterey, to the States.

EXPLORATION OF BVT. CAPT. W. H. WARNER, TOPOGRAPHICAL ENGINEERS, 1847 to 1849.

Very little of the results of the exploration of Brevet Captain Warner, after he was relieved from duty with Major Emory, have been published. He made extensive examination of routes along the Pacific and in the Coast Mountains, from San Diego to San Francisco, and had nearly completed his map of that then unknown section of country when he was directed to make the exploration in the Sierra Nevada, on which he lost his life in an Indian ambuscade. His notes and papers passed into the possession of his assistant, Lieutenant Williamson, Topographical Engineers, and were thus available to him in his examinations made in 1853–'54, in connection with a route for a railroad to the Pacific.

The only portion of Captain Warner's explorations, to my knowledge, of which a map and report were published, was that of his last expedition. This was prepared by Lieutenant Williamson, and forms a portion of Senate Ex. Doc. No. 47, first session Thirty-first Congress. The map of the route is on a scale of 15 miles to an inch. * * * In about latitude 42° Captain Warner was surprised on the march by an ambush of Pit River Indians, and he and several of his party were killed. This rendered the further prosecution of the reconnaissance impossible, and Lieutenant Williamson returned to Benicia. Captain Warner's note-books were saved, and from them a sketch of his route, with a report, was made by Lieutenant Williamson.

GEOLOGICAL EXPLORATIONS IN THE LAKE SUPERIOR REGION LAND DISTRICT, BY J. W. FOSTER AND J. D. WHITNEY, 1847 TO 1849.

These explorations to obtain a knowledge of the physical geography, climate, and geology of the copper and iron regions bordering on Lake Superior were made by Messrs. Foster and Whitney in or about the years 1848, 1849, and 1850. It would appear that the U. S. Land Office surveys were the basis upon which the work proper of this survey was compiled. Messrs. Foster and Whitney were in charge of the survey a little more than two years, and were aided by Messrs. James Hall, of New York, E. Desor, of Massachusetts, and Charles Whittlesey, of Ohio; also for a part of the time by Mr. S. W. Hill, of Michigan, and Mr. John Burt, for many years a surveyor in that region, who placed his notes at their disposal.

The report is addressed to Hon. Justin Butterfield, Commissioner of the Land Office. It is in two parts.

Part I, made in 1850 and published in 1851, gives a historical sketch of the explorations, a description of the physical geography and climate, and so much of the geology as was necessary to the full elucidation of the copper-bearing rocks and their relation to the sedimentary formations.

Part II forms Senate Ex. Doc. No. 4, special session, March, 1851, and has title, "The Iron Regions," together with the general geology; ordered to be printed March 13, 1851. Printed by A. Boyd Hamilton, Washington, 1851. In this a detailed and systematic description, as far as the materials would permit, is made of the geology of the whole of the Lake Superior region, commencing with the bed formations and ascending to those which are now in process of accumulation.

The report was accompanied with sections, illustrations, and a general map on which the range and extent of the general systems of rock are defined. The observations were extended over an area of little less than 100,000 square miles.

Chapter IX, on Magnetic Variations, Comparison of Terrestrial and Astronomical Monuments, by Charles Whittlesey, General Warren states, "will have a permanent geographical interest and value as long as the United States land surveys form the basis of our maps."

GEOLOGICAL EXAMINATION OF WISCONSIN, IOWA, AND MINNESOTA, AND PORTIONS OF NEBRASKA, BY DAVID DALE OWEN.

The published results of this investigation appear in the form of a "*Report of a Geological Survey of Wisconsin, Iowa, and Minnesota, and incidentally of a portion of Nebraska Territory, made under instructions from the U. S. Treasury Department by David Dale Owen, U. S. Geologist. Philadelphia: Lippincott, Grambo & Co.*—1852." (1 vol., 4°, pp 638.)

This work made large additions to geographical as well as geological information. The final report made to Hon. J. Butterfield, Commissioner of the Land Office, embraces in a connected and revised form the substance of all the preliminary reports made from time to time and of the annual reports for 1848, 1849, together with a full statement of the result of the last year's operations. It is accompanied by condensed reports of the assistant geologist and of the heads of sub-corps, which contain detailed distributions of the districts assigned to each, together with generalizations deduced therefrom. The names of the following gentlemen are acknowledged: J. G. Norwood, assistant geologist; J. Evans, B. F. Shumard, B. C. Macy, C. Whittlesey, A. Litton, and R. Owen, heads of sub-corps; G. Warren, H. Pratten, F. B. Meek, and J. Beal, sub-assistants.

Accompanying the report is a general map, 1 to 1,200,000, on which the different geological formations are represented by distinct colors. It includes latitude 38° to 49°, longitude 89° 30′ to 96° 30′.

The report contains many illustrations in scenery, sections, diagrams, plates of fossils, and detail maps. Among the latter may be enumerated a map of the north shore of Lake Superior; of the Mississippi from the mouth of the Wisconsin River to the Falls of St. Anthony; of the Wisconsin River from the mouth up to Whitney's Rapids; of the Missouri River from its mouth to the Big Sioux River, in two sheets; of the Des Moines River from its mouth up to Lizard Fork, in two sheets. These maps of rivers exhibit sections showing the geological formations of the bluffs. There is also a map of the Bad Lands, which is imperfect in its representation.

A party under Dr. Evans examined the Missouri River in 1849 as high up as Fort Berthold, the Fox Hills north of the Cheyenne River, and the Bad Lands on the White River.

A party under Dr. Shumard ascended the Minnesota River as far as the mouth of Red Wood River, a tiny stream. Dr. Owen ascended the Mississippi as high as Crow Wing; thence by that river and Otter Fort River he passed into the valley of the Red River of the North, and along it to Fort Garry in the British Provinces.

Many barometrical observations were made and altitudes deduced.

RECONNAISSANCE IN CALIFORNIA BY LIEUT. G. H. DERBY, TOPOGRAPHICAL ENGINEERS, 1849.

A report of certain of these examinations forms a part of Senate Ex. Doc. No 47, first session, Thirty-first Congress, and is accompanied by a map of the Sacramento Valley from the American River to Butte Creek, surveyed and drawn by order of General Riley, commanding Tenth Military Department, by Lieutenant Derby, Topographical Engineers, September and October, 1849, on a scale of 10 miles to an inch.

SURVEY OF THE MOUTH OF RIO GRANDE, BY LIEUT. J. D. WEBSTER, TOPOGRAPHICAL ENGINEERS, 1847.

The report of this forms Senate Ex. Doc. No. 65, first session Thirty-first Congress. The map is on a scale of an inch to a mile and exhibits the windings of the river from Matamoras to its mouth.

SURVEY OF A ROAD FROM FORT SMITH TO SANTA FÉ, BY LIEUT. J. H. SIMPSON, TOPOGRAPHICAL ENGINEERS, 1849.

The report of this survey forms Senate Ex. Doc. No. 12, first session Thirty-first Congress, and is accompanied by a map of the route, in four sheets, on a scale of one inch to 10 miles. The survey was made with chain and compass, checked by astronomical observations made with a sextant and chronometer.

* * * * * * * * *

RECONNAISSANCE IN THE NAVAJO COUNTRY, BY LIEUT. J. H. SIMPSON, TOPOGRAPHICAL ENGINEERS, 1849.

Lieutenant Simpson's report of this expedition forms part of Senate Ex. Doc. No. 64, first session, Thirty-first Congress, and is accompanied by a map of the route pursued, on a scale of an inch to 10 miles.*

This expedition, the object of which was the chastisement of the Navajo Indians, was under the command of Bvt. Lieut. Col. J. M. Washington. Lieutenant Simpson was assisted in his duties by Messrs. E. M. Kern and R. H. Kern, and was provided with a sextant and chronometer for astronomical observations. The whole command left Santa Fé on the 16th August, 1849.

* * * * * * * * *

* This report is also published as part of House Ex. Doc. No. 45, Thirty-first Congress, first session.

EXPEDITION OF CAPT. R. B. MARCY, FIFTH INFANTRY, 1849.

The report of Captain Marcy forms Senate Ex. Doc. No. 12, first session Thirty-first Congress,* and is accompanied by a map drawn on a scale of an inch to 36 miles, embracing the country from the Arkansas River south to the 31st parallel, between the 94th and 108th meridians. Captain Marcy went from Fort Smith to Santa Fé over the route surveyed by Lieutenant Simpson, Topographical Engineers. Of the remainder of his journey he prepared a map from notes taken by his command. He was not supplied with instruments for astronomical observations; his distances were measured with an odometer.

* * * * * * * * *

EXPEDITION TO GREAT SALT LAKE, BY CAPT. H. STANSBURY, TOPOGRAPHICAL ENGINEERS, 1849-'50.

The report of this expedition forms Senate Ex. Doc. No. 3, special session, March, 1851, and is entitled: "*Exploration and Survey of the Valley of the Great Salt Lake of Utah, including a reconnaissance of a New Route through the Rocky Mountains. By Howard Stansbury, Captain Corps of Topographical Engineers, United States Army. Philadelphia: Lippincott, Grambo & Co.*—1852." It is accompanied by a map of the routes from the Missouri River to the Great Salt Lake, on a scale of 1 to 1,000,000 (about an inch to 16 miles), and by another of the Great Salt Lake and vicinity, on a scale of 1 to 240,000 (about 4 miles to an inch).

* * * * * * * * *

MARCH OF RIFLE REGIMENT TO OREGON, 1849.

An account of this march by Maj. Osborne Cross, A. Q. M., forms an appendix to the Quartermaster-General's report to the Secretary of War. It is printed in House Ex. Doc No. 1, second session Thirty-first Congress.

This regiment, under Colonel Loring, marched from Fort Leavenworth to the Columbia River, with wagons.

* * * * * * * * *

EXPEDITION TO THE RED RIVER OF THE NORTH, 1849.

The report of the commander of this expedition, Bvt. Maj. S. Woods, Sixth Infantry, U. S. Army, forms House Ex. Doc. No. 51, first session Thirty-first Congress. That of Capt. John Pope, Topographical Engineers,

---

* This report appears also as part of House Ex. Doc. No. 45, Thirty-first Congress, first session.

who was attached to the command, is to be found in Senate Ex. Doc. No. 42, first session Thirty-first Congress, and is accompanied by a map of the route, on a scale of an inch to 20 miles, based on the map of the Hydrographical Basin of the Upper Mississippi, by Mr. Nicollet, most of which latter map is here repeated. On the outward journey, Captain Pope measured the road with an odometer, took courses with a compass, and made observations for latitude with a sextant.

* * * * * * * * *

RECONNAISSANCES IN TEXAS, BY BVT. LIEUT. COL. J. E. JOHNSTON, LIEUTS. M. L. SMITH, WILLIAM F. SMITH, F. T. BRYAN, AND N. MICHLER, TOPOGRAPHICAL ENGINEERS, AND LIEUT. H. C. WHITING, ENGINEERS, IN THE YEARS 1849 TO 1851.

No reports have as yet been published giving the whole extent of the explorations made in Texas by the above-mentioned officers. The following notice of such data as have come to my knowledge will therefore be the more acceptable. The reports of explorations that have been published form part of the Senate Ex. Doc. No. 64, first session Thirty-first Congress. The report of Capt. S. G. French, A. Q. M., of the southern route from San Antonio to El Paso, forms also a part of this document, which is accompanied by a map of the routes described, on a scale of an inch to 20 miles.

Lieut. William F. Smith, in February, 1849, started to explore a road from San Antonio to El Paso.

* * * * * * * * *

Lieut. F. T. Bryan left San Antonio June 14, 1849, for El Paso, and taking nearly the same route as Lieutenant Smith to the San Saba River, crossed it, and traveled north to the north branch of Brady's River, where he struck west along the head of the Rio Concho, and thence to the Pecos at the Horse-head Crossing. Fording the river he traveled up its right bank to Salinas Creek; thence he struck northwestward to Delaware Creek, ascended it to its source, and crossed the Guadalupe Mountains, through the Guadalupe Pass; thence he proceeded to the Sierra de los Alamos, and thence through the Sierra Hueco to El Paso.

Colonel Johnston, in 1849, directed the construction of a road for the troops over the route discovered by Lieut. William F. Smith. * * *

On arriving at El Paso Colonel Johnston and Lieutenant Bryan surveyed the valley of the Rio Grande to Doña Ana, while Lieut. William F.

Smith examined the Organ Mountains north to Salina de San Andres, and the Sacramento Mountains between the Cañon del Perro and La Cienega.

Colonel Johnston and party returned to the Pecos by the route that Lieutenant Bryan had explored through the Gaudalupe Pass; thence they passed down the Pecos River to the mouth of Live Oak Creek, from which point they examined the direct route to Fort Inge, across the heads of the San Pedro and Nueces Rivers. During Colonel Johnston's reconnaissance the roads were measured with an odometer, and numerous observations were made with the sextant.

Lieut. N. Michler, in 1849, made a reconnaissance of the country from Corpus Christi to Fort Inge, along the valleys of the Nueces, Leona, and Frio Rivers, for the purpose of opening a military road.

Lieutenant Michler then examined the route from San Antonio to Fort Washita, passing through Austin, Navarro, Dallas, and Preston, and thence to the emigrant crossing of the Pecos. The return route from Fort Washita lay up the Red River to the mouth of the Little Washita, thence west to the Big Washita, thence southwest to the Double Mountain Fork, thence to the Big Springs of the Colorado, and thence through the White Sand Hills to the Pecos. From this point he returned to San Antonio over nearly the route previously explored by Lieutenant Bryan as far as the head of the Concho, where he struck southwest to the San Saba, and thence by Forts Mason and Martin Scott to San Antonio. The distances along the route from Fort Washita to the Pecos were chained. No mention is made of astronomical observations being taken on this journey.*

Capt. R. B. Marcy, Fifth Infantry, had just passed over the portion of the route from the Pecos to the Double Mountain Fork, and gave Lieutenant Michler information concerning it.

* * * * * * * * *

An examination was also made of the Colorado, with the view of improving its navigation, by Lieut. William F. Smith, assisted by Messrs. R. A. Howard and J. F. Minter.

Lieutenant Whiting reconnoitered the route between San Antonio and Preston, via Fredericksburg, Fort Croghan, Fort Gates, Fort Graham, and

* See House Ex. Doc. No. 67, Thirty-first Congress, first session.

Fort Worth. This route was also examined by Lieutenant Bryan, Topographical Engineers.

The above items are mainly from the printed reports or maps. The following information in regard to the unpublished maps of the explorations in Texas in 1850–'51 have been obtained from the officers engaged in the surveys. In the Topographical Bureau there are two maps, both incomplete, of these explorations; and each contains routes not upon the other.

In January, 1849, Lieutenants Bryan and Michler, Topographical Engineers, examined Aranzas and Corpus Christi Bays, and the road from Corpus Christi to San Antonio, via San Patricio and Calaveras. In February, 1849, they made a reconnaissance of the lower road from San Antonio to the crossing near Presidio de Rio Grande, via Fort Inge; and also of a road from the San Fernando Crossing to San Antonio.

In May, 1849, Lieutenant Michler examined the road from San Antonio to Port Lavacca; and in June and July, 1849, the road between Corpus Christi and Fort Inge, along the Nueces, Frio, and Leona Rivers.

In May, 1850, Lieuts. William F. Smith and F. T. Bryan, Topographical Engineers, surveyed the Rio Grande with boats from El Paso to Presidio del Norte.

* * * * * * * * *

From August to November, 1850, Lieut. M. L. Smith and N. Michler examined a road from San Antonio to Ringgold Barracks, via Fort Merrill, of which we have no map. They also surveyed the Rio Grande from Ringgold Barracks to a point 80 miles above the mouth of the Pecos.

In April, 1851, Lieutenant Bryan laid out and made a road from Austin to Fort Mason, of which we have no map.

In April, 1851, Colonel Johnston reconnoitered the western frontier of Texas from the headwaters of the Nueces to Fort Belknap, via the headwaters of the Llano, San Saba, Concho, and Clear Fork of Brazos.

* * * * * * * * *

There were other surveys and reconnaissances made by these officers; but the maps are not available, and I have experienced more difficulty in compiling the map of Texas than that of any other portion. Throughout most of the above examinations astronomical observations were made for latitude. The longitude of San Antonio was determined by Colonel Johnston by moon culminations.

In April, 1851, Lieuts. W. F. Smith and N. Michler were placed on duty on the United States Mexican Boundary Survey. Lieutenant Bryan left Texas in the spring of 1852; Lieut. M. L. Smith in November, 1852; Colonel Johnston in the spring of 1853.

MAP OF THE TERRITORY OF THE UNITED STATES WEST OF THE MISSISSIPPI RIVER, ETC., 1850.

To this map the following title was affixed: "*A map of the United States and their Territories, from the Mississippi River to the Pacific Ocean, and of part of Mexico; compiled in the Bureau of the Corps of Topographical Engineers, under a resolution of the United States Senate, from the best authorities which could be obtained.*"

This map was published on a scale of 50 miles to an inch, and contained material from the greater portion of the maps I have already described.

RECONNAISSANCE ON THE PECOS, BY MR. R. H. KERN, 1850.

A military reconnaissance of the Rio Pecos, as far south as the Bosque Grande, was made in 1850 by Mr. R. H. Kern, who was attached to the command of Capt. H. B. Judd, Third Artillery. It was probably made with a compass and estimated distances, and without any astronomical observations; but of this I have no positive information. The map of the reconnaissance was used by Lieutenant Parke in his compiled map of New Mexico in 1851.

MAP OF NEW MEXICO, COMPILED BY LIEUT. J. G. PARKE, TOPOGRAPHICAL ENGINEERS, IN 1851.

This map, by Lieutenant Parke, was a careful compilation of all the available and reliable information in relation to New Mexico which could be obtained at that date from trappers and hunters, as well as from actual survey. It was prepared by him, while in that country, by order of Bvt. Col. John Munroe, U. S. Army, commanding Ninth Military Department, and was drawn by R. H. Kern in 1851. It was subsequently reduced in the Bureau of Topographical Engineers, and published on a scale of 36 miles to an inch.

RECONNAISSANCE FROM SANTA FÉ TO FORT LEAVENWORTH, IN 1851, BY CAPT. J. POPE, TOPOGRAPHICAL ENGINEERS.

Captain Pope traveled on the Cimarron route as far as Cedar Creek, where he turned north and struck the Arkansas at the Big Timbers. Crossing this river he took a northeast course to the Smoky Hill Fork, and came upon it near where Captain Fremont struck it in 1844. From this point he traveled down the stream.

* * * * * * * * *

SURVEY OF CREEK BOUNDARY, BY CAPTAIN SITGREAVES AND LIEUTENANT WOODRUFF, TOPOGRAPHICAL ENGINEERS, 1850-'51.

The report and map of this survey form printed House Ex. Doc. No. 104, first session Thirty-fifth Congress. The map is on a scale of 1 to 600,000, or about an inch to 9½ miles. Chain and compass were used in the survey, and the longitude of Fort Gibson was determined by moon culminations. A sextant was used to determine the latitudes.

The northern line begins on the parallel which passes near the mouth of the Red Fork of the Arkansas, at a point a little west of north from Fort Gibson, and continues west on the parallel to the 100th meridian.

RECONNAISSANCE DOWN THE ZUÑI AND COLORADO RIVERS, BY CAPT. L. SITGREAVES, UNITED STATES TOPOGRAPHICAL ENGINEERS, IN 1851.

The report of this forms Senate Ex. Doc. No. 59, second session of Thirty-second Congress, and is accompanied by a map of the routes pursued, on a scale of 10 miles to an inch. The reconnaissance was made with a compass and estimated distances, and checked by astronomical observation made with a sextant.

This expedition, under Captain Sitgreaves, assisted by Lieut. J. G. Parke, Topographical Engineers, Mr. R. H. Kern as topographer, and Dr. S. W. Woodhouse, surgeon and naturalist, was organized at Santa Fé, New Mexico, and consisted of about twenty persons, including packers and servants; pack-mules being used for transportation of provisions, etc. The party accompanied an expedition against the Navajos as far as Zuñi, which point they reached by the usual road from Albuquerque on the 1st of September, 1852.

* * * * * * * * *

RECONNAISSANCE OF THE COLORADO RIVER, BY LIEUTENANT DERBY, TOPOGRAPHICAL ENGINEERS, 1852.

The report of this forms Senate Ex. Doc. No. 81, first session Thirty-second Congress, and is accompanied by a map, on a scale 4 miles to an inch, of the Colorado River from its mouth to Fort Yuma. Lieutenant Derby was supplied with a sextant and chronometer.

* * * * * * * * *

RECONNAISSANCE OF LIEUTENANT WOODRUFF, TOPOGRAPHICAL ENGINEERS, 1852.

Lieut. I. C. Woodruff, Topographical Engineers, made a reconnaissance, in 1852, of a portion of the Kansas River; of Walnut Creek; of Pawnee Fork; and of other streams lying between the Smoky Hill Fork of the Kansas and the Arkansas Rivers. These examinations were made for the purpose of selecting proper sites for military posts. The map and report prepared by Lieutenant Woodruff have never been published The former was made from compass notes and estimated distances, checked by the astronomical determinations of Captain Fremont and Major Emory.

EXPEDITION TO THE SOURCES OF RED RIVER, BY CAPT. R. B. MARCY, UNITED STATES INFANTRY, 1852.

The report of this expedition forms Senate Ex. Doc. No. 54, second session Thirty-second Congress, House Ex. Doc., first session Thirty-third Congress, and is accompanied by numerous illustrations and by two maps, one of which exhibits the country from the 91st to the 114th meridian, lying between the 31st and 38th parallels, drawn on a scale of 24 miles to an inch; the other, on a scale of 10 miles to an inch, shows the country surrounding the sources of Red River.

Captain Marcy was assisted by Bvt. Capt. G. B. McClellan, Engineers, who made astronomical observations for latitude and longitude by means of a sextant and "pocket lever watch." The routes were mostly measured with an odometer, and observations were taken with a barometer. Dr. G. G. Shumard accompanied the expedition as surgeon and geologist.

* * * * * * * * *

CHAPTER IV

EXPLORATIONS FROM A. D. 1852 TO A. D. 1857.

Gov. I. I. Stevens and Capt. G. B. McClellan, U. S. Engineers, exploring and surveying railroad route, 1853-'54-'55.—Lieut. R. Arnold, U. S. A., survey, 1854.—F. W. Lander, C. E., reconnaissance, 1854.—Capt. G. W. Gunnison, T. E., and Capt. E. G. Beckwith, U. S. A., exploring and surveying railroad route, 1853.—Capt. E. G. Beckwith, U. S. A., exploring and surveying railroad route, 1854.—Capt. A. W. Whipple, T. E., exploring and surveying railroad route, 1853-'54.—Lieut. R. S. Williamson, T. E., survey for railroad route, 1853-'54.—Lieut. J. G. Parke, T. E., exploring and surveying railroad route, 1854.—Capt. J. Pope, T. E., exploring and surveying railroad route, 1854.—Lieut. J. G. Parke, T. E., exploring and surveying railroad route, 1854-'55.—Lieut. R. S. Williamson, T. E., and Lieut. H. L. Abbott, T. E., exploring and surveying railroad route, 1855.—Maj. W. H. Emory, U. S. A., United States and Mexican boundary survey, 1849 to 1855.—Capt. J. L. Reno, U. S. A., survey, 1853.—Capt. R. B. Marcy, U. S. A., exploration, 1854.—Alexander Ross, fur hunters of the far West, 1855.—March of Colonel Steptoe's command to California, 1854-'55.—Lieut. J. Withers, U. S. A., survey of road, 1854.—Lieut. G. H. Derby, T. E., survey roads, 1854-'55.—Lieut. G. H. Mendel, T. E., reconnaissance, 1855.—Capt. J. H. Simpson, T. E., survey roads, 1855.—Lieut. G. K. Warren, T. E., reconnaissance, 1855.—Lieut. F. T. Bryan, T. E., reconnaissance, 1855.—Lieut. J. C. Amory, U. S. A., reconnaissance in 1855.—Major Merrill, U. S. A., reconnaissance, 1855.—Lieut. I. N. Moore, U. S. A., map part of New Mexico, 1855.—Lieut. E. L. Hartz, U. S. A., reconnaissance, 1856.—Lieut. F. T. Bryan, T. E., survey of road, 1856.—Capt. J. H. Dickerson, U. S. A., survey road, 1856.—Lieut. W. D. Smith, U. S. A., route, 1856.—Capt. A. Sully, U. S. A., reconnaissance, 1856.—Lieut. G. K. Warren, T. E., reconnaissance Missouri and Yellowstone, 1856.—Explorations ordered in 1857.

EXPLORATION AND SURVEY FOR A RAILROAD ROUTE NEAR THE FORTY-SEVENTH AND FORTY-NINTH PARALLELS, 1853 to 1855.

The report of this exploration and survey will be found in Vol. I,* Senate Ex. Doc. No. 78, second session Thirty-third Congress, and House Ex. Doc. No. 91, second session Thirty-third Congress. Quarto edition.

They are accompanied by a map, in three sheets, drawn on a scale of 1 to 1,200,000, exhibiting the entire exploration; and a sheet of profile on

---

*Vol. I also contains the report of the Secretary of War and Capt. A. A. Humphreys on the comparative advantages of the routes examined. These are accompanied by a map of the territory of the United States, from the Mississippi to the Pacific, on a scale of 1 to 3,000,000, and a sheet of profiles of all the routes on a horizontal scale of 1 to 3,000,000, and a vertical scale of 1 to 60,000.

a horizontal scale of 1 to 3,000,000, the vertical scale being 1 to 60,000, or fifty times greater.

A brief report of the progress of the survey was published in Senate Ex. Doc. No. 29, first session Thirty-third Congress, which is accompanied by a map of the route from St. Paul to Fort Union, drawn on a scale of 1 to 1,200,000.

A nearly complete report is contained in House Doc. No. 129, first session Thirty-third Congress, accompanied by a profile and map, in three sheets, showing the entire route, drawn on a scale of 1 to 1,200,000. This map is, however, not so complete as the one in the quarto edition.

An additional report has also been made by Governor Stevens, which will appear in a subsequent volume with numerous landscape illustrations.†

This expedition, as first organized, consisted of four separate parties. The one under Governor Stevens's personal supervision operated from St. Paul westward towards the mouth of White Earth River; thence on the prairies lying along the Missouri River to the Rocky Mountains, and then among the passes of that region. Another, under Bvt. Capt. G B. McClellan, Engineers, began at Fort Vancouver, on the Columbia, operated northeastward, examining the passes of the Cascade Range, and then eastward to join Governor Stevens's party. Another party, under Lieut. A. J. Donelson, Engineers, examined the Missouri River from its mouth to the Yellowstone, where a junction was made with that under Governor Stevens. The fourth party, under Lieut. R. Saxton, United States artillery, conducted a reconnaissance from Fort Walla Walla to the Bitter Root Valley, where a depot was established.

The party under the immediate supervision of Governor Stevens took the field at St. Paul's on the 8th June. The principal engineer and scientific assistants consisted of Lieut. C. Grover, United States artillery; Dr. George Suckley, surgeon and naturalist; Messrs. F. W. Lander and A. W. Tinkham, civil engineers; Mr. J. Lambert, topographer; Mr. J. M. Stanley, artist; Mr. G. W. Stevens, assistant astronomer, and Mr. J. Moffett and Mr. J. Doty, meteorologists. Governor Stevens failed in securing the services of the officer designed to take charge of the astronomical observations.

† Ordered by the Senate at the second session Thirty-fifth Congress.

The party was well supplied with suitable instruments. Odometers, compasses, barometers, thermometers, sextants, chronometers, and a portable astronomical transit of twenty-six inches focal length (which latter was not used).

* * * * * * * * *

Lieutenant Saxton arrived at Fort Benton on the 12th of September. He had been charged with establishing a depot of supplies at St. Mary's village, and left The Dalles on the 18th of July, 1853. His party consisted of Lieuts. Robert Macfeely and Richard Arnold, Messrs. Arnold and Hoyt, and forty-nine enlisted men, packers, etc. They were provided with barometers, compasses, sextants, and chronometers. The distances were estimated.

* * * * * * * * *

The party on the western division, under the command of Capt. George B. McClellan, consisted of Lieut. J. K. Duncan, Third Artillery, Lieut. S. Mowry, Lieut. H. C. Hodges, Mr. J. F. Minter, civil engineer, George Gibbs, geologist, and Dr. J. G. Cooper, naturalist. Captain McClellan left Fort Vancouver in July, 1853.

* * * * * * * * *

A large map of the Cascade Range, north of the Columbia, was prepared by Lieutenant Duncan on a scale of 1 to 400,000.

* * * * * * * * *

Lieutenant Mullan, being left at Cantonment Stevens, on the Bitter Root River, to make observations in the mountains during the winter, made several reconnaissances. He was assisted by Mr. Adams as topographer and artist. The maps of the routes were made from compass courses and generally estimated distances.

* * * * * * * * *

The reports of each of the reconnaissances made by the subordinates of Governor Stevens's expedition will be found with his printed report; and the various maps of these routes were compiled by Mr. Lambert on the map that accompanies it. Governor Stevens also made additional examinations in 1855, in connection with his official duties with the Indians, and the results will be published in a supplementary volume.

SURVEY BY LIEUT. R. ARNOLD, 1854.

In the summer of 1854 Lieut. R. Arnold, Third Artillery, made an odometer survey and map of a road which he opened from Puget Sound to Walla Walla, through the Nachess Pass, over nearly the same route reconnoitered by Lieutenant Hodges, of Captain McClellan's party, in 1853. His report will be found as an appendix to the annual report of Col. J. J. Abert, Topographical Engineers, forming part of Senate Ex. Doc. No. 1, first session Thirty-fourth Congress.

EXAMINATIONS BY MR. F. W. LANDER, CIVIL ENGINEER, 1854.

The report of Mr. Lander forms part of House Ex. Doc. No. 129, First Session Thirty-third Congress, and is reprinted in the quarto edition of Pacific Railroad Reports, Vol. II, Senate Ex. Doc. No. 78, and House Ex. Doc. No. 91, second session Thirty-third Congress. The report is unaccompanied by maps or sketches.

Mr. F. W. Lander returned to the States in 1854 by the emigrant road up the valley of the Columbia; thence across the Blue Mountains through the Grande Ronde; thence up Snake River and across to Bear River; and thence by the usual traveled road through the South Pass and down the Platte River to Missouri.

The journey was undertaken by him at the request of citizens of Oregon and Washington Territories, to endeavor to find a railroad route in this direction. Although he examined several approaches to the Blue Mountains from the west, he found no practicable railroad route, as time and means did not permit him to reconnoiter this portion as fully as he intended. It was also his design to examine a route from the source of Snake River over the mountains to the head of Green River, but an accident to himself prevented this. His examinations tended to confirm the opinion of the difficult nature of the route west of the South Pass.

EXPLORATION AND SURVEY FOR A RAILROAD ROUTE TO THE PACIFIC, NEAR THE THIRTY-EIGHTH AND THIRTY-NINTH PARALLELS, UNDER CAPT. J. W. GUNNISON, TOPOGRAPHICAL ENGINEERS.

The report of this examination was made by Capt. E. G. Beckwith, United States Artillery, and forms part of Vol. II of the quarto edition of the Pacific Railroad Report, Senate Ex. Doc. No. 78; House Ex. Doc. No.

91, second session Thirty-third Congress. The maps were prepared by Mr. F. W. Egloffstein, and are in four sheets, on a scale of 12 miles to an inch.

The profile of this route is engraved on a horizontal scale of 30 miles to an inch, and a vertical scale $39\frac{1}{10}$ times greater than the horizontal. Numerous illustrations accompany the quarto edition. This report was also published in House Doc. No. 129, first session, Thirty-third Congress, and was accompanied by a preliminary map, on a scale of 50 miles to an inch, and profile on a horizontal scale of 15 miles to an inch, the vertical scale being 2,000 feet to an inch. A sketch of the portion of the route between the 104th and 110th meridian, on a scale of about 16 miles to an inch, accompanies the report of the Secretary of War—Senate Ex. Doc. No. 29, first session, Twenty-ninth Congress.

This expedition was composed of Captain Gunnison, Lieut. E. G. Beckwith, Third Artillery; Mr. R. H. Kern, topographer; Mr. S. Homans, astronomer; Dr. J. Schiel, surgeon and geologist; Mr. F. Creutzfeldt, botanist; and Mr. J. A. Snyder, assistant topographer; with the necessary teamsters and employés. They were escorted by Capt. R. M. Morris and Lieut. L. S. Baker, and about thirty soldiers of the regiment of mounted rifles. They were provided with sextants and artificial horizons, compasses, odometers, mercurial and aneroid barometers, and instruments for railroad surveying. Their supplies, etc., were transported in wagons.

* * * * * * * * *

Messrs. Beale and Heap passed over nearly this same route in advance of Captain Gunnison's party on their way to California. The journey of these enterprising travelers was a very trying one; and they lost nearly everything they had in attempting to cross Grand River on a raft during a high stage of water. They published a brief and interesting narrative of their journey, accompanied by a map.

Col. J. C. Fremont* also passed over nearly this same route during the winter of 1853–'54. He crossed the Sierra Blanca through the Sandy Hill Pass; thence his route was not materially different from Captain Gunnison's to the point where the latter left Grand River. Colonel Fremont con-

* See letters to the editors of the National Intelligencer, which form House Miscellaneous Document No. 8, second session Thirty-third Congress.

tinued further south, and crossed the Sawatch Mountains south of Gunnison's route. He had with him, as far as the Mormon settlement, Mr. F. W. Egloffstein, as topographer.

SURVEY FOR A RAILROAD TO THE PACIFIC NEAR THE FORTY-FIRST PARALLEL, BY LIEUT. E. G. BECKWITH, IN 1854.

The report of this route, by Lieutenant Beckwith, forms part of Volume II of the quarto edition of the Pacific Railroad Reports. The topographical maps are in four sheets, on a scale of 12 miles to an inch. The profiles are drawn on a horizontal scale of 16 miles to an inch, the vertical scale being $28\frac{16}{100}$ times larger. This report of Captain Beckwith was also published in House Document No. 129, first session Thirty-third Congress, and was accompanied by a preliminary map on a scale of 50 miles to an inch.

On the 3d of April Lieut. E. G. Beckwith, aided by Mr. F. W. Egloffstein and the surviving assistants of Captain Gunnison, started to examine the practicability of the Wasatch Mountains east of Great Salt Lake.

* * * * * * * * *

AN EXAMINATION TO ASCERTAIN THE MOST PRACTICABLE LOCATION FOR A WAGON ROAD ALONG THE CARSON VALLEY ROUTE, PASSING NEAR LAKE BIGLER,† (CALLED BY FREMONT, IN HIS MAP OF HIS SECOND EXPEDITION, "MOUNTAIN LAKE," AND ON HIS MAP OF THE THIRD EXPEDITION, LAKE BONAPLAND.)

This examination throws much light on the subject of the practicability of the route for a railroad.

The altitudes were determined by an aneroid barometer. The determination of the eastern boundary of California was another object in the examination, and for this purpose the party used an astronomical transit and sextant with chronometers. The report of these operations, by George H. Goddard, accompanies the annual report of the surveyor-general of the State of California, Assembly document No. 5, session of 1856.

SURVEY FOR A RAILROAD ROUTE TO THE PACIFIC, NEAR THE THIRTY-FIFTH PARALLEL, BY CAPT. A. W. WHIPPLE, TOPOGRAPHICAL ENGINEERS.

The final report of Captain Whipple forms Volumes III and IV of the quarto edition of the Pacific Railroad Reports, Senate Ex. Doc. No. 78, House Ex. Doc. No. 91, second session Thirty-third Congress. It is accom-

† Now known as Lake Tahoe.

panied by a topographical map in two sheets, drawn on a scale of 15 miles to an inch, and a sheet of profiles on a horizontal scale of 15 miles to an inch, and a vertical 50 times the horizontal. There are, besides, geological maps and numerous other illustrations. His preliminary report forms part of House Doc. No. 129, first session Thirty-third Congress. This edition is accompanied by a map in two sheets, and on a scale of 1 to 900,000, and a profile of the route on a horizontal scale of 1 inch to 79,500 feet, and a vertical scale of 1 inch to 3,000 feet.

Captain Whipple was assisted by Lieut. J. C. Ives, Topographical Engineers; Dr. J. M. Bigelow, surgeon and botanist; Jules Marcou, geologist and mining engineer; Dr. C. B. R. Kennerley, physician and naturalist; A. H. Campbell, principal assistant railroad engineer; H. B. Mollhausen, topographer and artist; Hugh Campbell, assistant astronomer; William White, jr., assistant meteorological observer; Mr. George G. Garner, assistant astronomer; Mr. N. H. Hutton, assistant engineer; John P. Sherburne, assistant meteorological observer; and Mr. T. H. Parke, assistant astronomer and computer. They were provided with a portable transit, sextants, and chronometers, for astronomical observations, and with the other instruments needful for reconnaissances. They were escorted by a company of the Seventh Infantry, under Capt. J. M. Jones, and began the survey with a train of wagons. Lieutenant Ives proceeded, with an astronomical transit and other instruments, from Washington, D. C., to Albuquerque, by way of San Antonio and El Paso, where he joined the party.

* * * * * * * * *

SURVEY FOR A PACIFIC RAILROAD THROUGH THE PASSES OF THE SIERRA NEVADA AND COAST RANGE, BY LIEUT. R. S. WILLIAMSON, TOPOGRAPHICAL ENGINEERS, 1854.

The final report of these surveys and reconnaissances forms Volume V of the quarto edition of the Pacific Railroad Reports. It is accompanied by a general map on a scale of 1 to 600,000; one of certain passes on a scale of 1 to 240,000, and several detailed maps. There are, too, sheets of profiles drawn on a horizontal scale of 1 to 120,000 and a vertical scale five times greater. The report is also accompanied by geological maps and profiles. The report and general map were also in House Document No. 129, first session Thirty-third Congress.

Lieutenant Williamson was assisted by Lieut. J. G. Parke, Topographical Engineers; Lieut. G. B. Anderson, Second Dragoons; Dr. A. L. Heerman, physician and naturalist; Mr. W. P. Blake, geologist; Mr. Isaac W. Smith, civil engineer; Mr. Charles Preuss, topographer; and Mr. Charles Koppel, artist. His escort was commanded by Lieut. G. Stoneman, First Dragoons. Continuous topographical sketches of the routes traversed were taken, and the work checked by astronomical observations with the sextant. Two of the passes were surveyed with chain and spirit level. On the map Lieutenant Williamson embodied some of the explorations of Captain Warner which had not before been published.

* * * * * * * * *

RECONNAISSANCE FOR A RAILROAD ROUTE BETWEEN PIMAS VILLAGE AND EL PASO, BY LIEUT. J. G. PARKE, TOPOGRAPHICAL ENGINEERS, IN 1854.

The report of this reconnaissance forms part of Volume II, quarto edition of the Pacific Railroad Reports. This report is printed in House Ex. Doc. No. 129, first session Thirty-third Congress, and is there accompanied by a map on a scale of 5 miles to an inch, and profile on the same horizontal scale, the vertical being 1,000 feet to an inch.

Lieutenant Parke, assisted by Mr. H. Custer, topographer, and Dr. A. L. Heerman, physician and naturalist, and provided with barometers, odometers, and compass, on the 24th of January, 1854, left San Diego with a party of twenty-three men, exclusive of an escort, under Lieutenant Stoneman, of twenty-eight dragoons

* * * * * * * * *

RECONNAISSANCE FOR A RAILROAD ROUTE FROM EL PASO TO PRESTON, BY BVT. CAPT. JOHN POPE, TOPOGRAPHICAL ENGINEERS, 1854.

The report of this reconnaissance will be found in Volume II of the quarto edition of the Pacific Railroad Reports, and is accompanied by a map, on a scale of 15 miles to an inch, and a profile on the same horizontal scale, the vertical being fifty times greater. The report, with a map and profile, on a scale of 10 miles to an inch, also forms part of House Doc. No. 129, first session Thirty-third Congress.

Capt. J. Pope was assisted by Lieut. Kenner Garrard, First Dragoons; Dr. J. Mitchell, surgeon and naturalist; Mr. C L. Taplin, and J. H. Byrne, with an escort of twenty-five men under Lieut. L. H. Marshall, Third Infantry. The party, including teamsters, etc., numbered seventy-five men. They were provided with sextant, chronometer, odometer, and compasses. The grades were determined by measuring the vertical angle with a theodolite. The expedition left Doña Ana February 12, 1854.

* * * * * * * * *

Captain Pope made additional explorations in the vicinity of the Guadalupe Mountains during the years 1855, 1856, and 1857, while engaged in the experiment for obtaining water by artesian wells, but his final report has not yet been made.

EXPLORATION AND SURVEY FOR A RAILROAD ROUTE FROM BENICIA, CALIFORNIA, TO FORT FILLMORE, NEW MEXICO, BY LIEUT. J. G. PARKE, TOPOGRAPHICAL ENGINEERS, 1854-'55.

The report of these examinations forms part of Volume VII of the quarto edition of the Pacific Railroad Reports, and is accompanied by two topographical maps, on a scale of 12 miles to an inch, and profiles of his routes on the same horizontal scale, and a vertical scale fifty times larger. On the same sheet is a profile of the route from Fulton to San Diego, on a horizontal scale of 36 miles to an inch, and a vertical scale fifty times greater. There are also geological maps and profiles.

Lieutenant Parke was assisted by Mr. Albert H. Campbell, civil engineer; Dr. Thomas Antisell, geologist; and Messrs. Custer and N. H. Hutton, topographers. They were provided with sextants and chronometers, barometers, compasses, and odometers. On the 20th November, 1854, they left Benicia with a party of about thirty persons.

* * * * * * * * *

EXPLORATION AND SURVEY FOR A RAILROAD ROUTE FROM THE SACRAMENTO RIVER TO THE COLUMBIA RIVER, BY LIEUT. R. S. WILLIAMSON, TOPOGRAPHICAL ENGINEERS.

The report of this expedition, owing to the illness of Lieutenant Williamson, was written by Second Lieut. H. L. Abbot, Topographical Engineers. It forms Volume VI of the quarto edition of the Pacific Railroad Reports, and is accompanied by a topographical map, in two sheets, on a scale of 12 miles to an inch, and two sheets of profiles, on the same horizontal scale, but with the vertical scale fifty times greater.

The party consisted of Lieut. R. S. Williamson, Topographical Engineers, assisted by Lieut. H. L. Abbot, Topographical Engineers, with Dr.

J. S. Newberry, as geologist; Dr. E. Sterling, as physician and naturalist; Mr. H. C. Fillebrown, as assistant engineer; Mr. C. D. Anderson, as computer; and Mr. John Young, as draughtsman. A light cart was taken for the instruments, but everything else was transported by pack mules. The party was supplied with sextants and chronometers, odometers, compasses, and barometers.

The expedition left Benicia, California, on July 10, 1855, and proceeded up the Sacramento Valley to Fort Reading, crossing the river at Fremont. At the fort it was joined by the escort, consisting of Lieut. H. G. Gibson, Third Artillery; Lieut. G. Crook, Fourth Infantry; Lieut. J. B. Hood, Second Cavalry, and one hundred soldiers

* * * * * * * * *

In making the map of this exploration, Lieutenant Abbot embodied various unpublished military reconnaissances made in Oregon and northern California, which he duly acknowledges. These were: That by Major Alvord, in 1853, from Myrtle Creek, in Umpqua Valley, to Rogue River Valley; that by Mr. G. Gibbs, in 1852, from Humboldt Bay to the head of Scott's River; that of Lieutenant Chandler, in 1856, near the mouth of Rogue River; that of Lieutenant Kautz, in 1854, near Coos Bay; those of Lieutenant Williamson from Yreka, east of Shasta Butte, to Fort Reading; from Yreka to lower Klamath Lake, and from Port Orford to Coquille and Rogue Rivers, made while on military duty in the Department in 1851–'52.

UNITED STATES AND MEXICAN BOUNDARY SURVEYS.

These surveys began in 1849, and continued, with various interruptions, till 1856. During the establishment of the boundary line agreed upon by the treaty of Guadalupe Hidalgo, four different appointments were made of United States commissioner, four of astronomer, and two of surveyor. Delays were caused by these changes, by a want of means to properly carry on the work, and by differences of opinion as to the proper initial point on the Rio Grande.

The following-named reports can be consulted in relation to it:

1st. The reports of the Secretary of the Interior, one dated February 27, 1850, printed Senate Ex. Doc. No. 34, first session Thirty-first Congress;

and another dated July, 1852, which is printed Senate Ex. Doc. No. 119, first session Thirty-second Congress.

These contain various letters from different individuals and sketch maps in reference to the initial points of the boundary line on the Pacific shore, at the juncture of the Gila and Colorado Rivers, and on the Rio Grande.

2d. Extract from a journal of an expedition from San Diego, California, to the Rio Colorado, from September 11 to December 11, 1849, by A W. Whipple, Lieutenant United States Topographical Engineers; printed Senate Ex. Doc. No. 19, second session Thirty-first Congress

3d. Report of Lieut Col. J. D. Graham, Topographical Engineers, Senate Ex. Doc. No. 121, first session Thirty-second Congress.

This is a narative by Colonel Graham of his connection as astronomer with the establishment of this line, and is accompanied by numerous letters from different persons, one of which is Lieutenant Whipple's report to Colonel Graham on the survey of the Gila. This report of Colonel Graham is also accompanied by a "barometric profile of the route from San Antonio via Castorville, Fort Inge, Howard's Spring, Ojo Escondido, Eagle Spring, El Paso del Norte, and Doña Ana, to the copper mines of Santa Rita, in New Mexico, in 1851; from observations by and under the direction of Bvt. Lieut. Col. J. D. Graham, United States Topographical Engineers, assisted by Lieut. W. F. Smith, Togographical Engineers, and Mr. J. Lawson, and computed by Lieut. G. Thom, Topographical Engineers" The profile is on a horizontal scale of 20 miles to an inch, the vertical scale being $105\frac{6}{10}$ times greater.

Colonel Graham acknowledges, in terms of commendation, the aid received by him from Lieutenant Whipple, Topographical Engineers, and Lieutenants Tillinghast and Burnside, U. S. Army.

4th. "*Personal Narrative of Explorations and Incidents in Texas, New Mexico, California, Sonora, and Chihuahua, connected with the United States and Mexican Boundary Commission, during the years* 1850–'51–'52, *and* '53. *By John Russell Bartlett, United States Commissioner during that period; in two volumes, with maps and illustrations. Published by D. Appleton & Co., Nos.* 346 *and* 348 *Broadway, New York, and No.* 16 *Little Britain, London*—1854."

In page 11 of the preface to this work, Mr. Bartlett says: "The maps of the survey, as well as the astronomical, magnetic, and meteorological observations, with all that strictly appertains to the running and marking the boundary line, were, by the instructions of the Secretary of the Interior, placed in charge of the surveyor, Bvt. Maj. W. H. Emory, who alone is held responsible for the faithful performance of these duties. From the high character of that officer as an engineer, the public may expect, in proper season, a satisfactory account of his labors in these departments. Some time must elapse before the maps to illustrate the whole boundary from one ocean to the other can be completed; I have therefore been compelled to construct, meanwhile, the map prefixed to this work from my own itinerary and from the most authentic information that could be obtained."

This work contains, among other things of interest, an account of the country south of the boundary, on the route from El Paso via the Guadalupe Pass to Guaymas; and also of a journey through Chihuahua, Coahuila, and New Leon to the Rio Grande.

5th. "Report on the United States and Mexican Boundary Survey," made under the direction of the Secretary of the Interior, by William H. Emory, Major First Cavalry and United States Commissioner. Washington: Cornelius Wendell, printer."

The report of Major Emory was published in 1858, and forms Senate Ex. Doc. No. 108, first session Thirty-fourth Congress, and, with the appendices, makes two volumes. There are four topographical maps on a scale of 1 to 600,000, "showing the boundary line and the country contiguous, as far as information has been obtained from actual survey or reconnaissance." There is also a topographical map on a scale of 1 to 6,000,000, entitled a "Map of the United States and their Territories between the Mississippi River and the Pacific Ocean and part of Mexico, compiled from surveys made under the order of W. H. Emory, Major First Cavalry, United States Commissioner, and from the maps of the Pacific Railroad, General Land Office, and the Coast Survey, projected and drawn under the supervision of Lieut. N. Michler, Topographical Engineers, by Thomas Jekyll, C. E., 1857–'58." This map (of all the country north of the surveys of the Mexican boundary) is a reduction from the map which I have compiled for the Pacific Railroad office.

Major Emory's report is also accompanied by a geological map of the same country, and on the same scale as that just mentioned, prepared by James Hall, assisted by J. P. Leslie, esq. This map is without date.

There is also a barometrical and geological profile along the Rio Grande from its mouth to El Paso, and thence across the country to the Pacific. The report contains numerous illustrations of scenery, and geological, botanical, and zoological plates.

Assistance is acknowledged to have been received in the field from Lieut. A. W. Whipple, Topographical Engineers; Bvt. Capt. E. L. F. Hardcastle, Topographical Engineers; Mr. G. C. Gardner, Dr. C. Parry, Messrs. E. Ingraham, C. Radziminski, Arthur Schott, J. H. Clark, S. W. Jones, E. A. Phillips, J. H. Houston, J. E. Weiss, H. Campbell, F. Wheaton, W. White, and G. G. Garner.

The line, as finally determined and established under the treaty of Guadalupe Hidalgo, extended up the Rio Grande from its mouth to latitude 31° 54′ 40″ north; thence west along that parallel to the meridian of 109°37′ west; thence due north to the Rio San Domingo; thence down that stream to the Gila; thence down the Gila to its mouth; thence in a straight line to the point on the Pacific in latitude 32° 32′ north.

Numerous reconnaissances were made by different parties in going to and from various points on the line; and the Rio Grande was surveyed as far up as the parallel of 32° 22′ north, and a portion of that parallel run by Lieutenant Whipple as directed by Mr. Bartlett, commissioner at the time.

The treaty of 1853, by which the tract of territory known as the Gadsden purchase was acquired from Mexico, changed the boundary line so as to make it commence on the Rio Grande at latitude 31° 47′ north; thence due west 100 miles; thence south to latitude 31° 30′ north; thence due west to the 111th meridian; thence in a straight line to a point on the Colorado 20 miles below its junction with the Gila; thence up the Colorado to the former line.

To establish this boundary Major Emory (then brevet major, Corps Topographical Engineers) was appointed commissioner and astronomer on the part of the United States; and the work was accomplished during the years 1855–'56. Major Emory was assisted in this work by Lieut. N. Michler, Topographical Engineers; Lieut. C. N. Turnbull, Topographical Engineers; Messrs. C. Radziminski, M. T. W. Chandler, J. H. Clark, H. Campbell, W. Emory, M. Von Hippel, C. Weiss, F. Wheaton, A. Schott, J. Houston, D. Hinkle, B. Burns, E. A. Phillips, and J. O'Donoghue. Capt. G. Thom, Topographical Engineers, had charge of the office in computing the work and projecting the maps of both boundary surveys.

SURVEY OF ROAD FROM BIG SIOUX TO MENDOTA, BY BVT. CAPT. J. L. RENO, UNITED STATES ORDNANCE, IN 1853.

Captain Reno was assisted in this survey, which was made with chain and compass, by Mr. James Tilton (now surveyor-general of Washington Territory) and Mr. A. Cross.

The map now in the Topographical Bureau has never been published. The report forms printed House Ex. Doc. No. 97 first session Thirty-third Congress.

EXPLORATIONS OF THE SOURCES OF THE BRAZOS AND BIG WICHITA RIVERS, BY CAPT. R. B. MARCY, FIFTH INFANTRY, IN 1854.

The report of this forms Senate Ex. Doc. No. 60, first session Thirty-fourth Congress. It is accompanied by a map of the region explored, on a scale of 8 miles to an inch. Captain Marcy was accompanied by Major Neighbors, Indian agent, and Dr. G. G. Shumard, geologist, and escorted by forty-five men of the Seventh Infantry, under Lieuts. N. B. Pearce and G. Chapin. An odometer, compass, aneroid barometer, and thermometer composed his main instruments.

The object of the expedition was to find suitable lands to reserve for the Indians.

*   *   *   *   *   *   *

No astronomical observations being made, he adopted the positions of Forts Belknap and Phantom Hill, from Johnson's map of Texas.

FUR HUNTERS OF THE FAR WEST, BY ALEXANDER ROSS, IN TWO VOLUMES; PUBLISHED BY SMITH, ELDER & CO. LONDON: 1855.

This book begins with the transfer of Astoria to the British Northwest Company, and gives the history of this company down to its union with the Hudson's Bay Company in 1821, which closes the first volume. The second volume is a narrative of some expeditions conducted by the author for the Hudson's Bay Company in 1825 and previous years. On one of these he led a large trapping party into the Snake country, and visited the sources of Salmon, Malade, Goddin's, and Reid's or Boisé Rivers, giving a very interesting account of much country as yet unexplored by any surveying expedition, and I believe undescribed in any other book. The information concerning it is of great value and interest.

The author, in speaking of the great amount of information required by the members of these fur companies, and the little that has been given to the public, says that it has not been kept secret from design, but merely from inability to make it public.

There are many works of travels and adventures on the prairies mentioned in this memoir, but I have endeavored to refer to most of those containing accurate information of country not covered by the official surveys.

MARCH OF THE COMMAND UNDER COLONEL STEPTOE, FROM FORT LEAVENWORTH TO CALIFORNIA, 1854-'55.

The report of Capt. Rufus Ingalls, who was quartermaster to this command, forms a portion of the printed annual Executive Document of 1855, part two. A map showing the routes of portions of the command from Salt Lake City west is also a part of the same document, and was furnished by Captain Ingalls. The command started from Fort Leavenworth during the first part of June, 1854, and traveled the usual route via Fort Kearny, Fort Laramie, South Pass, and Bear River to Great Salt Lake City, where they spent the winter.

* * * * * * * * *

Lieut. S. Mowry, who accompanied Colonel Steptoe, was detached at Great Salt Lake City in the spring of 1855 to conduct some dragoon recruits and animals by the Santa Fé trail to Fort Téjon, in California.

This duty he performed. His report was rendered to the Adjutant-General, but has not been published. It was not illustrated by any topographical sketches.

SURVEY OF MILITARY ROAD IN OREGON, BY LIEUT. JOHN W. WITHERS, IN 1854.

The map, with descriptive notes, is on file in the Topographical Bureau. It is drawn on a scale of 2 miles to an inch. The road is located along the valley of Umpqua River, between Scottsburg and Myrtle Creek. The report of Lieutenant Withers accompanied the annual report of the Colonel of Topographical Engineers for 1855.

SURVEYS AND RECONNAISSANCE BY LIEUT. G. H. DERBY, TOPOGRAPHICAL ENGINEERS, IN OREGON AND WASHINGTON TERRITORIES, 1854 AND 1855.

The principal of these examinations were for a road from Salem to Astoria, in Oregon, and from Columbia Barracks to Fort Steilacoom, in Washington Territory. The maps are on file in the Topographical Bureau, drawn on a scale of 1 to 48,000. There are also reductions of these (made in the Topographical Bureau) to a scale of 4 miles to an inch. These surveys and maps were made by direction of Maj. H. Bache, Topographical Engineers, by Lieutenant Derby, assisted by Mr. George Gibbs and C. M. Bache. A brief report in relation to these routes will be found in the annual report of the Colonel of Topographical Engineers for 1855.

RECONNAISSANCE OF THE ROUTE OF THE SNAKE RIVER EXPEDITION, BY LIEUT. G. H. MENDELL, TOPOGRAPHICAL ENGINEERS, 1855.

I have never seen Lieutenant Mendell's report. The reconnaissance was probably made by means of compass courses and estimated distances, checked by astronomical observations for latitude. A tracing from his original map is in the Topographical Bureau.

This expedition, consisting of about two companies, all mounted, under the command of Bvt. Maj. G. P. Haller, Fourth Infantry, was organized by General Wool in the summer of 1855, for the purpose of chastising the Indians who had killed some emigrants near Fort Boisé.

* * * * * * * * *

SURVEYS OF ROADS IN MINNESOTA, UNDER CAPT. J. H. SIMPSON, TOPOGRAPHICAL ENGINEERS.

Captain Simpson's annual report for 1855, with a map, on a scale of 24 miles to an inch, showing all the General Government roads under his charge, forms a part of the annual Executive document for that year. One of these roads extends from Point Douglas, on the Mississippi, to the mouth of St. Louis River; another from Point Douglas to Fort Ripley; another from Fort Ripley, on Crow Wing River, to Otter Tail Lake; and another from the Mendota to the mouth of the Big Sioux River. These are the principal roads. The one last mentioned was surveyed by Captain Reno in 1853.

RECONNAISSANCE IN THE DAKOTA OR SIOUX COUNTRY, BY LIEUT. G. K. WARREN, TOPOGRAPHICAL ENGINEERS, IN 1855.

The report of this forms Senate Ex. Doc. No. 76, first session Thirty-fourth Congress. It is accompanied by a map on a scale of 1 to 600,000, giving the detailed topography of the routes explored, and a general map of Nebraska, on a scale of 1 to 3,000,000.

While making this reconnaissance I was attached to the staff of General Harney, commanding Sioux expedition, and was assisted by Mr. P. Carrey and J. H. Snowden. Sketches of routes were also furnished me by Lieut. G. T. Balch, U. S. Ordnance, and Lieut. J. Curtiss, Second Infantry. The instruments used consisted of odometers, compasses, and barometers. I left St. Louis on the 7th of June. * * * Over the routes traveled the distances were measured with an odometer, and maps were made of all the routes traversed.

RECONNAISSANCE OF A ROAD FROM FORT LEAVENWORTH TO THE BIG TIMBERS ON THE ARKANSAS, BY LIEUT. F. T. BRYAN, TOPOGRAPHICAL ENGINEERS, IN 1855.

The map of this is in the Topographical Bureau, but neither it nor the report have been published.

The party under Lieutenant Bryan consisted of Mr. J. Lambert, topographer; Mr. C. Lombard, road surveyor; Mr. C. F. Larned and S. M. Cooper, assistant topographers. Their instruments consisted of compasses and odometers. Having surveyed the route from Fort Leavenworth to Fort Riley, they were joined there by an escort under Maj. L. Armistead.

* * * * * * * * *

RECONNAISSANCE BY LIEUT. J. C. AMORY, FROM FORT GIBSON TO BENT'S FORT, IN 1855.

Lieutenant Amory was attached to the command of Lieutenant-Colonel Morrisson, who left Fort Gibson and traveled up the Verdigris as far as the Kansas boundary. Here they left that river and proceeded northwest, gradually approaching the Arkansas until they struck it at the mouth of Walnut Creek; thence they proceeded over the usual road to Bent's Fort. Their route from Fort Gibson to the mouth of Walnut Creek was through country previously unexplored.

RECONNAISSANCE BY MAJOR MERRILL, UNITED STATES DRAGOONS, IN 1855.

This consists in a sketch of the route of a portion of the Second Dragoons from Fort Belknap direct to Council Grove and Fort Riley.

MAP COMPILED BY LIEUT. I. N. MOORE, UNITED STATES DRAGOONS, IN 1855.

This map embraces the country between the Rio Grande and Pecos, from the thirty-second parallel to the thirty-sixth, and is compiled from examinations, sketches, and notes taken by himself, Major Carlton, Lieutenant Higgins, and other officers of the Army while traversing this region on Indian scouts, etc. The positions of the main points along the Rio Grande, Canadian route, and upper El Paso route are taken from the published maps of the Topographical Engineers.

RECONNAISSANCE BY LIEUT. E. L. HARTZ, EIGHTH INFANTRY, U. S. ARMY, 1856.

Lieutenant Hartz, with a command of three non-commissioned officers and twenty-four men, with two wagons, started on the 16th of August from Fort Davis to intersect the El Paso road. His general course was nearly west, but with many détours to obtain water. He passed through the Carisso Pass, which is difficult for wagons, and struck the El Paso road 25 miles west of Eagle Springs. A map of this route was made by Lieutenant Hartz, on a scale of 1 inch to 5 miles. It is not stated in his report or map what instruments were employed in reconnoitering.

EXPLORATIONS FOR ROAD FROM FORT RILEY TO BRIDGER'S PASS, BY LIEUT. F. T. BRYAN, TOPOGRAPHICAL ENGINEERS, 1856.

The report of this will be found in the annual documents accompanying the President's message for 1857. The original map, on a scale of 1 to 600,000, is in the Topographical Bureau, and was not published with it Lieutenant Bryan was assisted by Mr. J. Lambert, Mr. C. F. Larned, Mr. S. M. Cooper, assistant topographers, and Mr. H. Englemann, as geologist. They were provided with odometers, compasses, barometers, and sextant. They were accompanied by thirty men, and protected by an escort of one company of the Sixth Infantry under Maj. L. A. Armistead.

* * * * * * * * *

SURVEY OF ROAD FROM OMAHA CITY TO FORT KEARNY, BY CAPT. JOHN H. DICKERSON, A. Q. M., IN 1856.

The report of Captain Dickerson is published with the documents accompanying the President's annual message for 1857, but without the map, which is in the Bureau of Topographical Engineers, under the direction ot which the survey was made. This survey from Omaha to the Platte, and along that river to Fort Kearny, was made with a chain and compass and spirit level.

A survey was made with compass and odometer of the route up the Loup Fork, on the south side, leaving it near the mouth of Beaver Creek.

RECONNAISSANCE FROM FORT RANDALL TO FORT KEARNY, BY LIEUT. W. D. SMITH, SECOND DRAGOONS, IN 1856.

A reconnaissance was made of this route during the march of a squadron of the Second Dragoons under Lieut. W. D. Smith. The report is accompanied by a sketch map made from the measured distances, but without compass courses. The report has not been printed.

RECONNAISSANCE FROM FORT RIDGELY TO FORT PIERRE, BY CAPT. A. SULLY, SECOND INFANTRY, IN 1856.

A reconnaissance was made of this route by Captain Sully, whose company formed part of the command of Lieutenant-Colonel Abercrombie, in making the movement between these two posts. Topographical sketches were made with a pocket compass and estimated distances. Captain Sully determined the source of the Big Sioux River to be in Lake Kampeska. This map and the report are not yet published.

RECONNAISSANCE ON THE MISSOURI AND YELLOWSTONE RIVERS, BY LIEUT. G. K. WARREN, TOPOGRAPHICAL ENGINEERS, IN 1856.

A map on a scale of 1 to 600,000 has been prepared and the material reduced from it to the Pacific Railroad map. The detailed report and map are not yet published.

On this reconnaissance I was assisted by Mr. N. H. Hutton and Mr. J. H. Snowden, assistant topographers, Dr. and F. V. Hayden, geologist and natūralist, and was provided with an astronomical transit, a sextant, chronometers, barometers, odometers, and compasses. We started on a steamboat from St. Louis, April 16, to join General Harney at Fort Pierre, and on our way made a map of the Missouri from the mouth of the Big Nemeha. At Fort Pierre I received orders from General Harney to proceed on board the American Fur Company's boat *St. Mary* and examine the Missouri River as far as she should go, and then to return down the stream by Mackinac boats. The Missouri River was thus mapped as far up as the mouth of the Big Muddy, 60 miles above Fort Union. The party consisted, in addition to the assistants, of about thirty men, seventeen of whom were enlisted men of the Second Infantry.

* * * * * * * * *

BRIEF STATEMENT OF THE EXPEDITIONS THAT TOOK THE FIELD IN 1857.

The United States astronomical and surveying parties for establishing the boundary line (49th parallel) between the United States and Great Britain, of which Archibald Campbell, esq., was commissioner, and Lieut. J. G. Parke, Topographical Engineers, astronomer, was organized under the State Department and started for the field of operations on the Pacific coast in April, 1857.

The party under Mr. W. H. Nobles, organized in the Interior Department for making a road from Fort Ridgely to the South Pass, examined the route during the summer as far west as the Missouri at the mouth of Crow Creek.

The party under Lieutenant Warren, Topographical Engineers, organized by the War Department, started in June in two divisions—one from Omaha City, the other from Sioux City. They united at the mouth of Loup Fork, examined this stream to its source, and thence proceeded by way of the valley of the Niobrara River to Fort Laramie. Thence they proceeded north, explored the Black Hills, and, returning by way of the Niobrara River examined it to its mouth.

The wagon-road expedition, organized under the Department of the Interior, of which Mr. F. W. Lander was the engineer, made reconnaissances of the mountains between Green River and Bear River.

The wagon-road expedition under Lieutenant Bryan, this year, was confined to routes which he had previously mapped and explored.

The expedition against the Sheyenne Indians, commanded by Colonel Sumner, explored a portion of the country between the Platte and Arkansas Rivers.

The party commanded by Colonel Johnston to survey the southern boundary of Kansas, and of which Mr. J. H. Clark was astronomer and Mr. Weiss surveyor, was organized by the War Department. It accomplished that work and reconnoitered the country south of the line.

The party for constructing a wagon-road from Fort Defiance to the Colorado River was organized by the War Department and placed in charge of Mr. E. F. Beale. He examined the line of the proposed road during the summer and winter.

The party for the construction of a wagon-road from El Paso to Fort Yuma, of which Mr. Leach was superintendent and Mr. N. H. Hutton was engineer, passed the summer and winter in the operation, and have not yet returned.

The expedition of Captain Pope for making of experiments in artesian well-boring is still in the field.

A party under Mr. Major, for establishing that part of the 98th and 100th meridians between the Canadian and Red Rivers, was organized by the Interior Department and is still in the field.

The expedition under Lieutenant Ives for ascertaining the navigability of the Colorado of the Gulf of California, was organized under the War Department and is still in the field.

The Land Office surveys along the whole frontier are advancing steadily, as in former years.

The foregoing is an epitome of the expeditions taken direct from Warren's Memoir, Pacific Railroad Reports, Vol. XI. In Chapter V he gives the method of compiling the map of the territory west of the Mississippi, with a list of the principal longitude determinations. This general map, first published immediately before the outbreak of the war, was drawn and engraved to the scale of 1 to 3,000,000 (1″=47.35 miles) and contained all the then known topographic and general geographic information of this territory, and with revisions was issued up to 1867, when a recompilation was commenced.

NOTE.—As instances, more particularly of general geological exploration work, or publication not appearing on page 490 of House Ex. Doc. 270, Forty-eighth Congress, second session (Venice Geographical Report), notes of which have kindly been furnished by Jules Marcou, the following may be mentioned, which, though not furnishing data valuable for map compilation (especially in original geographical co-ordinates), are of interest at least from a bibliographical point of view:

Gabriel Franchère, 1819–'46–'54.—Narrative of a voyage to the northwest coast of America in the years 1811–'12–'13–'14. First edition (French), Montreal, 1819; second edition (English), New York.

M. Nuttal, 1821.—A journal of travels into the Arkansas Territory during the year 1819.

J. K. Townsend.—Narrative of a journey across the Rocky Mountains to the Columbia River. Philadelphia: 1839.

Prince Maximilian de Wied, Neuwied, 1840.—Voyage in the interior of North America, 1832–'33–'34. Three volumes with atlas. Paris. (Published also in German.)

Duflat de Mofras.—(Exploration du territoire de l'Orégon, des Californies, etc.) Exploration of the Territory of Oregon, of California, etc., 1840–'41–'42, in two volumes, 8°, 1844. Published by order of the King, under the auspices of the President of the Council and the Minister of Foreign Affairs. Vol. I, p. 521, four plates; Vol. II, p. 387, four plates; accompanied by an atlas of twenty-six sheets (maps and plans). On page 475 *et seq.* of Vol. I will be found a list of latitudes and longitudes of eighty-six places, with authorities.

De Smeth (the Jesuit Father), 1846 (?).—Letters upon the Rocky Mountains. (These first appeared in the Annals of the Propaganda at Rome.)

G. F. Ruxton, 1848.—Adventures in Mexico and the Rocky Mountains.

Ferdinand Romer, 1849.—Texas. (Contains a geological and geographical map.)

P. T. Tyson, 1850.—Geology of California. His report forms a part of Senate Ex. Doc. No. 47, Thirty-first Congress, first session, which also contains several maps, especially one by Lieut. (afterwards General) E. O. C. Ord, with two reports of this officer to General Riley.

Jules Marcou, 1855–'58.—Geology of North America, p. 144, with three maps and seven plates. Zurich: 1858. This publication contains a compiled general geologic map of the country west of the Mississippi River (no scale); also a general geological map of New Mexico (compiled), scale 1 to 900,000.

In 1880 General G. K. Warren had proposed to furnish notes of "some interesting early explorations" of which he had learned since his memoir was published (and also additional bibliography), as soon as his duties should permit, which he had not, however, been able to do before his death in 1882.

In the same category are the following voyages and travels, taken from a manuscript kindly furnished by Amos Bowman, now an assistant of the Canadian Geological Survey:

In 1806 Simon Frazer, a partner in the Northwest Company, explored westward from the Red River settlement, reaching Fraser Lake, between the great bend of the Fraser River and the mouth of Sheena River, in latitude 54° N., and established a fort.*

* See Greenhow's Memoir, p. 155.

David Thompson, a partner and geographer of the Northwest Company, set out from the Selkirk settlement on Lake Winnipeg in 1810, for the purpose of crossing the Rocky Mountains to the Columbia River. In the spring of 1811 he constructed a cedar canoe, near the sources of the Columbia (probably at the boat encampment in latitude 52° N.), and descended that river, arriving on July 15 at Astoria. He was the first white man to descend the northern or upper main branch of the Columbia. Finding the Astor Company already in possession he returned the way he came.*

He made a map of the previously unexplored and unsurveyed Northwest Territory, which is preserved in the Crown lands department of Canada.

In 1824–'25 Dr. McLoughlin established a post at Fort George (Astoria) and at Vancouver.

Rev. Samuel Parker's exploring tour beyond the Rocky Mountains in 1835–'36–'37, with map, is written in narrative, but has separate chapters on geology, zoölogy, ethnology, and climatology. Mr. Parker entered the Rocky Mountains, and traveled by the usual trappers' (afterwards the Oregon emigrant) route via Black Hills, Jackson's Hole, the Three Tetons, Pierre's Hole, Fort Hall, Grande Ronde, and Walla Walla to Vancouver.

In 1841 Sir George Simpson crossed the Rocky Mountains via the Saskatchewan and Kootenay Rivers, and came down the Columbia to the Hudson Bay establishment at Vancouver, of which there is a published account.

McLeod's Santa Fé expedition left Austin, Tex., in June, 1841, and proceeded over the Llano Estacado and was captured by the Mexicans.

Fremont made a fourth expedition in 1848, at his own expense, assisted by the public-spirited citizens of St. Louis, including Dr. George Engleman. He left St. Louis October 9, 1848, and went via Kanses River to headwaters of the Colorado and the Wahsatch Mountains into California by a southern pass.†

Humboldt, in his "Aspects of Nature," attempts to present the progress of discovery in the Far West.

---

* See Irving's Astoria, pp. 96, 97.

† See Upham's Life of Fremont. Boston: 1856.

PART III.

EXPLORATIONS AND SURVEYS.—1857-1880.

CONTENTS.

NOTE.

The authorities consulted, and upon which this memoir of expeditions between 1857 and 1880 depends, are the published reports of the several expeditions and works, communications from Messrs. King, Hayden, Powell, and G. K. Gilbert (the latter regarding Black Hills exploration by Jenney), replies to Engineer Department circular of February 8, 1875, and from notes compiled in the fifth division of the office of the Chief of Engineers, by whose order all the manuscript matter collected at the Engineer Department has been placed in my hands for examination and digest.

In order that a route should be considered as possessed of sufficient geographical information to be embraced in the following lists, especially of expeditions subsequent to the war, the criterion followed has been that there should have been established at its terminal points, or along its course from original and independent observations and computations, latitudes and longitudes, one or both.

Hence it has been necessary to omit many worthy military expeditions of no little magnitude and importance, that have added to the store of general geographical and topographical knowledge, that has often in map compilation been utilized by connecting with known points the geographical co-ordinates of which had been established, as also the great number of scouts, meritorious in themselves, but not provided with the means or instruments for determining independent geographical latitudes and longitudes.

To do full justice to the efforts of the Army, as a fixed, as well as a moving nuclei in the pioneer settlement of our western region would require a special memoir, and while the large number of important military expeditions are not here traced out, as not within the scope of this compilation, yet no one more than the author is alive to the great importance of all these movements, not alone as the bulwark upon which the early settlement has leaned, but as gatherers of facts, topographical detail and allied data. The Army has on one occasion and another threaded nearly every main and minor route in the West and scouted myriads of lesser streams to their very source, thus producing a vast fund of truthful and practical information that in various forms has been available to the Government, the settler, and the public.

It is not by any means certain that my examination has developed all the expeditions that come within the schedule, the available time having been short and my health broken; therefore, conscious of the imperfections, the result is submitted with diffidence, and with the hope that where errors and omissions are found that I may be notified of them.

G. M. W.

PRINCIPAL AUTHORITIES CONSULTED IN PREPARATION OF MEMOIR.

Annual Reports, Chief of Topographical Engineers, 1857 to 1862, inclusive.

Annual Reports, Chief of Engineers, 1866 to date; also manuscript and other maps at Engineer Department.

Professional Papers No. 24, Corps of Engineers, U. S. Army.

Primary Triangulation of the Lake Survey, Comstock.

Published reports and maps of the geological exploration of the 40th parallel.

Published reports and maps, geographical surveys west of the 100th meridian.

Published reports and maps of the geological and geographical survey of the Territories.

Published reports and maps of the geological and geographical survey of the Rocky Mountain region.

Published reports and maps of the geological exploration of the Black Hills.

Annual reports of the General Land Office, 1857 to date.

Annual reports of the Coast Survey from 1852 to date.

Annual reports of the Naval Observatory, and report under Nautical Almanac Office of 1869; total solar eclipse 1869.

Executive documents mentioned under the several headings: Report of the survey of the northern boundary; report of exploring expedition from Santa Fé to junction of Grand and Green Rivers, 1859, Macomb; report of explorations across the Great Basin of Utah, 1859, Simpson; report of Owen's geological survey of Iowa, Wisconsin, and Minnesota; report of exploration of Oregon Territory by M. Duflot de Mofras, two volumes, 1845; Northwestern Wyoming, including Yellowstone National Park, Jones, 1873; Nebraska and Dakota, Warren, 1855 to 1857; military wagon-road from Fort Walla Walla to Fort Benton, Mullen, 1858 to 1862; exploration of Yellowstone River, Reynolds, 1858; Texas boundary, Senate Ex. Doc. No. 70, first session Forty-seventh Congress, geological report, Hayden, Engineer Department, 1859 and 1860; Ives's Colorado River expedition, 1857 and 1858; Barlow and Heap, Yellowstone region, 1871; Ludlow, Black Hills, 1875; Ruffner, Ute country, 1873 and 1874; Raymond, Yukon River, 1869; Symons, Columbia River; Geology of the Black Hills of Dakota, Newton and Jenney, 1880.

Letters of several engineer officers to the Chief of Engineers, from archives of the Department, and maps compiled at headquarters divisions and departments; manuscript notes prepared in Division V, Office of the Chief of Engineers, U. S. Army; summary list of boundaries run by the General Land Office, in manuscript; manuscript maps of Northwest Boundary Survey, from State Department.

From manuscripts and letters kindly furnished by Messrs. Hayden, Powell, King, Hague, Gilbert, the General Land Office, and others.

CHAPTER I.

EXPLORATIONS FROM A. D. 1857 TO OUTBREAK OF WAR OF THE REBELLION.

WAR DEPARTMENT.

EXPLORATION OF LIEUT. G. K. WARREN, T. E., IN 1857. LOUP FORK, BLACK HILLS, BETWEEN FORKS OF SHEYENNE RIVER, NIOBRARA RIVER, ETC.

The survey was made under the direction of Capt. A. A. Humphreys, in charge of Office of Exploration and Survey, and for which the sum of $25,000 was set apart. Organized at Omaha, and left there June 27, 1857. The objects sought were to gain knowledge of the Territories of Nebraska and Dakota generally in both practical and scientific matters, and among the former was specially desired the nature of the routes pursued as to their being favorable or otherwise to the construction of common roads or railroads.

The expedition divided at once into two parts, one going direct to the Loup Fork of the Platte, the other up the east bank of the Missouri to Sioux City, where an escort was obtained, and thence as directly as possible to the rendezvous at the Loup Fork. Thence the whole expedition proceeded up the main Loup Fork to its source, in longitude 104° 35′, in the Great Sand Hills, making occasional side examinations some 10 miles on each side of the river.

Thence the expedition tried to proceed directly north to the Niobrara River, but the sand ridges compelled it to take a westerly course through a country with occasional alkaline and fresh-water lakes, but scantily watered, till it struck the Indian trail between the Platte and Niobrara, in longitude 102° 30′. Thence it easily reached the Niobrara River, which it followed to where the trail turns off to Fort Laramie, and thence to that point, the longitude of which was determined to be 104° 30′.

In two parts the expedition left Fort Laramie September 4, 1857, one portion proceeding down the Niobrara to about longitude 101° 30′, and there awaiting the other, which proceeded nearly due north to the neighborhood of Rawhide Butte, which was examined; thence to the Indian agency of the Dakotas, on the Niobrara, and from there by a well-marked trail to the Old Woman's Fork; down this to the Sheyenne, along this some distance, thence to Beaver Creek, and along the east branch of that into the Black Hills. Entering these from the west the Inyan Kara Creek was reached; thence southeast by a peak named in honor of General Harney to Bear Butte and the North Fork of the Sheyenne; thence southeast to the South Fork of the Sheyenne, where connection was made with the route of 1855; thence up this fork two days, then through a portion of the "Bad Lands" to the White River; thence southerly to the Niobrara River, and thence to the rendezvous with the other party at the mouth of Reunion Creek.

The whole expedition then proceeded down the Niobrara River to the junction of Turtle Creek, when the main party proceeded directly to Fort Randall, while a special party continued the reconnaissance of the river to the Missouri. At Fort Randall a longitude was determined, and thence the expedition went to Sioux City, where it closed.

Lieut. G. K. Warren, T. E., commanded the expedition, escorted by 30 enlisted men of the Second Infantry under Lieut. James McMillan. The civil assistants were J. H. Snowden and P. M. Engel, topographers; Dr. F. V. Hayden, geologist; W. P. C. Carrington, meteorologist; and Dr. S. Moffatt, surgeon.

The instruments were a portable transit of 26 inches focal length, pocket and box chronometers, sextants, prismatic and pocket compasses, odometer, mercurial barometers and thermometers, and a full outfit of everything necessary for collecting and preserving objects of natural history.

Only a preliminary report of Lieutenant Warren to Capt. A. A. Humphreys has been published in the Report of the Secretary of War accompanying the President's Message to Congress at the session beginning December, 1858. A selection from this was published in No. 9, Vol. I, of the publications of the American Geographical and Statistical Society of New

York, November, 1859, and is also quoted by the English traveler, Burton, in his "Journey across the Rocky Mountains to California," published by Harper & Brothers, New York, 1862. A number of these preliminary reports (1 vol, 8°, pp. 173, 1859), printed for special distribution by the War Department, were accompanied by a military map of Nebraska and Dakota by Lieutenant Warren, which embodied his own results and those of earlier explorers, on a scale of 1 to 120,000. This map was published by resolution of the Senate, first session Thirty-fifth Congress.

The above report was reprinted in 1875 (1 vol., 8°, pp. 125).

A letter dated January 29, 1858, by Lieutenant Warren to Senator G. W. Jones, of Iowa, by direction of the Hon. J. B. Floyd, Secretary of War, was also published (8°, pp. 15), with a small sketch map, scale 1 to 6,000,000.

SOUTHERN BOUNDARY OF KANSAS, LIEUT. COL. JOHNSTON, 1857.

This boundary was established by Lieut. Col. Joseph E. Johnston, First Cavalry, under the War Department during the summer and fall of 1857. He was assisted by J. H. Clark, H. Campbell, and J. E. Weyss.

A reconnaissance was also made for a railroad route from the southeast corner of Kansas to the Rio Grande. A practical route was found commencing at Neosho, Mo.; thence southwestwardly, crossing the Grand and Little Verdigris Rivers and the Arkansas at approximate latitude 36° 20′; thence south of west to the Canadian, connecting with Lieutenant Whipple's route of 1853 near the one-hundredth meridian; thence via head of Canadian to Anton Chico on the Pecos; thence westward to Albuquerque, on the Rio Grande. A report to the Secretary of War of the latter appears in House Ex. Doc. No. 103, Thirty-fifth Congress, first session, accompanied by a printed copy of the general map, scale 1 to 1,000,000.

The original maps of this boundary determination, in one general sheet, scale 1 to 1,000,000, and 9 detailed sheets, 8 of which are at scales 1 to 100,000, and one at scale 1 to 25,000, are now on the files of the Engineer Bureau.

From a note indorsed on Map No. IX of the vicinity of the terminal point, scale 1 to 25,000, it would appear that this point, ascertained by assuming the west boundary of Missouri at longitude 94° 38′ 03″.6 west from Greenwich and measuring 462.7 miles, was found upon revision and full comparison of the moon culmination observations, taken at this point, to be 11,582 feet too far west, which places (by this authority) the west boundary of Missouri at 94° 40′ 26″. No field-notes are on record in the Engineer Bureau.

The act of July 8, 1856, authorizing the survey directs the line "to be surveyed and distinctly marked, and a plat of said survey shall be deposited in the office of the Secretary of the Interior, and another plat of said survey shall be deposited in the office of the Secretary of the Territory of Kansas. The sum of $35,400 was appropriated to carry out the above.

EXPEDITION FOR THE EXPLORATION OF THE COLORADO OF THE WEST, BY LIETT. J. C. IVES, CORPS OF TOPOGRAPHICAL ENGINEERS, 1857-'58.

The work of this expedition was commenced at "Robinson's Landing," near the mouth of the river, on or about December 1, 1857.

The party ascended the river in an iron steamer fifty feet long, constructed in sections, and shipped from the east to the mouth of the river via San Francisco. Fort Yuma was reached January 9, 1858, where the entire party (two sections approaching from San Diego and old Fort Tejon, respectively) were assembled.

The principal object of the expedition was to ascertain how far the river was navigable for steam-boats, and whether it might not prove an avenue for the economical transportation of supplies to newly occupied military posts in Utah and New Mexico.

The steamer exploration was conducted as far as "Explorers' Rock" at foot of Black Cañon, from whence by skiff the head of the cañon was reached, and probably Las Vegas Wash. Here the further exploration of the river was abandoned, a return to the steamer made, the foot of Black Cañon assumed to be the practical head of navigation, and a reconnaissance conducted to connect this point with the road to the Mormon settlements A land party under Lieutenant Tipton also followed the banks of the river from Yuma to Pyramid Cañon. The entire expedition returned to the Mohave villages, where a division was made, a portion returning on the little iron steamer, the *Explorer*, to Fort Yuma; the remainder, including Lieutenant Ives, Dr. Newberry, Messrs Egloffstein,

Mollhausen, and Peacock, laborers, packers, and twenty soldiers as escorts under Lieutenant Tipton, took up a further land exploration. This party proceeded to the eastward, reaching by a détour the Grand Cañon at the mouth of Diamond Creek, thence along the Colorado Plateau to the northeast. The Grand Cañon was again pierced at the "Yampais villages," near the mouth of Cataract Creek; thence south and eastwardly San Francisco Mountain was reached, and eastwardly the little Colorado, from whence a northern détour brought them to the Moquis villages; thence eastwardly to old Fort Defiance, where the party was disbanded.

The expedition was in command of Lieut. Joseph C. Ives, Corps of Topographical Engineers, and under the direction of the Office of Explorations and Surveys, Capt A. A. Humphreys in charge. Lieutenant Ives was assisted by Messrs. Egloffstein and C. Bielawski as topographers, Messrs. P. H. Taylor and C. K. Bockert, assistants; Dr. J. S. Newberry, geologist, with Mr. Mollhausen as assistant. The engineer and constructor of the steamer *Explorer* was Mr. A. J. Carroll, with Robinson as pilot. The escort consisted of twenty-five enlisted men under Lieutenant Tipton, Third Artillery. The chief of land transportation was Mr. G. H. Peacock. The party were supplied with astronomical transits, sextants, and chronometers, theodolites and transits, cistern barometers, prismatic clinometer, and pocket compasses, chains, tapes, etc. Transit observations, coupled with occultations for longitude, were made at initial and check points; the latitudes were obtained by daily sextant observations and the elevations by barometric hypsometry. Hydrographic and topographic data were separately recorded. The report was made to the Office of Exploration and Survey and published in 1861 as Senate Ex. Doc., Thirty-sixth Congress, first session. It makes one volume quarto, aggregating 365 pages. It comprises also a geological report by Dr. Newberry, one on botany by Profs. Gray, Torrey, Thurbert, and Dr. Engleman, and one on geology by Prof. S. F. Baird. The appendices are devoted to the discussion of the astronomical and barometrical observations, with lists of distances, latitudes, longitudes, etc., and to the construction of the maps. There are two topographical maps: one from mouth of the Colorado to head of navigation, scale 1 inch to 6 miles; another from head of navigation to Fort Defiance, 1 inch to 12 miles. Upon these maps as a base Dr. Newberry has shown the general geological formations in colors. The report is well illustrated by an abundance of panoramic views, engravings, Indian portraits, and wood-cuts.

The party reached Fort Defiance for disbandment May 23, 1858.

This appears to have been one of the most careful, complete, and interesting of the reconnaissance expeditions prior to the war.

A preliminary report appears in the annual report of Captain Humphreys, in charge of Office of Explorations and Surveys, War Department, 1858, from pages 31 to 42, inclusive.

EXPEDITION FROM SANTA FÉ, N. MEX., TO THE JUNCTION OF THE GREEN AND GRAND RIVERS, BY CAPT. J. N. MACOMB, TOPOGRAPHICAL ENGINEERS, 1859.

The survey was commenced in July, 1859, to develop an unexplored region to the northwest. The route was from Santa Fé to Cañada, and thence crossing the Rio Grande up the valley of the Chama via Abiquiu, the then outpost of civilization in this direction, across the continental divide to the headwaters of the San Juan via "Horse Lakes," crossing the Navajoe and Blanco, reaching Pagosa Springs; thence to the valley of the Rio Dolores, crossing the streams known as Piedras, Los Pinos, Las Animas, La Plata, and Mancos, and thence northwestward to the Grand River, to a point whence could be seen the junction of its valley with that of the Green River. To Ojo Verde the route followed sensibly the old "Spanish Trail."

Returning, a southerly direction was taken till the San Juan was struck, near the mouth of Rio de la San Abaso, the right bank of which was followed up to a crossing opposite Cañon Largo, which cañon was followed up to the divide, which was crossed to the valley of the Rio Grande; thence to the pueblo of Jemez, to the crossing of the Rio Grande at San Domingo, and to Santa Fé.

The expedition was commanded by Capt. J. N. Macomb, Topographical Engineers, the escort a detachment of Company E, Eighth Infantry, by Lieut. M. Cogswell. The civil assistants were: J. S. Newberry, geologist; C. H. Dimmock, topographer; F. P. Fisher, as time and astronomical observer; Messrs. Dorsey and Vail, meteorologists. Captain Macomb was the astronomical observer and computer.

The instruments were sextants and artificial horizons, a refracting telescope of about 6 feet focal length and 4 inches aperture, prismatic and pocket compasses, sidereal chronometers, barometers, and thermometers.

A report was made November, 1860, to Capt. A A. Humphreys, Topographical Engineers, in charge of Office of Explorations and Surveys, and printed (page 149, Senate Ex. Doc. No. 1, second session Thirty-sixth Congress).

Subsequent duty with the Army in the field prevented a more full report on the part of the officer in command.

A map* of the route was prepared on a scale of 2 inches to 1 mile or 1 to 31,680, a reduction from which was incorporated in the map of explorations and surveys in New Mexico and Utah, 1860, scale 1 inch to 12 miles, constructed and engraved on a steel plate by F. W. von Egloffstein.

The survey was completed in September, 1859.

The Geological Report was published by the Engineer Department, U. S. Army, 1876 (1 vol., 4°, 152 pp) While the map was engraved in 1860, the publication of this report, in common with others on western surveys, was arrested by the war of the rebellion, each and every available military officer and man being called to the field.

Captain Macomb, while en route east, proceeded to the southwest corner of the then Territory of Kansas and retraced that part of the boundary along the thirty-seventh parallel from the old monument to the one hundred and third meridian, and erected a stone monument at the intersection of the above meridian and parallel in November, 1859.

EXPLORATIONS AND SURVEYS FOR WAGON-ROADS ACROSS THE GREAT BASIN OF UTAH FROM CAMP FLOYD TO GENOA, BY CAPTAIN SIMPSON, T. E., 1859.

This exploration and survey, ordered by Bvt. Brig. Gen. Albert S. Johnson, commanding Department of Utah, and having for its object the discovery of routes across the Great Basin of Utah more direct and practicable than the Fremont route—hitherto believed the only one possible—left Camp Floyd May 3, 1859. No itinerary is given, but the party reached the termination of the westward exploration June 12, started

*This map contains on its face the latitude and longitude of a number of points determined (astronomically) by the expedition.

on its return June 24, and reached Camp Floyd August 5, having discovered two practicable emigrant and military roads, either of which shortened the distance between Camp Floyd and Genoa 200 miles.

The party, in command of Capt. J. H. Simpson, Topographical Engineers, was accompanied by an escort of twenty men commanded by Lieut. Alexander Murray, 10th Infantry, and consisted of Lieut. J. L. Kirby Smith, Topographical Engineers, in charge of observations, with sextant for latitude and time or longitude; Lieut. H. L Putnum, Topographical Engineers, in charge of compass survey of route and topography, observations with astronomical transit for longitude and of dip-circle and magnetometer; Henry Engleman, geological, meteorological, and botanical collector; Charles S. McCarthay, collector of specimens of natural history and taxidermist; C. C. Mills, photographer; Edward Jagiello and William Lee, assistants to astronomer, meteorologist, and photographer; H. V. A. von Beckle, a soldier, as artist to take sketches. Asst. Surg. Joseph C. Bailey accompanied the expedition. The entire party, including the escort and employés, numbered sixty-four persons. The expedition was provided with three sextants, three artificial horizons, one astronomical transit, four chronometers, two barometers, and several prismatic and pocket compasses.

The report of Captain Simpson, made to the Chief of Topographical Engineers, February 5, 1861, is accompanied by reports from his assistants on the topographical, geodetic, magnetic, geological, mineralogical, botanical, ethnological, and pictorial character of the country traversed, by a map drawn by J. P. Mechlin (scale 1 to 1,000,000), by profiles, diagrams, and sketches. An important result of the expedition was the establishment by Captain Simpson of a new and more accurate longitude of Salt Lake City, differing largely from certain previous determinations, which has since been substantially verified by the telegraphic determination of the Coast Survey. The report of Simpson was published by the War Department at the Government Printing Office in 1876, and appears as one volume, quarto, 495 pages, accompanied by maps and other illustrations. There is a geological report by Henry Engleman, one on paleontology by Prof. F. B. Meek, a list of birds by Professor Baird, a chapter on ichthyology by Theodore Gill, with botany by Dr. George Engleman.

The entire report consists of an "Introduction, Report, and Journal" and nineteen appendices. It is accompanied by a map (scale 1 to 1,000,000) of the wagon-roads explored and opened by Captain Simpson, which contains original topographical data of parts of the Great Interior Basin, then (1859) but little known. Captain Simpson in 1858, prior to his western trip, examined and surveyed a new wagon route (the itinerary of which appears in the above volume) from Camp Floyd to Fort Bridger, which was constructed also under his direction, and a report of which appears in Senate Executive Document No. 40, Thirty-fifth Congress, second session.

RECONNAISSANCE, FORT DALLES, OREGON, TO GREAT SALT LAKE VALLEY, LIEUT. JOSEPH DIXON, T. E., 1859.

A command was organized for the purpose of exploring and opening a wagon-road from Fort Dalles, Oregon, on the Columbia River, to Great Salt Lake Valley, by special orders No. 40, Headquarters Department of Oregon, dated April 27, 1859, Brig. Gen. W. S. Harney, commanding. Capt. H. D. Wallen, Fourth U. S. Infantry, was in command of the expedition, and Bvt. Second Lieut. Joseph Dixon, Corps of Topographical Engineers, was assigned to duty with the command.

The route traveled commences at Fort Dalles and runs nearly due south, crossing Deschutes River, at the mouth of Warm Spring Creek, to Crooked River, following the same to its headwaters, and from thence to Lake Harney; from thence northeasterly, crossing the Blue Mountains to Malheur River; crossing which, meandering mountain passes and adjacent valleys, Malheur River is again crossed, to Snake River and along this stream to Raft Creek, which is followed to its source at Cedar Spring; thence crossing the dividing ridge to Bear River, which it crosses near mouth of Roseaux River, and from thence nearly due south to Salt Lake City and Camp Floyd.

Another route commences at Fort Dalles and runs easterly to Umatilla River, which it crosses and follows for about 30 miles, thence southeasterly crossing the Blue Mountains to headwaters of Burnt River, which it follows to its mouth on Snake River; thence to Malheur River where the first route crosses that river the second time.

Another route was traversed by Lieutenant Bonnycastle, of the expedition, from Crooked River to Fort Dalles, crossing the Deschutes at its mouth on the Columbia.

Still another route, by Mr. L Scholl, was also traveled, from vicinity of the mouth of the Owhyee near where the first route crosses Snake River, following the course of the Owhyee to near mouth of Kearney River, which it follows to its source, thence passing headwaters of Cañon Creek, Bruneau, and Salmon Falls River, etc., to Rock Creek, connecting with first-mentioned route.

The instruments used on this exploration consisted of sextants, chronometers, barometers, compasses, odometers, etc.

The reconnaissance was completed as far as Lake Harney, and on October 20, 1859, the command returned to Fort Vancouver.

The report of Lieutenant Dixon was submitted to the Chief of Topographical Engineers and published in Senate Executive Document No. 1, second session Thirty-sixth Congress, accompanied by a map, scale 1 inch to 20 miles, compiled under the direction of Capt. George Thom, Topographical Engineers.

A general report of this expedition, accompanied by reports of Lieutenant Dixon and Lewis Scholl, guide and topographer, appears as Senate Executive Document No. 34, Thirty-sixth Congress, first session. In the appendices are found (pp. 46–49) tables of latitudes, longitudes, variations of the needle, altitudes, and distances.

SURVEY OF THE NORTHWESTERN BOUNDARY OF THE UNITED STATES, 1857–'61.
STATE DEPARTMENT.

The United States Commission, authorized to determine and mark the boundary line between the United States and the British Possessions, from the crest of the Rocky Mountains to the Pacific Ocean, according to the treaty of June 15, 1846, and to act conjointly with a similar English commission, was created by act of Congress of August 11, 1856.

A commission, consisting of Captains Prevost and Richards, Royal Navy, was appointed by the British Government to determine that part of the line which runs through "the channel which separates the continent from Vancouver's Island."

In the summer of 1858 Col. J. S. Hawkins, Royal Engineers, appointed as British commissioner to determine the land portion of the boundary, arrived with a party organized for field operations. In February, 1857, Mr. Archibald Campbell was appointed commissioner for the United States; Lieut. John G. Parke, Topographical Engineers, chief astronomer and surveyor, and G. Clinton Gardner, assistant astronomer and surveyor. Other members of the expeditionary force were William J. Warren, secretary to the commission; John J. Major, clerk to the chief astronomer; J. S. Harris, general assistant; C. B. R. Kennerly, surgeon and naturalist; Henry Custer and Francis Herbst, topographers; George Gibbs, assistant geologist; J. N. King, quartermaster and commissary; R. V. Peabody, guide and interpreter; Prof. James Nooney and F. Hudson, computers; Charles T. Gardner, surveyor; E. Ross, assistant; and James M. Alden, artist; also, the requisite number of packers, laborers, etc.

The United States Commission was duly organized and repaired to Fuca Straits in the spring of 1857;—from whence, because of the inability to co-operate of the British Commission, the United States Commission established a depot and located an observatory at the western land terminus of the forty-ninth parallel, and continued reconnaissances and explorations in the vicinity of the boundary eastward as long as the season permitted. Four astronomical points on the forty-ninth parallel were determined. A meeting of the joint commission was held in the summer of 1858, and a plan for the field operations for the survey of the land boundary was agreed upon.

The reconnaissance at the close of this season had extended as far east as the valley of the Skagit, and the astronomical observations necessary for marking the three points of the parallel in the valley of the Chiloweyuck were completed.

The following is the work done during season of 1859: Completion of the determination and marking the parallel from three points fixed the previous year; observations for latitude at six stations, between which the parallel has been determined, and seven points marked at crossings of streams; chronometer-trip for difference of longitude between Camp Simiahmoo and Chiloweyuck Depot; longitude determined at two of the latitude stations; triangulation covering an area of 50 square miles; route survey (chained) connecting astronomical stations of about 370 miles; reconnaissance for developing the topography along and adjacent to the boundary line and for communications; magnetic observations at one station and meteorological registers at all the stations occupied.

It is understood that the commission remained in the field during the seasons of 1860 and 1861, but no report is available from which to trace its operations and results for these seasons. The commission passed the winter of 1859–'60 at Fort Colville.

United States troops for the protection of the parties were furnished by General Harney from the Department of Oregon. In 1859 an additional escort, under Captain Archer, met the parties in the valleys of the Similkameen and Okinakane.

The route of the United States Commissioner in 1859 commenced at Fort Langley, thence running down Fraser's River by water to mouth of Chiloweyuck River; thence along the latter to its source, crossing the divide to head of Similkameen River, thence following its northern bank to Lake Osoyas; thence via valley of the Ne-hoi-al-pit-gua River to Fort Colville; thence via Slavoutchas and Chemikana Rivers to the Spokane River; thence to Lewis Fork or Snake River, at the mouth of the Peloux, and to Walla Walla; thence due south to the Umatilla; thence to Fort Dalles; from the Dalles by water to Monticello, thence along the Cowlitz River and the headwaters of the Chehalis to Olympia on Puget Sound.*

The transportation was largely by mules and pack-trains on land, and whale-boats on the water. Bridging streams, corduroying and grading rough roads, with ferryings at river crossings, was constantly done.

The instruments used were astronomical transits, heliotropes, zenith telescopes, transit theodolites, telescopes, sextants, chronometers, magnetic theodolites, dip-circles, compasses, pocket levels, chains, tapes, camera-obscura, barometers, hygrometers, and thermometers.

Monuments marking stations on the parallel were constructed of pyramidal piles of stones 6 to 8 feet high, or earthen mounds, covering wooden posts.

*This route is indicated in manuscript on a printed map of Oregon and Washington Territories, 1859. Scale 1 to 1,500,000, Bureau of Topographical Engineers.

These stations were established at nearly every accessible point from which the line was ascertained, and traced along vistas crossing valleys and trails. The reconnaissance line connecting stations was 800 miles, embracing an area of 30,000 square miles. Within this space over 800 barometric heights were obtained. The boundary line exceeds 9° in longitude, or about 410 miles, and the amount expended (see Senate Ex. Doc. No. 86, Fortieth Congress) for its survey and demarkation, including the preparation of results, was $569,223.79, or at the rate of $1,388.34 per mile. Magnetic observations were made over an arc of 3° 20′ in latitude, and 4° in longitude.

Reports upon the geology, botany, and natural history of the reconnaissance area were prepared. Glaciers were discovered and perpetual snow found in the cascades (2 feet of snow found on the route in July, 1859). Much of the line ran through a heavy growth of pine and fir, with much fallen timber.

A progress report of the marking of the boundary, made November 12, 1859, appears as Senate Ex. Doc. No. 16, Thirty-sixth Congress, first session. The expenditures made appear in House Ex. Doc. No. 86, Fortieth Congress, second session, in which a letter from Mr. Campbell to the Secretary of State gives data concerning the nature and extent of the services performed, but I have been unable to trace the manuscript of the final report, including that of the chief astronomer and the specialists, which it is believed was made. According to the Journal of the Senate of February 9, 1871, this report was called for by the Senate, but a search of the Senate records, and also those of the State Department, made at my request by Mr. Dwight, librarian of the State Department, remained unavailing on June 15, 1887. Mr. William J. Warren, secretary of the commission, now chief clerk of the Engineer Department, recollects to have seen the manuscript of this report at the office of the Northern Boundary established in 1873, as does also Maj. J. F. Gregory, Corps of Engineers, a member of that commission, but it could not be found by Mr. Dwight in the records transmitted at the close of the latter survey to the State Department. The original manuscript maps are on file in the State Department, photographic copies of which were furnished the General Land Office.

Captain Prevost, R. N., visited the 49th parallel in October, 1857, and in absence of Captain Richards proposed to proceed to the determination of the water boundary. He claimed Rosario Straits (the channel nearest the continent), and Mr. Campbell the Canal de Haro (the channel nearest Vancouver's Island), as the boundary channel intended by the treaty. The British commissioner, after correspondence, proposed to compromise by running the boundary through an intermediate channel, thereby securing the island of San Juan to Great Britain, which the United States commissioner declined.

Senate Ex. Doc. No. 29, second session Fortieth Congress, contains the correspondence above referred to; also a geographical memoir of the islands in dispute, and a map and cross-section of the channels.

In pursuance of the fifth section of the act creating the commission the superintendent of the Coast Survey was directed to place the steamer *Active* and brig *Fauntleroy* at the disposal of the commission. Both of these vessels were employed for the survey and soundings of the various channels and islands between the continent and Vancouver's Island, co-operating with Captain Richards of the British surveying steamer *Plumper*, as a result of which a thorough survey of these channels and islands south of the 49th parallel was made during the several seasons, which was shown on the map above mentioned.

Maps.—The following maps were constructed and compiled under the supervision of Archibald Campbell, commissioner, and Lieut. John G. Parke, Topographical Engineers, by Assistants L. D. Williams, Theo. Kolecki, and Ed. Freyhold, in 1866, and found reproduced, as follows:

"Survey of the northwest boundary, 1857–'61, from Point Roberts, along the forty-ninth parallel to the Rocky Mountains between the British Possessions and the United States," fourteen sheets, scale 1 to 60,000, photo-lithographed on double the scale of the originals; also, maps showing the boundary line from the western coast of the continent to the middle of the channel which separates the continent from Vancouver's Island, and thence southerly through the middle of said channel, etc., to Fuca Straits, scale 1 inch to 4 miles (engraved); also, map embracing the country between the parallels 46° and 49° 30′, and from the Pacific to 110° west longitude (all in Washington Territory), scale 1 inch to 17 miles (photographic copies); also, a series of cross-sections from Vancouver's Island on parallels 49°, 48° 45′, 48° 35′, and 48° 25′, respectively, to the mainland, were also prepared (engraved).

MILITARY ROAD, FORT WALLA WALLA TO FORT BENTON, BY CAPT. MULLAN, 1858-'62.

The purpose of this expedition, which took the field in 1858, was to survey, locate, and build a wagon-road from Fort Benton, on the Missouri, to the Oregon country at Walla Walla, thus completing a northern line of road communication to the Pacific.

The route commenced at Walla Walla and ran northeast to Snake River at the mouth of Palouse Creek, crossing on the way Dry Creek and Ponchet River; along Palouse River, Cow Creek to Aspen Grove; from thence northeast crossing the head of Rock Creek, a tributary of the Oray-tayons River, to Hangman's Creek and to Spokane River, which it crossed and followed to Cœur d'Alêne Mission and the river of that name; thence crossing summit of Bitter Root Mountain and striking the source of St. Regis Borgia River, the valley of which and also that of Bitter Root River it follows to Hell's Gate; thence along the Big Blackfoot River to Hell's Gate River; thence along Deer Lodge River; thence northeast over hilly ground to Little Blackfoot, up which and over the west base of the Rocky Mountains at Mullan's Pass to Prickly Pear Creek, which it follows to near its mouth; thence due north to Dearborn River; thence via Bird Tail Rock to Blackfoot Agency on Sun River, and thence northeast to Fort Benton.

The expedition was under the command of Capt John Mullan, Second Artillery. He was assisted by C. R. Howard and Capt. W. W. de Lacey, civil engineers; P. M. Engel, topographical engineer; Theo Kolecki, topographer; John Weisner, meteorologist, and assistants; G. Sohon, guide and interpreter, and others in various capacities. The military escort consisted of 100 men, detailed from the Third Artillery, at Fort Vancouver, accompanying which were Lieuts. James L. White, H. B. Lyon, and James Howard, Third Artillery. The report made to the Chief of Corps of Topographical Engineers was published as Senate Executive Document No. 43, Thirty-seventh Congress, third session, accompanied by four maps: One, reconnaissance from Fort Dalles via Fort Walla Walla to Fort Taylor, on Snake River, scale 1 to 300,000; one from Fort Taylor to the Cœur d'Alêne Mission, scale 1 to 300,000; one from Cœur d'Alêne Lake to Dearborn River (tributary of the Missouri River), scale 1 to 300,000, and a general map of the entire route, scale 1 to 1,000,000. The field work closed in September, 1862. In the exploration and location of this road distances were measured by the odometer, longitudes determined by lunar culminations, latitudes by polaris and meridian altitudes and prime vertical observations (the astronomical transit and sextant being employed), bearings by the Schmalcalder compass, profiles by the barometer, together with variations of the needle from camp to camp. The resulting latitudes, longitudes, and altitudes appear in an appendix to the above document. Considerable topographical information regarding territory on either side of the route, especially from a reconnaissance northward to Fort Colville, Wash., appears for the first time on the resulting general map. During the Indian difficulties of 1858, Lieutenant Mullan commenced the exploration and location of this road from Fort Dalles as far as Cœur d'Alêne Mission, as acting topographical engineer on the staff of Col. Geo. Wright, Ninth Infantry, and his report forms Senate Executive Document No. 32, Thirty-fifth Congress, second session.

EXPEDITION TO THE HEADWATERS OF THE YELLOWSTONE AND MISSOURI, BY CAPT. W. F. RAYNOLDS, CORPS OF TOPOGRAPHICAL ENGINEERS, 1859-'60.

The expedition started from St. Louis, May 28, 1859, by steamer, passed up the Missouri to Fort Pierre, and left the river at that point June 28, 1859, having for its object the examination of the headwaters of the Yellowstone and Missouri Rivers, and of the mountains in which they have their sources.

Leaving Fort Pierre the expedition went westward, skirting the northern slope of the Black Hills to the waters of the Powder River; down that stream to within 40 miles of the Yellowstone; thence westward to that river, below the mouth of the Big Horn; thence southward to the Platte, by two routes, one up the Big Horn, skirting the eastern base of the Big Horn Mountains, the other from 20 to 50 miles farther east. The expedition wintered at Deer Creek, on the North Platte. From winter quarters to the three forks of the Missouri the expedition was divided. One party passed up the Wind River with the intention of reaching the headwaters of the Yellowstone, but was compelled by impassable mountains to cross to the headwaters of the Columbia, near the sources of the Colorado; thence along the west side to Henry Lake; thence down the Madison to the three forks of the Missouri. The second passed through the valley of the Big Horn to the lower cañon; thence westward, by the Yellowstone and Gallatin of the Missouri to the three forks; thence to the mouth of the Yellowstone by three routes—the first by way of the Yellowstone; the second overland, on the east side of the Missouri to Fort Benton, thence by the Missouri; and the third overland from Fort Benton, following approximately the line separating the waters of the Yellowstone and Missouri Rivers. From the mouth of the Yellowstone part of the expedition descended the Missouri in boats to Omaha, and the remainder reached that place by a route never passed over before on the west side of the Missouri.

The expedition was commanded by Capt. W. F. Raynolds, Corps of Topographical Engineers.

The escort for the year 1859 was commanded by First Lieut Caleb Smith, Second Infantry. The escort for the year 1860 was commanded by First Lieut. John Mullins, Second Dragoons, and First Lieut. Henry E. Maynadier, Ninth Infantry, was assistant.

Astronomical positions en route were determined with sextant and chronometer The topography was sketched with the use of prismatic compass and odometer The longitude of "winter quarters" was determined by observations ot moon culminations with transit instrument.

The report, delayed by the breaking out of the rebellion, was made to the Chief of Engineers in 1867. The narratives of Captain Raynolds and his assistants were published as Ex. Doc. 77, Fortieth Congress, first session (8vo, 174 pages).

A special geological report by F. V. Hayden was printed in 8vo, 174 pages, at the Government Printing Office in 1869. The report (Ex Doc. 77) was accompanied by a topographical map on the scale of 1 to 1,200,000, by profiles and sketches of routes, and by numerous illustrations, and the special geological report contains the above topographical map, geologically colored.

This exploration first pointed out a route for a wagon-road, which was subsequently opened from the Platte to the three forks of the Missouri, skirting the eastern base of the Big Horn Mountains, and first located correctly the Yellowstone River from where it leaves the mountains to the mouth of Powder River. Captain Raynolds was told by his guide, James Bridger, of the latter having visited and seen "burning plains, immense lakes, and boiling springs" near the sources of the Yellowstone, as also the "Two Ocean River;" but impracticable ridges and deep snows prevented the party from penetrating from the Wind River direction the region since so well known as the Yellowstone National Park.

NOTE.—Bridger also gave Lieutenant Gunnison, while the latter was associated with Stansbury on the Salt Lake Survey (1849–'50), a description of the natural wonders of the Upper Yellowstone, mentioning a lake 60 miles long; plains where the ground resounded to the tread of the horses; geysers spouting 70 feet high; waterfalls; mammoth hot, acid, and other springs. (See Gunnison, History of the Mormons, 1852, page 151.)

The following papers accompanying the report have not been published:

Tables of latitudes and chronometer errors.
Tables of meteorological observations and barometrical heights (two routes 1859, and two routes 1860).
Tables of meteorological observations at Deer Creek.
Tables of meteorological observations at Fort Prien.
Report on Fossil Plants, by Prof. J. S. Newberry.
Report on Fossil Birds, by Dr. Elliott Coues.
Report on Mammals.
Catalogue of Plants, by Dr. George Engleman
Report on Carices, by Prof. Chester Dewey.
List of Mosses and Liverworts, by Professor Sullivan.
List of Shells, by Professor Binney.

The party reached Omaha, where it disbanded, October, 1860.

HARNEY LAKE TO EUGENE CITY, OREGON, LIEUTENANT DIXON, TOPOGRAPHICAL ENGINEERS, 1860.

By special order No. 37, Headquarters Department of Oregon, April 6, 1860, a command was again organized for the purpose of opening a wagon road from Harney Lake to Eugene City, Oregon, in extension of the exploration made in 1859.

The expedition was commanded by Maj. Enoch Steen, First Dragoons; and Bvt. Lieut. Joseph Dixon, Corps of Topographical Engineers, was assigned to duty with it. The instruments used were the same as in 1859.

A preliminary report, dated September 24, 1860, was made of this expedition by Lieutenant Dixon to the Chief of the Corps of Topographical Engineers, and will be found in his annual report for 1860.

A map of this expedition by Lieutenant Dixon, scale 1 to 750,000, is to be found in Senate Executive Document No. 1, Thirty-seventh Congress, second session.

The reconnaissance was commenced May 24, 1860, and on June 16 it had reached Lake Harney. From thence it was continued in a northwesterly direction with satisfactory results for a distance of 105 miles, when, on account of Indian difficulties, it returned to Lake Harney, and September 14, 1860, to Fort Vancouver.

The area traversed by the expeditions of 1859 and 1860 embraces a great portion of the country between latitude 42° and 45° and longitude 117° and 119° W. from Greenwich, independent of the southeasterly routes reaching Great Salt Lake.

UNITED STATES AND TEXAS BOUNDARY COMMISSION; J. H. CLARK, UNITED STATES COMMISSIONER, DEPARTMENT OF THE INTERIOR, 1858, 1859, 1860.

The boundary line is the one-hundredth meridian west from Greenwich, between the main Red River and the parallel of 36° 30′ north latitude; this parallel between the one-hundredth and one hundred and third meridian, the latter meridian between the parallels of 36° 36′ and 32° and this parallel between the one hundred and third meridian and the Rio Grande.

This commission was organized and conducted by instructions of the Secretary of the Interior of July 9, 1858, pursuant to act of June 5, 1858. Mr. J. H. Clark (the commissioner for the United States) was assisted in the astronomic work by H. Campbell and for the topography by J E. Weyss and W. P. Clark.

No corresponding Texas commission was continuously in the field, and the only known published results appear in Senate Executive Document No. 70, Forty-seventh Congress, first session.

This document, which embraces the field-notes of the astronomic and topographic work, is accompanied by fourteen detailed photolithographic maps (incomplete), each showing a portion of the line, one having upon it the scale of 1 inch to 2½ miles, or 1 to 132,000. The general map, scale 1 inch to 15 miles 4,133 feet (reported as lost in the above document), was found and photolithographed at the Engineer Department, the original having passed into the office of the Commissioner of Public Lands. None of the maps are authenticated or approved, and one is missing.

The field work commenced on January 9, 1859, near the junction of the thirty-second parallel with the Rio Grande, connection being had with the longitude determination of the Mexican boundary near El Paso, and terminated September 7, 1860, the winter quarters of the commission being at Fort Smith, Ark. The latitudes of forty-six stations, resulting from zenith telescope and sextant observations, are found on page 143.

Lunar culmination observations for longitude were made near junction of one hundred and third meridian and thirty-second parallel and near northwest corner, results from which were used in the field, but no final longitude computations are given.

The northwest corner was established by the transfer of longitude from the Kansas boundary, checked by a lunar culmination longitude and independent zenith telescope latitude.

The eastern boundary was joined to that part of the one-hundredth meridian between the Red and Canadian Rivers, run (with the assistance of Daniel G. Major, astronomer) by Messrs. Jones and Brown, in 1859, for the Indian Bureau.

That part of the west boundary between, approximately, 33° and 33° 45′ north latitude was not traced and marked on the ground on account of the desert character of this portion of the Staked Plains.

No part of the line was officially agreed upon or accepted by the two Governments. The length of the boundary is about 800 miles, the determination of which, on account of physical obstacles, required a survey of more than 1,400 miles, checked by nearly 4,000 astronomic observations.

The latitude of Fort Cobb was determined, a part of the Pecos meandered, and considerable topography sketched on either side of the line.

The monuments were of cairns of stone or mounds of earth.

The appropriation of $80,000, made for field operations alone, was also available for the office work, so far as continued. The work was transferred to the General Land Office, and suspended on January 21, 1862, with the maps left, as stated, in a partially finished condition.

During the period from 1857 to the outbreak of the war officers of the corps of Topographical Engineers were engaged in the survey, location, and construction of military wagon-roads in the following States and Territories, viz: Minnesota, Kansas, Nebraska, New Mexico, southern and northern Oregon, Washington and Utah Territories.

While geographical data was not the principal object, the survey of each and every road added its details to the first topographical knowledge of a vast expanse of country, while sketches and maps were always available in compilation of general maps issued by the Topographical Bureau.

The Interior Department during this period were also engaged in the construction of what were termed "Pacific wagon roads," of which Albert H. Campbell was superintendent. (See House Ex. Doc. No. 108, Thirty-fifth Congress, second session, and Senate Ex. Doc. No. 36, Thirty-fifth Congress, second session, the latter accompanied by a number of compiled maps.)

The principal therein mentioned are the "Fort Ridgely and South Pass Road," the "Fort Kearney and South Pass and Honey Lake Road," the "El Paso and Fort Yuma Road," and the "Nebraska Road."

The Land Office or planimetric subdivision surveys, necessary for marking the legal townships and other divisions, were carried on steadily in the several States and Territories west of the Mississippi River during this period.

The Coast Survey operations (devoted principally to the hydrography and a narrow strip of topography adjacent to main harbors) commenced on the west coast in the year 1848. Their progress, which is not especially pertinent to this memoir, will be found in the several annual reports of this service.

The wagon-road examined from Fort Defiance to the Colorado River by E. F. Beale, under the War Department, during the summer and winter of 1857-'58, will be found reported upon in House Ex. Doc. 124, Thirty-fifth Congress, first session. This report is accompanied by a map and itinerary from Albuquerque to the Colorado.

The outbreak of the war of the rebellion called all available officers and enlisted men to duty with the army in the field. The officers of Topographical Engineers were one and all called from the scene of their geographical labors in the Far West for actual war military service.

This corps was merged with the present Corps of Engineers in 1863, and no duties of a topographical character were resumed till the close of the war, when, in 1865, such service was first resumed in the Military Division of the Pacific by Major Williamson, as will appear in the succeeding chapter. (See annual reports of the Chief of Topographical Engineers up to 1863, and all reports of the Chief of the Bureau of Exploration and Survey, accompanying the Secretary of War, for reference to details of wagon-roads, compiled maps, and various results of a topographical nature, concluding those of the ante-war period.)

CHAPTER II.

RECONNAISSANCES, EXPLORATIONS, AND SURVEYS, HEADQUARTERS, MILITARY DIVISIONS AND DEPARTMENTS A. D. 1865 TO A. D. 1880.

SUSANVILLE TO FORT BIDWELL, CALIFORNIA, AND FORT KLAMATH; MAJOR WILLIAMSON, CORPS OF ENGINEERS, 1865.

The survey made by order of Maj. Gen. I. McDowell, commanding Department of the Pacific, organized at Fort Crook, and left there July 18, 1865. It had for its object the examination of routes of communication from Susanville, California, to Idaho and Surprise Valley, and from there to Fort Klamath, and the exploration of such unknown localities as might be of military interest, and to report upon sites for military posts which might become necessary for the protection of the increasing settlements and mining interests.

The routes traveled were from Fort Crook to Susanville, to Smoky Creek Depot, to Summit Springs on the Idaho route, to Surprise Valley, and along its west side to Fort Bidwell, where a connection was made with the northeast boundary corner of California, as established by the surveyor-general of California, and Warner's Valley and Mountains located. From Fort Bidwell a route was surveyed across Warner's Range by Lassen's Pass to Pitt River, the south fork of which was explored to its headwaters in the range near Saddle Mountain, which was ascended and its altitude obtained; thence to Madeline Plains and Pass and to Susanville by Pine Creek. From Susanville a more direct route was examined by Eagle Lake across Madeline Plains to the south end of Surprise Valley; thence by its western side to Fort Bidwell; thence by Lassen's Pass to Hot Springs at the head of Goose Lake, to south fork of Sprague River, and down this to Fort Klamath; thence to Lost River, along this to Grass Valley, and thence by the Old Emigrant Trail to Fort Crook.

Maj. R. S. Williamson, Corps of Engineers, commanded the expedition, and Captain Tillinghast the escort. The civil assistants were John D. Hoffman, photographer, and G. S. Demeritt, barometric observer.

The prismatic compass was used for angles, the odometer for distances, and the barometer for altitudes. Latitudes by sextant were observed at nearly every camp.

The report was made to the General Commanding the Department, but was not subsequently printed. It was accompanied by a map on a scale of 1 inch to 3 miles. In 1866 a map of parts of California, Nevada, Oregon, and Idaho was compiled, comprising the results of the expedition, and published with the consent of the Commanding General by Britton and Rey, of San Francisco.

The survey was completed by the return to Fort Crook, September 28, 1865.

RECONNAISSANCE MADE BY MAJ. R. S. WILLIAMSON, CORPS OF ENGINEERS, IN 1866, FROM FORT CHURCHILL TO CAMP McDERMIT, THENCE TO RUBY AND SILVER CITY VIA CAMP LYON AND RETURN TO CHURCHILL.

The survey made by order of General Halleck, organized July 25, 1866, at Fort Churchill, Nevada, to examine the hitherto unknown portions of northern California and Nevada and southern Oregon and Idaho, with the special object of discovering more direct and easy routes of travel.

The route was from Fort Churchill to the bend of the Truckee River, down this river to where it empties into Pyramid Lake.

A curious discovery was here made of the forking of the Truckee, one branch emptying into Pyramid Lake, the second into Winnemucca Lake, some 3 miles distant and 50 feet lower, 15 miles long and 3 wide.

The shore of this lake was followed to its northern extremity; thence the route lay in a northeast direction to Camp McDermit, a number of springs being discovered on the way. From Camp McDermit the usual circuitous trail to Camp Lyon was followed, from whence an examination was made to Ruby City, Silver City, and vicinity, returning to Camp Lyon.

From there a direct route was examined back to Camp McDermit, passing by the forks of the Owyhee River, which flows for many miles through a cañon from 500 to 1,500 feet deep, which can be crossed in but few places. One of these crossings is at the forks, where wagons can ascend and descend. Thence in a southeast direction an elevated plateau was crossed, from the top of which the descent of several thousand feet was made to the valley of Quin's River, where Camp DcDermit is situated. An attempt was made to find a better and more direct route from this camp to Lassen's Meadows, but the country was found to be sandy, with water only at long distances. From Lassen's by another route to Winnemucca Lake and thence to Fort Churchill.

Maj R. S. Williamson, Corps of Engineers, commanded the expedition. There was no commissioned officer commanding the escort, but Lieut. W. H. Heuer, Corps of Engineers, was Major Williamson's assistant. G. C. Demeritt was the meteorologist.

The instruments used were the sextant, prismatic compass, and odometer. Sextant observations were made nearly every night.

The report was made to the assistant adjutant-general, Department of California, accompanied by tables of distances, altitudes, etc., and a topographical sketch. The report was never printed, but a map on a scale of 1 inch to 12 miles was subsequently lithographed by Britten and Rey, of San Francisco. It is now out of print.

INDIAN EXPEDITION FROM FORT RILEY TO FORT DODGE AND FROM FORT HARKER TO DENVER, COLORADO, 1867, UNDER COMMAND OF GEN. W. S. HANCOCK AND BVT. MAJ. GEN. G. A. CUSTER—LIEUT. M. R. BROWN, CORPS OF ENGINEERS.

The route was from Fort Riley via Smoky Valley and Smoky Hill River to Salina, thence to Fort Harker, thence to Fort Zarah, thence along Arkansas River to Fort Larned, thence up Pawnee Fork to Indian Village, thence to Fort Dodge to headquarters of Coon Creek, thence to Fort Larned; from Fort Larned to Walnut Creek, and crossing Smoky Hill River to Old Fort Hayes on Big Creek, thence via Smoky Hill Valley to Fort Harker.

The expedition left Fort Harker again via Smoky Hill River Valley to Fort Hayes; thence along Big Creek to its source; thence to the head of

Castle Rock Creek and Fort Wallace; thence along the South Fork of Smoky Hill River via Big Timber to Cheyenne Wells; thence via Deering's Wells, David's Wells, and Hugo Springs to Willow Springs; thence along Big Sandy Creek to River Bend. From here the command proceeded by two different routes. The first, north by way of Cedar Point, Fairmount, Benham Springs, Bijou, and Kiowa; the second, south via Reed Springs, Bijou Basin at the source of Bijou Creek, and crossing Kiowa River to Denver. A route was also pursued from Fort Wallace along the valley of the Smoky Hill to Chalk Bluff, thence to Castle Rock, thence to Downer's, and along the valley of Smoky Hill River to New Fort Hayes.

Lieutenant Brown had with him on this expedition a sextant, transit, and artificial horizons, and made observations for latitude, longitude, and variation of the needle.

Accompanying his manuscript report, dated Fort Leavenworth, October 19, 1867, to the Chief of Engineers, are tables of distances measured by odometer, detail journal sketches of the country passed over, its topographical and geological character, and information concerning wood, water, and grass.

REPUBLICAN FORK TO ONE HUNDREDTH MERIDIAN, KANSAS PACIFIC RAILROAD, CAPTAIN HOWELL, CORPS OF ENGINEERS, 1868.

A transit and level line with chain measurement was run by Capt. Charles W. Howell, Corps of Engineers, in 1868, from a point on the Kansas Pacific Railroad up the Valley of the Republican Fork (east side) and across the divide to the valley of the Platte, to connect with a monument erected on the Union Pacific Railroad to mark the crossing of the one hundredth meridian west of Greenwich. The topography was sketched in, and Capt. George D. Graham was in charge of the escort, consisting of two non-commissioned officers and ten privates, Tenth Cavalry. The longitude of the terminal point of the survey was determined by observations with a sextant and telegraphic communication with Chicago. The monument was first established by the engineers of the railroad company by measurement from old Fort Kearney, Nebraska.

RECONNAISSANCE IN NORTHERN DAKOTA, BY CAPT. W. J. TWINING, CORPS OF ENGINEERS. 1869.

The survey, made by orders from headquarters Department of Dakota, started July 1, 1869, having for its object a reconnaissance of the part of northern Dakota lying east of longitude 100° 30′.

The surveyed lines were as follows: (1) From Fort Abercrombie to Fort Totten; (2) from Fort Totten to St. Joseph, crossing the head-waters of the western tributaries of Red River, and returning to the west of Devil's Lake; (3) from Fort Totten to Mouse River and Turtle Mountain and return; (4) a direct trail from Fort Totten to the south bend of Mouse River; and (5) from Fort Totten to Georgetown, on the Red River.

The officer in command was Capt. W. J. Twining, Corps of Engineers. The party was escorted, after leaving Fort Totten (September 6), by Lieutenant Lacristo, Twentieth Infantry, thirty men, and four Indian scouts.

The routes traveled were surveyed with a small compass and odometer, and were checked in latitude by frequent astronomical observations.

The report was made to the department commander, February 20, 1870. The map of the reconnaissance, incomplete, was embodied in the maps of northern Dakota. The report, field-notes, and astronomical observations were also used in connection with the work of the United States Northern Boundary Commission (1872–'74).

RECONNAISSANCE OF THE YUKON RIVER, ALASKA, BY CHARLES W. RAYMOND, CAPTAIN OF ENGINEERS, 1869.

The survey was commenced July 1, 1869, having for its object to fix the geographical position of Fort Yukon (latitude 66° 33′ 47″ north, longitude 145° 17′ 47″ west), and generally to gain information concerning northern Alaska, its resources, the disposition of the native tribes, etc.

The following is the itinerary of the route: Sailed from San Francisco April 6, 1869, to Sitka; thence on the *Commodore* to San Michael's Island, Morton Sound, carrying their small stern-wheel steamer *Yukon*, to be used in the ascent of the river of that name, under deck, leaving Sitka May 9.

On July 1 the *Yukon* was launched, and on the 4th the voyage to the upper mouth of the Yukon River commenced. Fort Yukon was reached

July 31 (distance 1,040 miles). This was the first journey by steam that had been made on the Yukon.

On August 28 the return trip was commenced. Anvic River was ascended in canoes to the head of navigation, 50 miles from mouth, thence over a divide a portage was made to the valley of the Golsova Richka, thence over an almost impassable country, arriving September 24 at the native village of Ikikitoik, on the coast of Norton's Sound, whence, on the 5th of October, a messenger was sent to San Michael's Island for assistance, from whence a whale-boat was secured, in which the party were taken to the ship *Commodore*, which sailed for San Francisco and reached there November 6, 1869.

Capt. Charles W. Raymond, Corps of Engineers, commanded the expedition, Mr. John J. Major being assistant. For surveying, prismatic compasses and hand levels were used; for astronomy, a sextant and five chronometers, portable transit, and zenith telescope; for hypsometry, mercurial and aneroid barometers, wet and dry bulb thermometers; magnetic instruments, theodolite magnetometer, and dip-circle.

The report was made to Maj. Gen. H. W. Halleck, commanding Military Division of the Pacific, and was printed as Senate Executive Document No. 12, Forty-second Congress, and was accompanied by a map lithographed by Julius Bien, on a scale of 1 inch to 50,000 feet, or 1 to 600,000.

The geographical co-ordinates of Fort Yukon being determined, it was found to be on United States territory. Possession was taken and the United States flag raised.

EXPEDITION FOR A MILITARY RECONNAISSANCE THROUGH SOUTHERN AND SOUTHEASTERN NEVADA IN 1869.—LIEUTENANT WHEELER, CORPS OF ENGINEERS, U. S. ARMY.

This expedition started from Camp Halleck, Nevada, on the 27th of June, 1869, and had for its object, in accordance with instructions from headquarters Department of California, Brig. Gen. E. O. C. Ord, commanding, a thorough reconnaissance of the country to the south and east of the White Pine Mines, extending, if practicable, to the head of navigation on the Colorado River, with a view to opening a wagon road thereto from the White Pine or Grant mining district; obtaining correct data for a military map of the country, and for the selection of the site or sites for such military post or posts, to cover the mining country south and east of White Pine from hostile Indians, as might be required. Explorations and examinations in reference to the physical geography of the country, its physical resources in wood, water, agricultural, and mineral productions, were required, and notice was also to be taken of the character, habits, and number of Indian tribes, and their disposition toward miners and settlers.

The area embraced by the reconnaissance of this year was 24,428 square miles, including portions of southeastern Nevada and western Utah. The officer in command (Lieut. George M. Wheeler, Corps of Engineers, U. S. Army, chief executive officer and field astronomer) was assisted by an officer of Engineers as assistant executive officer and field astronomer, an assistant surgeon of the Army, one chief topographer, one assistant topographer and photographer, one surveyor and draughtsman, one assistant surveyor and recorder, one collector, one guide, and the requisite number of teamsters, packers, and laborers.

Personnel of expedition.—First Lieut. George M. Wheeler, Corps of Engineers, U. S. Army, in command, chief executive officer and field astronomer; First Lieut. D. W. Lockwook, Corps of Engineers, U. S. Army, assistant executive officer and field astronomer; John D. Hall, assistant surgeon, U. S. Army; P. W. Hamel, chief topographer; Carl Rahskopff, assistant topographer and photographer; Charles E. Fellerer, assistant topographer and draughtsman; William M. Ord, assistant surveyor and recorder; John Koehler, collector; Henry Butterfield, guide.

The escort consisted of two non-commissioned officers and twenty-five enlisted men, drawn principally from company H, Eighth U. S. Cavalry.

Besides the daily latitudes and chronometric longitudes, by means of which and trigonometric measurements all the lines of survey were checked, it was found practicable to determine, by telegraph, longitudes at the following stations: (1) Camp Halleck, (2) Peko, (3) Elko, (4) Camp Ruby, (5) Camp near Hamilton, and (6) Monte Christo Mill, White Pine district; the value and character of which appear in the preliminary report.

Instruments.—The instruments used were sextants, theodolites for observations upon peaks, and small Casella instruments with Schmackalder compasses for meandering. Comparison of time was had with members of the U. S. Coast Survey, and Maj. H. M. Robert, Corps of Engineers, San Francisco, Cal.

Transportation.—The train consisted of thirty-six persons, eight wagons, forty-eight mules, and thirty-one horses. Supplies were provided at specified points, to which they were transported by the above army wagons, from whence, as centers, they were taken when required by pack animals along the routes following trails, or across country.

Reports.—A special report of this reconnaissance was made to General Ord, commanding the Department of California, and printed at San Francisco in 1869 in a folio pamphlet, accompanied by a topographical map, separately issued, on a scale of 1 inch to 12 miles.

This report, with additions, was reprinted in quarto form (pp. 72) and without the map, at the Government Printing Office in Washington, in 1875. On account of absence in the field no annual report was made at the close of the fiscal year 1868–'69 to the Chief of Engineers.

During this survey eighteen mining districts were visited, viz: Cave, White Pine, Robinson, Patterson, Sacramento, Snake, Shoshone, Ely, El Dorado, Yellow Pine, Timber Mountain, Hercules, Tim-pah-ute, Pahranagat, Reveille, Hot Creek, Morey, and Grant, and notice was taken of their character. The examination showed that there were two distinct extended parallel lines of mineral deposits, both bearing southerly to the military road from Mohave to Prescott. The route for a through line of travel, shortest and most practicable for a rail or wagon road, was found to be the one which crosses the Colorado River at the mouth of the Virgin River, furnishing more wood, water, and grass, and having generally less barren land along its way. By this route loaded wagons can reach Camp Toll-Gate from the Central Pacific Railroad in twenty-one days. Four mineral belts, having a general north and south course, are contained in the region traversed, viz, the Hot Creek, Humboldt, Egan, and Schell Creek belts or ranges. The minerals found are gold, silver, copper, lead, antimony, iron, salt, gypsum, alum, and cobalt; silver being the principal one.

The highest mountains are in the Humboldt and Spring Mountain ranges, some of the peaks reaching 12,000 to 13,000 feet. The rivers are the Colorado, Humboldt, and Virgin, and of the numerous smaller streams many become absorbed in the plains.

A large portion of the region observed is unfit, from its mountainous and desert character, for agricultural purposes, and, where cultivation is possible it must be with irrigation usually. Timber and game are not abundant, and in portions of the valleys water and grass are scarce. The timber for use is white and yellow pine; the principal forage, bunch grass. Herds of cattle range in the principal valleys.

Besides the mining settlements or camps, seven Mormon settlements were encountered along the route surveyed. Indians of the following tribes, to the number of about 2,500, were found within the limits of the survey, viz: Shoshones, Gosiutes, Snakes, Pahvants, Utes, and Pah-Utes.

About 5 miles from where Muddy Creek enters Virgin River is a large deposit of rock salt, known as Salt Mountain. On the left bank of the Virgin, about 8 miles from its entrance into the Colorado, is a salt mine yielding 80 per cent. of salt; the yield of the mountain being 90 per cent. On an extensive mesa, near the mouth of the Virgin, there is a salt well, and saline water is found in pools along the river wash.

A cave in Cave Valley, 3,000 feet in extent, is found near the Patterson mining district.

The Colorado River formed the southern limit of the survey, and was noticed, with reference to practicability of navigation, at Black and El Dorado Cañons, and other points. It was found to be navigable at all seasons as far as El Dorado Cañon, above which point, until obstructions are removed, navigation is dangerous as far as it may ever be carried, viz, to the foot of the Grand Cañon. The part of the Colorado River touched upon was afterward traversed in boats during the exploration of the Grand Cañon in 1871.

This survey discovered that the body of water known as Preuss Lake in the memoirs of Fremont's explorations is the reservoir into which Sevier River empties, and, instead of being in Nevada, lies wholly in Utah. It is now known as Sevier Lake, and, with Salt, Utah, and Owen's Lakes, lies within the great interior basin embracing portions of California, Nevada, and Utah, the waters of which find no outlet to the ocean.

Field work terminated on the 28th of November, nearly six months having been occupied in preliminary and actual observations.

The reductions, necessary upon which the maps were based were made at San Francisco, California, at the headquarters of the Department of California, where the reports were also prepared.

Results.—The principal result of this reconnaissance was the topographic data gathered over an area of 24,428 square miles, and published in preliminary and also final form, the latter appearing on regular atlas sheet, 48 D, 49, 57, 58, 59, and 66. Many new latitudes, longitudes, and altitudes were added to those hitherto existing.

This reconnaissance, based principally on meander methods checked by principal and intermediate astronomic determinations (of the former of which there were six stations), was the precursor of more elaborate reconnaissance work in 1871 and subsequent years, until the introduction of triangulation methods in 1873, that subsequently were carried to the establishment of a complete trigonometric basis for the detailed topography in 1874 and subsequently.

RECONNAISSANCES IN MONTANA AND DAKOTA TERRITORIES, BY CAPT. D. P. HEAP, CORPS OF ENGINEERS, 1870.

Capt. D. P. Heap, Corps of Engineers, as engineer officer of the Department of Dakota in 1870, surveyed the trails from Pembina to Fort Totten, and from Fort Ransom to Fort Wadsworth. He also approximately determined the forty-ninth parallel and marked it from Red River to Pembina, and later in the season made a short reconnaissance of the country near the mouth of the Yellowstone, commencing at Fort Buford, thence up the Yellowstone for 50 miles and return; thence west between the Yellowstone and Missouri, a distance of 40 miles, turning north and striking the Missouri; thence southeast, reaching the outward trail at Nelson's Springs, returning to Buford by the outward route.

Mr. King acted as Captain Heap's assistant in these surveys, except the last, when Mr. Sturgis was engaged.

The instruments used were odometer, compass, chain, sextant, pocket chronometer, and engineer's transit. The distance traveled was about 184 miles. A report and map of the last reconnaissance, on a scale of 1 inch to 2 miles, were forwarded to department headquarters.

YELLOWSTONE EXPEDITION OF 1870, LIEUT. G. C. DOANE, U. S. ARMY.

Lieutenant Doane, in August, 1870, in accordance with instructions from headquarters military district of Montana, with one sergeant and four privates of Company F, Second Cavalry, escorted the surveyor-general of Montana (H. D. Washburn) and eight others to the falls, lakes, and hot springs and geysers of the Yellowstone.

While this expedition does not answer to the criterion of those coming within the scope of the memoir (no latitudes or longitudes having been determined), yet it is introduced as a link in the chain of exploratory endeavor that led to the discovery, exploration, location, survey, and physical examination of that wonderful region now known as the Yellowstone National Park, the probable existence of which was first made known to the scientific world by Captain Raynolds, of the Topographical Engineers, in his report on the exploration of the Yellowstone, published in 1868. This party started from Fort Ellis August 22 on the direct road to the Yellowstone River, which was reached near Butler's Ranch. The valley of the river was then followed to the "Great Falls," thence to Yellowstone Lake, thence via head of Yellowstone and Snake Rivers to Firehole River, a tributary of the Madison, which was followed to near the upper settlements, Lieutenant Doane reaching Fort Ellis in return via Sterling.

A descriptive report by Lieutenant Doane appears as Senate Ex. Doc. No. 51, Forty-first Congress, third session. The information gathered by him was also presented to the Philosophical Society of Washington during the winter of 1870-'71, by Prof. S. F. Baird, and doubtless stimulated the further exploration of this region during the season of 1871 by Prof. F. V. Hayden and party, under the Interior Department, and Captains Barlow and Heap, under the Engineer Department.

RECONNAISSANCE OF THE UPPER YELLOWSTONE, BY CAPT. J. W. BARLOW, CORPS OF ENGINEERS, AND CAPT. D. P. HEAP, CORPS OF ENGINEERS, 1871.

By order of Lieut. Gen. P. H. Sheridan, commanding Military Division of the Missouri, the survey took the field at Fort Ellis, Mont., July 16, 1871, having for its object the examination of the sources of the Yellowstone, Missouri and Snake Rivers, for the purpose of verifying the reports of extraordinary phenomena existing in that region. Crossing the Bozeman Divide it proceeded up the valley of the Yellowstone, discovering and examining the remarkable system of hot springs near the mouth of Gardner's River; thence the Great Falls, the Boiling Mud Springs and the Yellowstone Lake were visited; thence west to the wonderful geyser basin on Fire Hole River, a tributary of the Missouri; thence up the valley and across to the Yellowstone Basin. The western shore of the Yellowstone Lake was meandered, and then the party turned southward to the sources of the Snake River; thence eastward to the Yellowstone, down this valley to the lake, the eastern shore of which was surveyed; thence to the Great Falls on the east side; thence a detour to the east fork of the Yellowstone, which was descended to its mouth. Recrossing the Yellowstone the party returned to Fort Ellis, and disbanded September 1, 1871.

The expedition was in command of Capt. J. W. Barlow, Corps of Engineers, who was assisted by Capt. D. P. Heap, Corps of Engineers. The civil assistants were W. H. Wood and H. G. Prout, topographers; Thomas J. Hine, photographer. The small cavalry escort was commanded by Capt. G. L. Tyler.

The instruments were sextants, chronometers, barometers, compasses, and odometers.

The report forms Senate Ex. Doc. No. 66, second session Forty-second Congress, and is accompanied by a map of the route traversed on a scale of 1 to 300,000.

EXPLORATION IN UINTAH MOUNTAINS, UTAH, BY CAPT. W. A. JONES, CORPS OF ENGINEERS, 1871.

The object of this expedition, as determined by the instructions from headquarters Department of the Platte, was as follows:

(1) To ascertain the character and extent of the valleys of the streams and their adaptability to cultivation or grazing.

(2) To ascertain the character of the timber, its amount, location, and the feasibility of getting it to the railroad.

(3) If possible, to find a wagon road from Fort Bridger to the Uintah Indian Agency.

(4) If practicable, to examine the country on Green River with reference to the large mineral deposits reported there.

Generally, to give all useful information concerning the country examined, which is now comparatively unknown.

The party left Omaha June 11, 1871, and arrived at Fort Bridger June 29, proceeding south along the west branch of Smith's Fork (9 miles distant), thence ascending this stream 24 miles, thence to Gilbert's Pass, thence eastward 12 miles to the headwaters of a branch of Lake Fork called Big Spring Creek, which was followed for 12 miles to within 14 miles of its mouth on the Uintah River. After examination and survey in this vicinity the Uintah Valley Agency, on the North Uintah River, was reached via the valley of this stream.

From thence northeast across Tau-a-wah to Ashley Creek, tributaries of Green River; thence northerly to near the summit of the mountains; thence northwesterly via the heads of Hunting-Ground Creek, Sheep Creek, and Burnt Fork to Henry's Fork, near boundary between Utah and Wyoming; thence northwesterly through the "Bridger Bad Lands" to Sage Creek, northerly along valley of Cottonwood Creek, and due westerly across to Smith's Fork, arriving at Bridger August 19, 1871.

The country was minutely and carefully examined on either hand from the route pursued. On account of the poor character of the transportation furnished it was found impracticable to examine the Green River country as had been anticipated. The expedition was in command of Capt. W. A. Jones, Corps of Engineers, assisted by one topographer and one flagman, and with an escort of one corporal and six men, under Lieut. W. W. Wood, Thirteenth Infantry.

A practicable wagon route was found from Fort Bridger to the Uintah Valley Agency via the pass at the head of the main branch of Smith's Fork, discovered by Lieutenant-Colonel Gilbert, Seventh Infantry. The funds available admitted of only a simple reconnaissance.

The report on this reconnaissance appears as Appendix A A of the Annual Report of the Chief of Engineers for 1872, accompanying which a map was prepared of the "Uintah Mountains and vicinity," scale 1 to 627,264, drawn by L. von Froben, 1872.

RECONNAISSANCES BY CAPTAIN HEAP, 1872.

In 1872 Captain Heap made a reconnaissance of the right bank of the Missouri from Fort Rice to the mouth of Heart River, and surveys of the roads or trails from Fort Rice to the Northern Pacific Railroad crossing of the James River, and from there to Fort Abercrombie.

The instruments employed were of a similar character to those used by Captain Heap in 1870. Captain Heap, during same year, also reconnoitered the country between Beaver Dam and Buck Creeks, including that portion between these streams above and below present site of Fort Abraham Lincoln. A report and map (scale 1 inch to 4,000 feet) were forwarded to department headquarters. The instruments used were sextant, transit, and chain.

RECONNAISSANCE OF THE YELLOWSTONE AND MUSCLESHELL RIVERS, BY MAJ. J. W. BARLOW, CORPS OF ENGINEERS, 1872.

Major Barlow, assisted by Second Lieut. Henry A. Irgens, accompanied the Northern Pacific Railroad engineers in their surveys in 1872 eastward from Fort Ellis, which they left July 27, to the Yellowstone, thence after a few days' work northward to the Muscleshell, up this valley, across the Belt Range, and down Sixteen-Mile Creek to the Missouri. Maj. J. W. Barlow, Corps of Engineers, commanded the expedition.

The escort of three hundred and seventy-six men, cavalry and infantry, was commanded by Bvt. Col. E. M. Baker, major Second Cavalry. The survey disbanded at Fort Ellis about September 29, 1872.

The report was published in Ex. Doc. No. 16, third session Forty-third Congress. A map (scale 1 to 1,200,000) of the country and a survey of the camp where an Indian battle occurred were made, but not published with the report.

SURVEY OF THE YELLOWSTONE RIVER FROM FORT BUFORD TO A POINT TEN MILES ABOVE POWDER RIVER, BY CAPT. WILLIAM LUDLOW, CORPS OF ENGINEERS, JULY, 1873.

This reconnaissance was made in connection with the movements of the Yellowstone expedition of that year. Boats loaded with stores ascended the Yellowstone 85 miles to Glendine Creek, the point near which the Northern Pacific Railroad survey line struck the river, and Captain Ludlow, after departure of the expedition from Glendine Creek, overtook it 10 miles above the mouth of Powder River. The river was carefully mapped by means of compass bearings and estimated distances checked by daily observations with sextant and chronometer. The expedition which Captain Ludlow accompanied consisted of six companies of the Sixth Infantry, commanded by Capt. H. S. Hawkins, Sixth Infantry. A report and map (on a scale of 1 inch to 4 miles) were forwarded to department headquarters.

The astronomical determinations will be found of record at the headquarters of the department at St. Paul.

LAVA BEDS, CAPT. G. J. LYDECKER, CORPS OF ENGINEERS, 1873.

Captain Lydecker made a reconnaissance of the lava beds during the Modoc campaign in northern California in April and May, 1873.

The preliminary report was made to the commanding general of the division, together with sketches and stereoscopic views, and subsequently a general map (showing position of Jack's stronghold, lake shore and country between Hospital Rock and General Gillem's camp, scale 1 inch to 1 mile) was prepared and forwarded to the Engineer Department. Mention of this reconnaissance appears in Captain Lydecker's annual report. (See Annual Report Chief of Engineers, 1873, Appendix FF.)

UTE COUNTRY EXPLORATION, BY LIEUT. E. H. RUFFNER, CORPS OF ENGINEERS, 1873.

This exploration was organized by command of Brigadier-General Pope, commanding Department of the Platte. The expedition left Pueblo, Colo. (the longitude of which was determined by telegraph), May 7, 1873, and ran a line to Fort Garland, Colo., thence across the San Luis Valley and up the Rio Grande to its source, and down the Animas River. Retracing the line to the vicinity of longitude 107° the Pacific Divide was again crossed, the Lake Fork of the Grand River was followed down to its grand cañon, thence east via Los Pinos Agency and Cochetopa Pass to the San Luis Park, where the first line was joined at Del Norte.

Refitting at Fort Garland the expedition was continued over the Cochetopa Pass, up Taylor River and its tributaries, across the Red Mountain Pass to the head of the Arkansas River, and down it to Cañon City, Colo. A side line was run through Puncho Pass, ending at Fort Garland, to connect with the Land Office surveys in San Luis Park. This expedition was the outgrowth of the disturbed relations between the Uncompahgre Utes and the miners of the so-called San Juan region, the ascertaining of the position of the eastern boundary of the Indian reservation (107° west of Greenwich) being the principal object, which was supplemented by an examination of the various approaches from the Arkansas to the Ute country.

The personnel was as follows: Assistant Engineer H. G. Prout (in charge of field work); assistant engineer, James Bassett; recorder, Samuel Anstey; recorder, D. W. Campbell; geologist, F. Hawn; assistant geologist, L. Hawn; photographer, T. Hines and two sergeants of the Engineer Battalion. A small escort from Company F, Eighth Cavalry, commanded by a sergeant, accompanied the first part of the exploration, and Lieutenant De Lancy, with a detachment from Company D, Fifteenth Infantry, escorted the second party.

The line was run by theodolite, the angles being referred to meridians determined nightly; the distance was ascertained by the use of a stadia, and this is believed to be the first time this method has been used in mountain work. A report made to the Chief of Engineers of this exploration, accompanied by a lithographed map on a scale of 1 to 500,000, was printed in Executive document No. 193, Forty-third Congress, first session, House of Representatives, and separately as a pamphlet by the Engineer Department in 1874.

The expedition disbanded at Pueblo October 4, 1873.

Photographic copies of forty-six detail sheets (scale 1 to 50,000) are on files of the Engineer Department.

In appendixes to this report are found tables of distances with astronomically determined positions and altitudes.

RECONNAISSANCE OF NORTHWESTERN WYOMING, INCLUDING THE YELLOWSTONE NATIONAL PARK, BY CAPT. W. A. JONES, CORPS OF ENGINEERS, 1873.

The expedition, which took the field at Fort Bridger, Wyo., in June, 1873, had for its object "the reconnaissance of the country about the head-waters of the Snake, Green, Big Horn, Gray Bull, Clark's Fork, and Yellowstone Rivers;" also to find, if possible, a good route from the south, via the Wind River Valley and Upper Yellowstone, to the Yellowstone National Park and Montana. The route traversed was: leaving Fort Bridger June 12; thence northward to Camp Brown; thence northward across the Owl Creek Mountains into the valley of the Big Horn as far as the Stinking Water River; thence westward across the South Shoshone Mountains to Yellowstone Lake; thence northward, a portion of the expedition going to Fort Ellis, Mont., and making a wide detour to the westward, visiting all the noted phenomena in the park; thence southeast via the head of Wind River to Camp Brown, where the expedition disbanded.

Capt. W. A. Jones, Corps of Engineers, commanded the expedition, and Capt. Henry E. Noyes the escort, of Company I, Second Cavalry, and fifteen Shoshone Indians, who were accompanied by their families.

The assistants were Prof. T. B. Comstock, geologist; Dr. C. C. Parry, botanist and meteorologist; Assistant Surg. C. L. Heizman, U. S. Army, chemist; Second Lieut. S. E. Blunt, Thirteenth Infantry, astronomer; Second Lieut. R. H. Young, Fourth Infantry, acting assistant quartermaster and acting commissary of subsistence; Louis von Fröben and Paul Le Hardy, topographers.

The instruments were one large transit theodolite, one small transit theodolite, one chain, three odometers, pocket compasses, one reflecting circle, one sextant, two box and two pocket chronometers, two mercurial and two aneroid barometers, ordinary pocket maximum and minimum and radiation thermometers, and one medical test chest, with apparatus for the field analysis of waters and gases.

The report was made to Brig. Gen. E. O. C. Ord, commanding Department of the Platte, and with the maps form House of Representatives

Executive Document No. 285, first session Forty-third Congress; also House of Representatives Bill No. 2854, first session Forty-third Congress. The former document with additions, including geological report by Professor Comstock, was republished by the War Department in 1875 (1 vol., 8°, pp. 331, with maps and sketches).

The much-doubted "two-ocean water" was discovered where one stream forms the common source of two, running respectively to the Atlantic and Pacific flowing waters.

A very easy pass was found at the head of Wind River, thus opening a route to Montana from the southeast via Wind River and the Yellowstone National Park, the distance from Point of Rocks, Wyo., to Yellowstone Lake being 289 miles, and to Fort Ellis 437 miles.

The reconnaissance was completed in September, 1873.

FORT GARLAND TO FORT WINGATE, LIEUTENANTS RUFFNER AND ANDERSON, 1874.

Lieut E. H. Ruffner states that in June, 1874, Lieut. G B. Anderson, Sixth Cavalry, was detailed from Fort Lyon, Colo., to conduct a survey for a direct wagon route from Fort Garland, Colo., to Fort Wingate, N. Mex. A small detachment of Company M, Sixth Cavalry, accompanied the party, which consisted, in addition to Lieutenant Anderson, of Assistant Engineer D. W. Campbell and Recorder Samuel Anstey.

The instrumental work was done by azimuth and stadia, as in the prior surveys of this office. The line was run southwest from Fort Garland, the instrumental line commencing at a point on the land surveys at the junction of the Conejos River and Rio San Antonio. Two lines were thus carried across the high mountain spur separating the waters of the Conejos and the Rio Chama, one of the tributaries of the Rio Grande, during the month of July.

The report of Lieutenant Ruffner on the results of this examination and survey, accompanied by that of Lieutenant Anderson, is found in House Executive Document No. 172, Forty-fourth Congress, first session (with map, scale 1 to 1,000,000).

An "atlas of detail sheets" (fourteen in number; scale, 1 to 50,000) remain as originals on the files of the Engineer Department.

RECONNAISSANCE OF THE BLACK HILLS, CAPT. WILLIAM LUDLOW, CORPS OF ENGINEERS, 1874.

The expedition under command of Lieut. Col. G. A. Custer was organized in pursuance of special orders No. 117, Headquarters Department of Dakota, June 8, 1874, and had for its purpose the reconnoitering of a route from Fort Abraham Lincoln to Bear Butte, in the Black Hills, and exploring the country south, southeast, and southwest of that point.

The expedition consisted of ten companies of cavalry, two of infantry, and a number of Indian scouts, in all about 1,000 men, one guide, interpreters, and teamsters. Captain Ludlow was detailed as its engineer officer.

The line of reconnaissance (1,204 miles in length) commenced July 2, moving southwestwardly toward the bend of Heart River; thence across the north fork of the Cannon Ball; thence across the south fork, called also Cedar Creek; thence over the Belle Pierres Hills; thence into the valley of the North Fork of Grand River; following this valley for a distance, the trail bore to the southwest, across several bends of the South Fork of Grand River, to a camp on a small branch of the Little Missouri; from this point (called Prospect Valley) the trail led around the northern extremity of the Short Pine Hills, into the valley of the Little Missouri; thence southeasterly in the direction of Bear Butte, camp was made on a small branch of the Belle Fourche, the valley of which stream was reached at a point 292 miles from Fort Lincoln; thence by Redwater Creek, a tributary of Belle Fourche, into the Black Hills; thence to Myan Kara Creek, after the peak of that name, which was here ascended, and near the source of which exploring parties were sent out in various directions; thence camp was made in Castle Valley Creek; thence southeasterly to an unnamed creek (from whence Harney Peak was ascended); from this point reconnaissances were made to the south and southeast, toward the plains, rendezvous being again made in the heart of the Black Hills. On August 6 camp was broken for the return trip, which followed partly the incoming route, to determine the practicability of a road northward through the hills, emerging near Bear Butte. Castle Valley and Elkhorn Prairie were retraversed, whence the plains were reached, and a trail reconnoitered over a different route in 1875, returning to Fort Lincoln (see pp. 1128 and 1129, Annual Report Chief of Engineers), which point was reached August 30, the sixtieth day of the trip.

Captain Ludlow was assisted by W. H. Wood, topographer, and a detachment of Engineer soldiers. Prof. W. H. Winchell was geologist; Dr. Williams, surgeon, U. S Army; George Bird Grinnell, paleontologist and zoologist; a photographer also accompanied the party.

The instruments used were odometers, prismatic compasses, mean solar chronometers, barometers and thermometers, a Wurdemann transit, and a sextant.

The general topography along all routes and at all points visited was carefully recorded and the lines checked by astronomical latitudes and points in the hills checked from a measured base by trigonometric means.

A preliminary report of this expedition was made to the Chief of Engineers, and appears in his Annual Report for 1874 (Appendix KK). A subsequent report, including summaries of distances, latitudes, longitudes, and altitudes, and the result of geological examinations of W. H. Winchell, State geologist of Minnesota, and upon paleontological observations by George Bird Grinnell, representing Prof. O. C. Marsh, appears as Appendix PP, Annual Report Chief of Engineers for 1875. This report also, accompanied by maps, was subsequently reproduced in quarto in 1875 (pp. 121).

The latter document is accompanied by a map of the reconnaissance (scale 1 inch to 12 miles); one of the Black Hills, topographical (scale 1 inch to 3 miles), and a geological map, based on the same.

RECONNAISSANCE FROM CARROLL, MONTANA, TO THE YELLOWSTONE NATIONAL PARK AND RETURN, BY CAPT. W. LUDLOW, CORPS OF ENGINEERS, 1875.

The reconnaissance commenced at Carroll, Mont., July 13, 1875; thence the Carroll road was surveyed to Camp Baker, Mont.; thence to Fort Ellis; thence through Bozeman Pass and up the Yellowstone River to the Yellowstone Park, and return by same route to Ellis August 31; thence to the South Fork of Deep Creek; thence down the South Fork of the Musselshell to the forks; thence along the Carroll road to Armelis Creek. From this point an examination of the Judith basin was made by Lieutenant Thompson, under direction of Captain Ludlow; thence to Carroll, September 19, 1875.

Captain Ludlow commanded the expedition, assisted by Second Lieut. R. E. Thompson, Sixth Infantry. The escort from Carroll to Baker was

10 men, Second Cavalry, under command of Second Lieut. C. F. Roe, Second Cavalry, and from Ellis to Carroll of 2 non-commissioned officers and 8 men of Second Cavalry. The civil assistants were W. H. Wood and Edwin Ludlow, topographers; G. B. Grinnell, paleontologist and zoologist; Edward S. Dana, geologist, besides his detachment of engineer soldiers; and Charles Reynolds, hunter and guide.

The instruments used were transit, chain, sextant, reflecting circle, prismatic compass, odometers, and chronometers.

The report was accompanied by a map of the reconnaissance on a scale of 1 inch to 6 miles. The published report (Appendix NN, Report Chief of Engineers, 1876) is illustrated by three maps—of the reconnaissance, 1 inch to 12 miles; of the Judith Basin, 1 inch to 6 miles; and of the Geyser basin, 1 inch to 6 miles. This report was also separately published in quarto, 155 pages, in 1876.

BIG HORN AND YELLOWSTONE EXPEDITION, CAPT. W. S. STANTON, CORPS OF ENGINEERS, 1876.

This expedition, of fifteen companies of cavalry, five of infantry, one hundred and five wagons, and six hundred pack-mules, commanded in person by General George Crook, was organized at Fort Fetterman in May, 1876.

The expedition left Fetterman May 29, marching northward on the old Montana road, camping first on Sage Creek; thence on branch of Cheyenne; thence across two tributaries to headwaters of this stream; thence to Dry Fork of Powder River; thence to Clear Fork of Powder River; thence via old Fort Phil Kearney to camp on Little Piney Creek; thence to Hay Creek; thence to mouth of Prairie Dog Creek; thence returning along this creek, reaching camp on Goose Creek; thence to Rosebud Creek, where a successful engagement was had with the Sioux Indians; thence to a small stream in vicinity of Tongue River; thence by a devious route to new rendezvous camp on Goose Creek; thence to Camp Cloud Peak, on same stream; thence to main Fort Smith road, near Fort Phil Kearney, returning by the outward route and reaching Fort Fetterman June 21.

Captain Stanton, engineer officer to the expedition, was assisted by Mr. R. F. Koehneman, draughtsman and topographer; Private Henry Kehl, general service, and two infantry soldiers.

The instruments employed were sextants and chronometers for difference of time and latitude, mercurial and cistern barometers, prismatic compass and odometers. Careful topographical sketches of country adjoining the route were made.

A report of the reconnaissance will be found as Appendix PP, Annual Report Chief of Engineers, 1876, and it is also mentioned in Appendix QQ, Annual Report Chief of Engineers, 1877.

CAMPAIGN AGAINST THE HOSTILE SIOUX, LIEUT. E. MAGUIRE, ENGINEER OFFICER, 1876.

The expedition organized in the Department of Dakota was in command of Brig. Gen. A. H. Terry, and to which Lieutenant Maguire, U. S. Engineers, was attached as chief engineer.

It left Fort Abraham Lincoln May 17, 1876, marching almost due west to Heart River; thence to Sweet Brier Creek; thence to Crow's Nest, or Buzzard's Roost Butte; thence to Big Muddy Creek; thence via Big Muddy Valley to Thinfaced Woman's Creek; thence to north fork of Heart River; thence to valley of Powder River; thence to valley of Davis Creek; thence to the Little Missouri; thence via Sentinel Buttes to Beaver Creek; thence via head of Cabin Creek to O'Fallon's Creek; thence to Powder River; and thence to the Yellowstone—a total distance of 318½ miles.

The command with which Lieutenant Maguire moved was transferred by steamer up the Yellowstone, to near the mouth of the Big Horn, where the march to the Little Big Horn commenced, which was reached about 9 miles above its mouth, near the scene of the Custer massacre, which battle-field was mapped.

A return march was made to the Yellowstone, and a reconnaissance carried up the valley of the Rosebud and via Tongue River to Pumpkin Creek; thence to the valley of Powder River via a tributary of the Mizpah, and thence again to the Yellowstone, from whence movements were made in different directions. Astronomical observations, necessarily interrupted by the specially military necessities of the campaign, requiring moving by pack train at a moment's notice in any direction, without intervals of repose, were taken at a number of points, results from which appear on pages 1359 and 1360, Annual Report Chief of Engineers, 1877.

The instruments used were chronometers and sextants, with artificial horizons.

Transportation was both by wagon and pack-train. The elevations are barometric; the measurements are odometric.

Lieutenant Maguire was assisted by Second Lieut. E. J. McClernand, Second Cavalry, and Mr. W. H. Wood. His report appears as Appendix PP of Annual Report Chief of Engineers, 1877.

The original map, now on the files of the Engineer Bureau, drawn by Sergt. James E. Wilson, Battalion of Engineers, is to the scale of 1 inch to 12 miles.

RECONNAISSANCE OF ROUTES IN WYOMING, BY CAPT. W. S. STANTON, CORPS OF ENGINEERS, 1877.

The parties took the field at Cheyenne, Wyo., July 11, and proceeded first to Fort Laramie, 88 miles; thence to Hat Creek, 60 miles; thence to Deadwood, 126 miles; thence to Fort McKinney, 197 miles; thence to Fort Fetterman, 91 miles; thence to Rock Creek Station, Union Pacific Railroad, 83 miles; thence to Laramie Peak, 45 miles; thence to Fort Laramie, 60 miles; thence to Camp Robinson, 73 miles; thence to Deadwood, 157 miles; thence to Custer City, 55 miles; thence to Hat Creek, 87 miles; thence to Camp Robinson, 53 miles; thence to Sidney Barracks, 120 miles; where disbandment was made November 3.

The length of the reconnaissance was 1,328 miles. Forty-four latitudes and longitudes were determined, twenty-two magnetic declinations, and two hundred and seventy-one barometric altitudes.

The expedition was in command of Captain Stanton, who was assisted by Lieutenant Swigert, Second Cavalry; Lieut. Henry Seton, Mr. R. F. Koehsman, draughtsman and topographer; 10 enlisted men, one of whom acted as photographer. An escort of 1 sergeant and 9 men from Fort Laramie, and a like number from Camp Robinson, accompanied the expedition.

The instruments employed were sextants, chronometers, prismatic compass, cistern and aneroid barometers, and odometers.

Independent of latitude and longitude determinations by Captain Stanton, as well as magnetic variations, careful topographic sketches of country adjacent to the routes was recorded, and the usual hypsometric observations taken for altitudes.

The report of this extended instrumental reconnaissance will be found as Appendix RR, Annual Report of the Chief of Engineers for 1878, p. 1705. It is accompanied by a sketch map of the routes (scale 1 to 900,000).

The result of his explorations was availed of by Captain Stanton in compilation of a military map of the Department of the Platte.

The engineer officers at headquarters military divisions and departments have, from time to time, made surveys of military reservations and of wagon-roads, prior to the construction of the latter, the results of which appear in the Annual Reports of the Chief of Engineers; or, if unpublished, in the archives of the Engineer Department or at the headquarters offices respectively. It has been impossible to make an exhaustive study of these separate surveys, and doubtless some established latitudes and longitudes have been missed which would be developed upon a more complete and extended search, which should be done, when final working tabulated lists of latitudes and longitudes shall be made up, weighted and graded according to precision and reliability, with description of monuments, and with full bibliographical references.

The following are the authorities available for the compilation of a standard official list of latitudes and longitudes west of the Mississippi River:

1. Annual reports of Chief of Topographical Engineers (Graham, Lee, Poe); 1860, p. 341; 1860-'61, pp. 554 and 571.
2. Annual Reports Chief of Engineers U. S. Army to date (Lockwood, Bailey, Ruffner, Wheeler, Wisner, Ruffner, Hoffman, Major, Greene, Barlow, Safford, Maguire, and others); 1860-'61, pp. 576 and 581; 1866, p. 48; 1870, p. 546; 1873, p. 681; 1874, pt. 2, pp. 432 and 610-620; 1877, p. – ; 1879, p. –; 1881, Vol. III, p. 2844; 1882, pt. 3, p. 2833, and elsewhere.
3. U. S. Coast and Geodetic Survey to date (various observers).
4. U. S. Geographical Surveys. annual reports 1875 to 1879, inclusive; 1875, p. 11; 1876, pp. 6-35; 1877, pp. 1214-1217; 1878, pp. 6-14; 1879, pp. 114-122; 1880, p. 35.
5. Tables of geographic positions, etc., U. S. Geographic Surveys, 1885 (Wheeler, Lockwood, Hoxie, Marshall, Kampff, Safford, Clark, Austin, Eastman, Wheeler, and Roberts).
6. U S. Geographical Survey Reports, Vol. I, especially App. A, and Vol. II, pp. 488-491.
7. Vol I, Reports of fortieth parallel, p. 766.
8. Astronomic report, 1874; preliminary report, 4°, 1869; distances, etc., 4°, 1872; U. S. Geographic Surveys.
9. Hayden reports, Bull., Vol. III, No. 3, p. 713, 1877; annual reports 1872, p. 796, and annual report 1878, p. 463.
10. Final report Lake Survey (Professional Papers, Corps of Engineers, No. 24; Comstock, Adams, Lockwood, Price, Ruffner, Wheeler, Wisner, Maguire, and others).
11. General Land Office for State and Territorial boundaries.

12. Texas and United States (Clark). Senate Ex. Doc. No. 70, Forty-seventh Congress, first session.
13. United States and Mexican boundary reports (Emory, Whipple, and Michler).
14. United States and Northwestern boundary (Parke and Gardner). MSS. in State Department archives.
15. United States and Northern Boundary report (Twining, Gregory, Greene, and Boss); p. 198.
16. Warren, Vol. XI, Pacific Railroad reports.
17. Naval Observatory, annual report 1871, p. xvi and others.
18. Reports on transit of Venus and eclipse expeditions (Harkness, Newcomb, and others).
19. Yukon River (Raymond and Major); Jones, Wyoming (Blunt and Hitt); Mullan's wagon road, p. 360 (Wiesner and Kolecki); Ives, Colorado River; Simpson, Great Basin; Ludlow, Black Hills; Stanton, Nebraska; Livermore in Western Texas (unpublished), and others.
20. General records of the Engineer Department (see among others 305 and 2139 of 1879, 651 and 2664 of 1881, 3476, 4032 and 4900 of 1882).
21. General records of the Geological Survey (probably).

CHAPTER III.

GEOGRAPHICAL AND GEOLOGICAL EXPLORATIONS AND SURVEYS UNDER THE WAR AND INTERIOR DEPARTMENTS, 1865 TO 1880.

WAR DEPARTMENT.

GEOLOGICAL EXPLORATION OF THE FORTIETH PARALLEL. (KING.)

This expedition first took the field in 1867, and continued its observations therein during the seasons of 1868, 1869, 1870, 1871, and 1872.

The object of the exploration, as determined by the instructions of General Humphreys, Chief of Engineers (see Appendix V, Annual Report Chief of Engineers, 1869), was "to examine and describe the geological structure, geographical condition, and natural resources of a belt of country extending from the one hundred and twentieth meridian eastward to the one hundred and fifth meridian of longitude, along the fortieth parallel of latitude, with sufficient expanses north and south to include the lines of the Central and Union Pacific Railroads, and as much more as may be consistent with accuracy and a proper progress."

To "examine all rock formations, mountain ranges, detrital plains, mines, coal deposits, soils, minerals, ores, saline and alkaline deposits."

To "collect material for detailed maps of the chief mining districts, coal fields, salt basins, etc., as well as also for a topographic map of the region traversed, and to conduct a systematic series of barometric and thermometric observations, with constant study of the atmospheric conditions bearing upon the subject of refraction and evaporation."

To "make collections in botany and zoology, with a view to a memoir on these subjects, illustrating the occurrence and distribution of plants and animals."

The Union and Central Pacific Railroads were used as the base lines of operations, and thence north and south, generally to distances not exceeding 40 or 50 miles, such routes as were found necessary to reach the points occupied for geological or other purposes were visited.

The area embraced was about 86,390 square miles.*

EXPEDITION OF 1867.

The area embraced during this season was bounded by the one hundred and twentieth meridian on the west and 117° 30′ on the east, and latitude 39° 3′ north and 41° north, in western Nevada.

The expedition took the field in July 27, disbanding at Virginia City December 15, 1867.

During the succeeding winter investigations by Mr. King and one assistant on the Comstock Lode were prosecuted. A statement of progress for this season is found in Annual Report Chief of Engineers, 1868, pages 76 to 77.

The instruments employed for the topographic field work were zenith telescopes for latitude, 8 and 6 inch Wurdemann theodolites, each reading to 10″, for triangulation, and a zenith sextant and chronometers, and 4″ gradienter for topographic details, steel tapes and chains, cistern barometers and hygrometers.

The transportation consisted of army wagons, saddle animals, either riding mules or horses, and pack-mules.

The personnel was as follows: Clarence King, geologist in charge; James D. Hague, assistant geologist; Arnold Hague, assistant geologist; S. F. Emmons, assistant geologist, volunteer; James T. Gardner, chief topographer; H. Custer, assistant topographer; F. A. Clark, assistant topographer; Sereno Watson, assistant topographer; W. W. Bailey, botanist; Robert Ridgway, zoologist; T. H. O'Sullivan, photographer.†

*This area is shown on the general sketch map of the fortieth parallel atlas, and colored on each edition of the Annual Progress Chart of United States Geographical Surveys.

†The lists of personnel do not include such assistants as geological collectors, barometer observers, and persons employed from time to time as general assistants.

The following extract from a letter from Mr. King serves as a general reference to the principal field assistants, the class of work of each, with mention also of the published results:

"I can say to you, in general, that the geological work was under my own personal direction; that I was assisted in this department by Arnold Hague and S. F. Emmons; that the mining geology was executed in conjunction with myself by James D. Hague. The topographical work was under the general direction of James T. Gardner, who executed the road triangulation on which the map is

The escort consisted of 20 mounted enlisted men, with the proper number of non-commissioned officers, the necessary camp equipage, transportation, and subsistence, and also medical attendance. Supplies were also authorized to be purchased from the Quartermaster and Commissary Departments.

SEASON OF 1868.

The field observations required along the belt in question, commencing April 15, were carried until October 15 eastward, nearly as far as the Great Salt Lake, and to the westward limit of its immediate desert, making a belt of 100 miles wide and 500 miles long in Nevada and western Utah, with preliminary explorations in vicinity of Mono Lake, California, and continuation of investigation of the Comstock Lode.

The personnel was as follows: Clarence King, geologist in charge; James D Hague, assistant geologist; Arnold Hague, assistant geologist; S. F. Emmons, assistant geologist; James T. Gardner, chief topographer; H. Custer, assistant topographer; A. D. Wilson, assistant topographer; F. A. Clark, assistant topographer; Sereno Watson, botanist; Robert Ridgway, zoologist; T H. O'Sullivan, photographer.*

The escort consisted of one sergeant, three corporals, one bugler, and fourteen privates, Troop H, Eighth Cavalry.

SEASON OF 1869.

The season's labors were commenced May 1, and disbandment was had in September.

The area occupied was in the vicinity of Great Salt Lake, and adjacent to mountain ranges in Utah and to the eastward as far as the Green River Divide, between 111° to 114° west longitude, and 40° to 42° north latitude.

based, and measured the astronomical and check bases. The topographical assistants were A. D. Wilson, F. A. Clark, and Henry Custer.

"The legend sheet of the main atlas, the title-page of the mining atlas, and the title-pages of the various volumes, give in full the authorship of the publications of the survey."

*Work carried on in three parties in charge, respectively, of Messrs. King, Arnold Hague, and Emmons. James D. Hague conducted the investigation of mining districts of Nevada and Colorado, in preparation for Volume III on Mining Industry.

A reference to the progress for this season appears in Annual Report Chief of Engineers, 1870, page 87, Vol. III. The first of the quarto series was put to press during the winter of 1869 and 1870.

The following constituted the personnel: Clarence King, geologist in charge; James D. Hague, assistant geologist; Arnold Hague, assistant geologist; S. F. Emmons, assistant geologist; James T. Gardner, chief topographer; A. D. Wilson, assistant topographer; F. A. Clark, assistant topographer; Sereno Watson, botanist; Robert Ridgway, zoologist; T. H. O'Sullivan, photographer.*

There was also an escort of one sergeant, one corporal, and nine men, Company H, Eighth Cavalry, and ten men (all mounted), Company I, Ninth Infantry.

SEASON OF 1870.

The field period, extending from August 12 to November 15, was used in completing vacant spaces in the 1869 work, and special observations in volcanic and glacial phenomena in northern California, Oregon, and Washington Territory.

The personnel was as follows: Clarence King, geologist in charge; Arnold Hague, assistant geologist; S. F. Emmons, assistant geologist; James T. Gardner, chief topographer; A. D. Wilson, assistant topographer; F. A. Clark, assistant topographer.

An escort of one non-commissioned officer and two privates, Company D, Twenty-third Infantry, and such transportation as required and could be spared, was furnished by the military authorities.†

Only a commencement was made in this work, which was intended to furnish monographs on the volcanoes, but was never carried to completion.

A progress report appears as Appendix ZZ, Annual Report Chief of Engineers, 1871.

---

* Work carried on in three parties in charge, respectively, of Messrs. King, Arnold Hague, and Emmons.

† Preliminary examination of the volcanoes of the Pacific coast, Lassen's Peak, Mount Shasta in California, Mount Hood in Oregon, Mount Rainier in Washington Territory.

SEASON OF 1871.

The main exploration was continued to the eastward of longitude 111° west in Wyoming, northern Colorado, and a part of Utah, including the Uintah Mountains. The full complement of topographical work was prevented by forest fires of great extent. Volume III, quarto reports, appeared during 1871.

The personnel was as follows: Clarence King, geologist in charge; Arnold Hague, assistant geologist; S. F. Emmons, assistant geologist; James T. Gardner, chief topographer; A. D. Wilson, assistant topographer; F. A. Clark, assistant topographer.

The escort consisted of one sergeant, one corporal, and thirteen privates (mounted). Forage from the quartermaster's department for not exceeding forty animals was supplied.*

SEASON OF 1872.

During this field year the unfinished geologic and topographic observations in Wyoming and northern Colorado were completed, with a review of the whole field of exploration from the 105th to the 122d meridian, and further study of extinct volcanoes and glacial phenomena.

The party disbanded on November 13.

Omissions were supplied north of Humboldt River as far east as Humboldt Wells, and field work carried to the region east of the North Platte.

Special observations were conducted in the Sierra Nevada, and at and about Mount Humphreys and the San Francisco Mountain region of the Colorado plateau.

The following was the personnel: Clarence King, geologist in charge; Arnold Hague, assistant geologist; S. F. Emmons, assistant geologist; James T. Gardner, chief topographer; A. D. Wilson, assistant topographer; F. A. Clark, assistant topographer.

An escort of one sergeant and nine men of Company A, Second Cavalry, was detailed to accompany the party of Mr. Emmons.†

* The work was carried on in two parties under the charge of Messrs. Hague and Emmons, respectively, the former taking the eastern, the latter the western portion of the region embraced.

† The work was carried on in two parties under the charge of Messrs. Hague and Emmons, respectively, the former taking the eastern, the latter the western portion of the region.

Statement of progress for this year is found in Appendix DD and DD², Annual Report, Chief of Engineers, 1873.

Mr. King alone in 1873 made a field geological review between September 2 and December 13 of the archæan formations as well as classification of the important mining districts visited.

The balance of the year was taken up in office work by himself, two geological assistants, one topographer, one clerk, and one microscopist.

The office work,* with two geological assistants, one topographer, one clerk, and one microscopist, continued during the years 1874 to 1878, and Mr. King's services in connection with this duty terminated January 30' 1879, while the publication of Vol. VII, the last of the quarto series, is announced in the Annual Report Chief of Engineers for 1880. The main results connected with this work are seven quarto volumes and one atlas.

This atlas contains ten sheets, five alone showing topography proper,† while the geological representations are found in colors upon the above topographic sheets in contours as a base.

Contributions from Messrs. J. D. and Arnold Hague, Emmons, Watson, Eaton, Meek, Hall, Whitfield, Ridgway, Marsh, and Zirckel appear in the several volumes other than No. I, by Mr. King. Volume III (Mining Industry) was issued in 1870, V (Botany) in 1871, VI (Microscopic Petrography) in 1876, II and IV (Descriptive Geology and Ornithology and Paleontology) in 1877, I (Systematic Geology) in 1878, and VII (Odontornithes) in 1880.‡

The only published geographical co-ordinates are seven latitudes, found in appendix to Volume I, page 765.

It appears that the latitudes and longitudes of three stations (Verdi, Salt Lake, and Sherman) by the U. S. Coast Survey were utilized.

The following main or initial astronomical stations of the U. S. Geographical Survey fall within the fortieth parallel:

(1) Virginia City, (2) Austin, (3) Carlin, and (4) Winnemucca, Nev.;

* Reports of office progress toward completion appear as appendices to Annual Report Chief of Engineers, as follows: EE 1874, KK 1875, II 1876, MM 1877, and MM 1878.

† The hill work of the topographic sheets, instead of hachuress, is represented by brush shading with an oblique light.

‡ A reference to progress and results of this work may be found in House Ex. Doc. No. 88, Forty-fifth Congress, second session.

(5) Ogden, Utah; (6) Green River, (7)* Fort Steele, (8) Laramie, and (9) Cheyenne, Wyo.

Various altitudes are found on the maps, but no distances are given in figures. The methods employed for establishing the field data, upon which the topographic maps are based, is described by Mr. James T. Gardner, pages 764 to 769, appendix to Volume I, Systematic Geology.

The many collections in mineralogy, paleontology, and other branches of natural history were, upon the conclusion of the investigations, transferred finally to the National Museum.

The original field and manuscript records remain a part of the archives of the Engineer Department.

The following is a brief list of maps and reports resulting from this exploration:

MAPS.

1. General atlas. (Scales 1 inch to 60 miles and 1 inch to 4 miles.)	
1. General and preliminary	1
2. Topographic	5
3. Geologic	5
4. Sections	1
2. Atlas with Volume III (geological and mining maps):	
Geologic	3
Miscellaneous	3
Sections	7
Total	25

REPORTS.

1. Annuals separately published	4
2. Monographs, quarto	7
Total	11

The area examined and mapped was 86,390 square miles.

EXPEDITION FOR EXPLORATIONS AND SURVEYS IN NEVADA, CALIFORNIA, UTAH, AND ARIZONA, IN 1871, FIRST LIEUT. GEORGE M. WHEELER, CORPS OF ENGINEERS, COMMANDING.

This expedition took the field at Halleck Station, Nevada, May 3, 1871. Its main purpose, under detailed instructions from Brig. Gen. A. A. Humphreys, Chief of Engineers, was to obtain correct topographical knowledge of the country traversed and to prepare accurate maps of the region entered. Other objects of the survey were to gather as much information as possible relating to the physical features of the country; the number, habits, and

* Connection was made with this station (see Annual Report Chief of Engineers, 1873, p. 1206).

disposition of the Indians; the selection of sites for military operations or occupation; facilities for making rail or common roads; to make such examinations as were justifiable from their importance of the mineral resources of the region; and to note the climate, geological formations, areas valuable for agricultural and grazing purposes, and the relative proportions of woodland, water, and other qualities.

The latitude and longitude of as many important points as possible were also to be determined.

The area embraced was 72,250 square miles, including portions of central, southern, and southwestern Nevada; eastern California; southwestern Utah; northwestern, central, and southern Arizona. The area of the expedition of 1869 was again entered along certain lines.

The following personnel constituted the expedition of this year: First Lieut. George M. Wheeler, Corps of Engineers, U. S. Army, in command, chief executive officer and field astronomer; First Lieut. D. W. Lockwood, Corps of Engineers, U. S. Army, assistant executive officer and field astronomer; Second Lieut. D. A. Lyle, Second Artillery, U. S. Army, assistant executive officer and field astronomer; A. H. Cochrane, acting assistant surgeon, U. S. Army, medical officer; W. J. Hoffman, acting assistant surgeon, U. S. Army, medical officer and collector in natural history; Theodore V. Brown, hospital steward, U. S. Army, barometric observer and recorder; Frank Hecox, hospital steward, U. S. Army, barometric observer and recorder; E. P. Austin, astronomical observer and computer; Archibald R. Marvine, astronomical observer and assistant geological observer; P. W. Hamel, Louis Nell, Joseph R. Mauran, Frank R. Simonton, and Charles E. Fellerer, geodetic and topographic assistants; Francis Klett, assistant topographer and clerk; William J. Bradley, barometric recorder; Charles A. Ogden, barometric observer and recorder; Frederick W. Loring, barometric observer and recorder; John Smith, barometer and odometer observer and recorder; G. K. Gilbert, geological observer; F. Bischoff, zoological collector; John Kohler, zoological collector; T. H. O'Sullivan, photographer; E. M. Richardson, general assistant; W. D. Wheeler, clerk; E. Martin Smith, Charles King, Charles Spencer, Willard Rice, William Egan, and Charles Hahn, guides.

The permanent escort was composed of six non-commissioned officers and twenty-six privates, Company I, Third Cavalry. Additional temporary escorts were obtained from several of the posts in Arizona, also the requisite number of cargadores, packers, teamsters, mechanics, laborers, etc.

The transportation was in the main by pack-train, wagons in certain instances conveying supplies to rendezvous points.

The following were members of the boat parties engaged in exploration of the Colorado River, including a part of the "Grand Cañon" from Camp Mohave to mouth of Diamond Creek: (1) Lieut. George M. Wheeler; (2) Dr. W. J. Hoffman; (3) P. W. Hamel; (4) G. K. Gilbert; (5) Frank Hecox; (6) T. H. O'Sullivan; (7) Frederick W. Loring; (8) E. M. Richardson; together with six boatmen and mechanics, two enlisted men of expedition escort, one sergeant and five privates from Company G, Twelfth Infantry; also Captain Asquit and thirteen other Mohave Indians, to assist in towing and general work.

INSTRUMENTS.

The following instruments were used:

Astronomic.—At the main stations a combined meridian instrument, sextants with artificial horizons, and chronometers.

Topographic.—Six-inch theodolites, reading by vernier to $20''+30''$ in arc; 3-inch transit theodolites, gradienters, and pivot-levels (Wurdemann pattern), field, prismatic, and pocket compasses, steel and linen tapes, and odometers attached to vehicles. For the inclination of the magnetic needle a dip circle was employed. For hypsometric purposes, cistern, mountain, and aneroid barometers, hygrometers, maximum and minimum and pocket thermometers were used.

The instruments of the geologists were pick and hammer, clinometer compasses, aneroid barometers, and hand levels.

REPORTS.

A special preliminary report of this exploration and survey was made to Brig. Gen. A. A. Humphreys, Chief of Engineers, U. S. Army, early in 1872, and published by departmental authority. A preliminary topographic map on a scale of 1 inch to 24 miles accompanied the report, embracing a skeleton of the general topographic information collected, location of routes pursued, positions of mining camps, etc.

A few copies, expressly for office use, of a list of camps, distances, etc., of the expedition of this year, were printed in oblong folio.

On account of the urgency of other duties no regular annual report for the fiscal year 1870–'71 was submitted to the Chief of Engineers.

At the close of this expedition a plan for a systematic topographic survey of the territory of the United States west of the 100th meridian was, by request, prepared by Lieutenant Wheeler, approved by the Chief of Engineers and the honorable the Secretary of War, and sanctioned by act of Congress approved June 10, 1872.

To facilitate operations, initial main astronomic stations were established this season (longitude by telegraph) at the following points: Carlin, Battle Mountain, and Austin, Nev.; Camp Independence, Cal.; St. George, Utah; and Prescott, Ariz. Including the points determined in 1869, eleven main astronomic stations were established by the survey in the western interior, and the longitude of nine established by telegraph.

The majority of these stations was confined to the main lines of the survey. Minor astronomical stations were established daily along the routes, the prominent mountain peaks were occupied as subordinate triangulation stations, while the extent of the country to be traversed precluded the possibility of carrying out any connected net-work of triangulation.

The principal mountain passes were traversed and profiled, and topographic sketches made at both prominent and minor points. Elevations were obtained of most of the prominent features of the country, and tri-daily meteorological observations made constantly by all the different parties.

The portion of the area surveyed during this season, with the most topographic detail, was that embracing the Colorado River, and that receiving most attention in a physio-geographical view, was the Great American Desert region, which was found to vary in breadth from 75 to 250 miles. The Grand Cañon of the Colorado was explored in boats, occupying one branch of the survey, under the immediate command of Lieutenant Wheeler, thirty-three days in the ascent of the river from Camp Mohave to Diamond Creek, a distance of more than 200 miles. More than two hundred rapids were passed during the trip, and there was revealed the most striking cañon scenery in the world, of some of which photographic pictures were made. The trip was one of great hardship, and notwithstanding the loss of some of the instruments, which limited observations, and a part of the records, was highly successful.

In addition to the highly interesting exploration of the Colorado Cañon the extent and character of the great Colorado Plateau, first defined and named by myself, were determined, and its peculiar features delineated.

The expedition also determined the existence and limits of several inclosed basins without outward drainage, and separate from the Great Salt Lake and Humboldt basins. These are mostly in Nevada, the Amargosa or Death Valley Basin, being most extensive and characteristic, its lowest depression being below the level of the sea.

Ninety-two mining districts were embraced in the area surveyed, eighty-six of which were visited by one or more of the members of parties, and much information elicited in classified form. Notes of the principal features of the mines appear in the report. The mapping of mineral districts, showing their positions, direction of lodes, etc., was made a part of the work of the survey.

A full series of meteorologic observations was taken during the season. The geological information acquired enabled a plan to be projected of a final comprehensive report. The natural history collections, except of coleoptera and in botany, were small, owing to the desolate nature of the regions visited and rapid movements of the parties. Mineralogical specimens were collected mostly from the mining regions.

Observations were made with a view to the practicability of establishing north and south lines of communication, and one from Salt Lake southerly to the foot of the Grand Cañon of the Colorado; one from the Central Pacific Railroad through Washoe, east of the Sierras; and one from a central point on the Central Pacific across the Colorado River at the mouth of Virgin River, were recommended as practicable.

The navigability of the Colorado River to Camp Mohave was noted, and the practicability of navigation to Callville, a point 95 miles above Camp Mohave, has been proved in an instance mentioned; and it is concluded that steam navigation may ultimately be carried to the foot of the Grand Cañon, 57 miles above Callville, or 577 miles above the mouth of the river.

The areas inhabited by the Shoshones, Pah-Utes, Chemehuevis, Utes, Mohaves, Seviches, Hualapias, Apache-Mohaves, Cosninas, and Apaches, were accurately determined and mapped, and information respecting the numbers, manner of life, and disposition of these Indians towards the whites, collected. Three members of the expedition were murdered near Wickenberg, Ariz., by Indians, near the end of the season, while en route home. Remnants of the works of extinct aboriginals were met with during the exploration.

The expedition reached Tuscon, Ariz., for disbandment December 4, 1871, after a protracted field season of a little more than seven months. A temporary office for both business and reduction purposes was occupied for a brief period in San Francisco, the balance of the winter months being spent in Washington, D. C., in the preparation and publication of results.

EXPEDITION FOR EXPLORATIONS AND SURVEYS WEST OF THE ONE HUNDREDTH MERIDIAN IN UTAH, NEVADA, AND ARIZONA, IN 1872.

The survey of 1872 commenced July 7, and was completed on the 11th of December.

The chief objects were to establish main astronomic stations, in pursuance of a comprehensive system, at points available by telegraph and contiguous to the areas of survey, in addition, to obtain the topographic details of the sections visited, with sufficient accuracy to enable routes of communication necessary for military operations to be delineated, as well as to enable the general physical features of the country to be drawn to a scale of 1 inch to 8 miles, this projection having been determined upon for the atlas intended to cover that portion of the territory of the United States lying west of the 100th meridian.

As the survey progressed data were gathered for maps of the scale of 1 inch to 4 miles, 1 inch to 2 miles, 1 inch to 1 mile, and 1 inch to 1,500 feet, the latter at prominent mining districts.

Meteorologic observations were made hourly at the main astronomic stations, and such geologic and mineralogic examinations as could be prosecuted were made to determine the physical structure, with its geographic and allied characteristics, and incidentally an examination of the condition of the mining industry in the region visited.

Collections in the remaining branches of natural history were also made. Photographs representing geologic formations and other peculiar natural features were taken. Such general data bearing upon the subjects of irrigation, agriculture, sites for military posts, etc., as could be had were also obtained.

Observations upon the varied native resources of the soil and underlying rock, in accordance with formal instructions, were undertaken for the first time.

The main astronomical stations occupied were at (1) Beaver, Utah; (2) Cheyenne, (3) Fort Fred. Steele, and (4) Laramie, Wyo.; (5) Pioche, Nev.; (6) Gunnison, Utah, and (7) Green River, Wyo., independent of the secondary and daily latitude stations.

Reports upon results at these stations will be found in (1) Preliminary Report for 1872, (2) Special Astronomic Report, 1874, and (3) Vol. II, Quarto Reports.

The area embraced was 47,366 square miles, including portions of central, western, and southwestern Utah, eastern Nevada, and northwestern Arizona.

The areas of the expeditions of 1869 and 1871 were entered along certain lines.

The following constituted the personnel of the year: First Lieut. George M. Wheeler, Corps of Engineers, U. S. Army, in command, chief executive officer and field astronomer; First Lieut. R. L. Hoxie, Corps of Engineers, U. S. Army, assistant executive officer and field astronomer; First Lieut. W. L. Marshall, Corps of Engineers, U. S. Army, assistant executive officer and field astronomer; Second Lieut. W. A. Dinwiddie, Second U. S. Cavalry, commanding cavalry escort; Second Lieut. Wallace Mott, Eighth U. S. Infantry, commanding infantry escort; H. C. Yarrow, acting assistant surgeon, U. S. Army, medical officer and zoological observer; Theodore V. Brown, hospital steward, U. S. Army, barometric observer and recorder; E. P. Austin, John H. Clark, William W. Marryatt, astronomic observers and computers; Louis Nell, John E. Weyss, Gilbert Thompson, Frank R. Simonton, and Henry Cruger, geodetic and topographic assistants; Francis Klett, assistant topographer and clerk; William M. Ord, assistant surveyor and recorder; William Kilp, C D. Gedney, Mark S. Severance, barometric observers and recorders; G. K. Gilbert, geological observer; Edwin E. Howell, assistant geological observer; H. W. Henshaw, ornithologist and collector; William Bell, photographer; George W. Bean and ——— Adams, guides.

The escort consisted of one sergeant, two corporals, and twenty privates from Company D, Second Cavalry, under the command of Second Lieut. William A. Dinwiddie, Second Cavalry, and three non-commissioned officers and thirty privates from Companies B, C, D, E, F, H, and I, Thirteenth Infantry, under the command of Second Lieut. Wallace Mott, Eighth Infantry.

The requisite number of chief packers, cargadores, packers, herders, teamsters, laborers, etc., were also a part of the expedition.

Instruments.—The astronomical instruments used were the same as those of 1871, with the addition of cylinder chronographs (Harkness pattern), for recording observations and signals, and break-circuit chronometers.

Signals for time comparisons were sent from the main and secondary stations in the field to the observatory in Temple Square, Salt Lake City.

With the addition only of compensated steel tapes, the topographic instruments used were the same as those employed in 1871, and the meteorologic instruments were identical with those employed during the previous year. The geologist used the same implements as those of 1871, while the photographer introduced the dry-plate process with success.

Reports.—A special report in quarto of this expedition was made to the office of the Chief of Engineers and printed by departmental authority. The report was accompanied by a skeleton map of the region west of the 100th meridian, on a scale of 1 to 6,000,000, illustrative of a scheme for mapping the entire area on a scale of 1 inch to 8 miles.

An annual report of operations for the fiscal year 1871–'72 was submitted to the Chief of Engineers, and appears as Appendix DD to his report for that year. (See also p. 101, Annual Report Chief of Engineers, 1872.)

A table of camps, distances, altitudes, etc., was published for office use, being a preliminary rather than completed work, and will contribute its quota to the geographic positions, distances, azimuths, altitudes, etc., to be specially prepared. (See Appendix LL, Annual Report Chief of Engineers for 1875.)

Besides the labor bestowed upon the principal objects of the survey this year, as above indicated, considerable attention was given to the subject of irrigation in connection with observations upon the agricultural resources of the country traversed.

Twenty-five mining districts in Utah, twelve in Nevada, and eleven in Arizona, forty-eight in all, were examined this season, and most of them described in the annual report to the Chief of Engineers.

A route of proposed communication from the head of the Sevier Valley, Utah, to Prescott, Ariz., was examined this year and found practicable even for a railroad, the point offering the most severe profile being that of descent into the basin of the Virgin River. The distance by the shortest of these routes from Salt Lake to Prescott is 585 miles. Other routes from Salt Lake south were partially examined during the season. The establishment of a military camp not far from St George upon the route most fully examined was suggested.

Two parties visited special points of the lower Grand Cañon of the Colorado. Some striking topographic details were gathered and photographic pictures taken.

Over one hundred and ninety species of birds were represented in the collections this year, and the specimens of reptiles and fishes numbered over four hundred. A description of them is contained in Vol. V of the regular series of quarto reports.

The area covered by the survey at the close of 1872 was a little over 155,000 square miles, an area as large as New England and the Middle States; and 6,137 miles were traversed beside the routes of the supply parties—2,067 miles in length. The large amount of geographic and topographic information collected is presented in the regular atlas sheets.

EXPEDITION FOR GEOGRAPHICAL AND GEOLOGICAL EXPLORATIONS AND SURVEYS IN COLORADO, NEW MEXICO, UTAH, AND ARIZONA, IN 1873.

The expedition took the field in three divisions, organized, respectively, at Santa Fe, N. Mex.; Salt Lake City, Utah, and Denver, Colo. The first, under immediate command of Lieut. G. M. Wheeler, left the rendezvous camp early in June; the second, under Lieutenant Hoxie, on May 30; and the third, under Lieutenant Marshall, about June 1, 1873.

The object of the survey was to gather data for topographic and geologic maps of the area explored, in accordance with the systematic plan submitted the year previous, and to gather information in the various branches of natural history. The data necessary to an approximate land classification, such as arable and irrigable, timber, grazing, etc., was gathered incidentally to the main objects of the survey more in detail than for the previous year.

The routes traversed were numerous and such as would lead the various parties from point to point in the fields of their labors in the political divisions named in the title hereof.

The area embraced was 72,500 square miles, including portions of central and southern Utah; northern, central, eastern, and southeastern Arizona; southwestern, western, northwestern, and central New Mexico; and central, southern, and southwestern Colorado. The area of the expedition of 1872 was entered along certain lines.

The personnel of the expedition was as follows: First Lieut. George M. Wheeler, Corps of Engineers, U. S. Army, in command, chief executive officer and field astronomer; First Lieut. R. L. Hoxie, Corps of Engineers, U. S. Army, assistant executive officer and field astronomer; First Lieut. W. L. Marshall, Corps of Engineers, U S. Army, assistant executive officer and field astronomer; First Lieut. Samuel E. Tillman, Corps of Engineers, U. S. Army, assistant executive officer and field astronomer; Second Lieut. A. H. Russell, Third U. S. Cavalry, assistant executive officer; Second Lieut. L. H. Walker, Fifteenth U. S. Infantry, commanding escort; J. T. Rothrock, acting assistant surgeon, U. S. Army, medical officer and botanical observer; C. G. Newberry, acting assistant surgeon, U. S. Army, medical officer; Theodore V. Brown, hospital steward, U. S. Army, barometric observer and recorder; Prof. T. H. Safford, Dr F. Kampf, John H. Clark, William W.

Marryatt, and Prof. H. B. Herr, astronomic observers and computers; Louis Nell, John E. Weyss, Gilbert Thompson, E. J. Sommer, John J. Young, Max. E. Schmidt, Robert J. Ainsworth, and Edgar Schroeder, geodetic and topographic assistants; Francis Klett, assistant topographer and clerk; W. D. Wheeler, assistant surveyor and recorder; Frank M. Lee, C. D. Gedney, Bernard Gilpin, and William Looram, barometric observers and recorders; G. K. Gilbert, Prof. John J. Stevenson, and Edwin E. Howell, geological observers; Dr. Oscar Loew, mineralogic observer and chemist; H. W. Henshaw, ornithologist and collector; George M. Keasby, collector in paleontology; John Wolf, botanical collector; A. H. Wyant, artist; T. H. O'Sullivan, photographer; Charles Herman, A. A. Aguirre, and John C. Lang, draughtsmen (office); George M. Lockwood, clerk (office).

The escort for the branch of the expedition leaving Santa Fe consisted at different times during the season of ten non-commissioned officers and forty-five privates of the Eighth Cavalry and Fifteenth Infantry, while Lieutenant Marshall, of the Colorado section, was escorted by three non-commissioned officers and thirteen soldiers of the Fifth Infantry, and Lieutenant Hoxie, of the the Utah section, had at his command one corporal and six privates.

Six privates were detailed from the Engineer Battalion who did service principally with the astronomic parties.

The usual number of chief packers, cargadores, packers, herders, teamsters, and laborers were also employed.

Reports.—The usual annual report for the fiscal year ending June 30, 1873, was made to the Chief of Engineers of the Army, and printed as Appendix EE of his annual report for 1873, a part being also contained in Appendix EE of the report of that office for 1874, the reports of the survey being for fiscal years ending June 30, parties of the several expeditions often being in the field at the date of the several reports.

The report for 1873 was reproduced in a pamphlet of 11 pages, being only a résumé of field operations, accompanied by a plan of publication of results of the survey, and a skeleton map on a scale of 1 to 6,000,000.

Division No. 1 of the expedition, assisted during a part of the season by Division No. 2, surveyed about 11,000 square miles in New Mexico and 17,500 in Arizona, in areas enjoying remarkable topographic features.

Division No. 2 occupied about 1,500 triangulation and topographic points, and meandered more than 1,000 miles, besides making special detours in Utah, and connected the meridian of Provo with that of the observatory at Great Salt Lake.

Six thousand square miles of difficult mountain and cañon country were mapped. This party was delayed by snow in the mountains and by the desertion of two packers with thirty mules, which were recovered after a chase of 400 miles, the delay forcing the party to subsist upon corn alone for seven days.

A party of Division No. 3 examined the mines at Central City, Black Hawk, Georgetown, Oro City, etc., and another party those at Hardscrabble and Rosita, and the Cañon City coal mines, Colorado. A main party surveyed the mountain ridges surrounding South Park, the headwaters of the Gunnison River, the drainage areas of the upper Arkansas and Gunnison and tributaries, and made numerous triangulation stations, thirty-six peaks over 13,000 feet high and many of less altitude being occupied. The area covered was nearly 21,000 square miles in extent.

The total area occupied during the field season approximated 72,500 square miles, and the number of main triangulation points occupied was eighty.

The geologic investigations determined that the Sam Pitch coal beds of Utah are of the Tertiary age; the coals of Castle Valley and southern Utah, of the Cretaceous; and that the disputed age of the coal series of Colorado is also Cretaceous.

A further study of the great lake regions of Utah was prosecuted during the season, and facts relating to the glacial period gathered. Considerable attention was given by some of the assistants to ethnologic researches with much success; and the subject of minerals, soils, etc., received attention also by competent observers.

Several regular topographic atlas sheets were completed, and certain specially interesting localities, as the San Juan mining region, in Colorado, published on larger scales.

An advance sheet issue of a portion of the topographic atlas was photolithographed during the year, and an edition of 2,000 copies printed, consisting of the following sheets, viz: Title, legend, and four atlas sheets and a drainage basin on a scale of 1 inch to 8 miles or 1 to 506,880 sheet, and a progress map, were also printed, each on a scale of 1 to 6,000,000

The latitudes and longitudes, the latter telegraphically, of the following main stations were determined by field astronomic observations of the first order of value, viz: (1) Bozeman, Mont.; (2) Virginia City, Nev.; (3) Winnemucca, Nev.; (4) Ogden, Utah; (5) Green River, Wyo.; (6) Denver, Colo; (7) Hughes, Colo.; (8) Colorado Springs, Colo.; (9) Cañon City, Colo.; (10) Trinidad, Colo.; (11) Fort Union, N. Mex.; and (12) Santa Fe, N. Mex. This vigorous campaign is duly reported in the Annual Report (1874), volume II, and special astronomical report (1874).

In addition to the advance made during the year toward placing the survey upon a geodetic basis, the preliminaries to a scheme of triangulation covering the entire region having been inaugurated, and the further development of observations looking to the approximate classification of the lands according to their agricultural and mineralogical characteristics, large advances were made in the geological examinations needed to determine the general structure of extended areas, and collections in the various branches of natural history were greatly amplified.

Although the expedition assembled at three rendezvous, the operations of the season were so conducted, by following converging lines, as to connect the areas of the branches and cement together those entered in prior years.

The area in which the heads of the Gila and its northern tributaries, the Little Colorado and Salt River, intertwine, was for the first time explored, and a reservoir lake discovered nearly in the center of this amphitheatre of 4,000 or 5,000 square miles, nestling in a frame of high and rugged ranges.

The presence of mines was noted in the Tonto Basin, below the volcanic beds, and adjacent to the crystalline rocks and the sedimentaries, although scarcely opened.

The presence of garnets, rubies, emeralds, etc., was noted north and east of old Fort Defiance, in placer ground worked from a dyke said to be persistent in a northerly direction for scores of miles. The presence of coal, noted by early explorers in the northern part of New Mexico, was corroborated at specified localities.

Parts of the southeastern extremity of the great Colorado plateau forest were traversed and their extent made known. The reservation of the Navajos and the Mescalero Apaches, together with the tracts set aside for the sixteen Pueblo tribes of New Mexico, were included in part by the examinations of the year, that embraced large areas in the Rio Grande Basin.

The explorations of the year assist in making clear routes that may practically be utilized, reaching from the valley of the Arkansas to northeastern Arizona, near Camp Apache in the Salt River Basin.

The survey parties disbanded at Santa Fe and Fort Union, N. Mex., and Denver, Colo., between December 5 and 10, 1873.

EXPEDITION FOR GEOGRAPHICAL AND GEOLOGICAL EXPLORATIONS AND SURVEYS WEST OF THE ONE HUNDREDTH MERIDIAN IN COLORADO, NEW MEXICO, ARIZONA, AND NEBRASKA, IN 1874.

The several parties of the expedition took the field this year from the camp of organization at Pueblo, Colo., previous to and on the 6th of August.

The object was a continuation of the topographic survey of the mountain regions in the political divisions above mentioned, in pursuance of the previously established plan, and the measurement of a number of bases connected with main astronomic positions then or subsequently fixed, the development of triangulation from the plains to the mountains, making a connected system of surveys, having a sufficient number of geodetic points well determined upon which to base a mathematically constructed map. The various field parties, nine in number, were not confined to special routes, but advanced in parallel areas as nearly as the conformation of the areas of drainage would permit westward except one party, which operated on the east of the summit line of the Rocky Mountains. The territory embraced in the field of operations is bounded on the north by the latitude of the Spanish Peaks, and on the south by a latitude line passing through Santa Fe; on the east by longitude 104° 07′ 30″ west, and on the west by the western boundary of Colorado and New Mexico, approximately.

A special photographic party from this division visited the Pueblo ruins on the Chaco, and at adjacent points.

This year the work was developed into a completely connected survey resting on a geodetic base, referred to the initial geographic points constantly being established at selected points within and adjacent to the area of any given year.

A still more systematic classification of the lands was this year begun.

The area embraced was 23,281 square miles, including portions of central, southern, and southwestern Colorado, and central, northern, and northwestern New Mexico. The area of the expedition of 1873 was again entered along certain lines.

The personnel as follows: First Lieut. George M. Wheeler, Corps of Engineers, U. S. Army, in command, chief executive officer and field astronomer; First Lieut. William L. Marshall, Corps of Engineers, U. S. Army, assistant executive officer and field astronomer; First Lieut. Philip M Price, Corps of Engineers, U S. Army, assistant executive officer and field astronomer; First Lieut. Rogers Birnie, jr., Thirteenth Infantry, U. S. Army, assistant executive officer and field astronomer; First Lieut. Stanhope E. Blunt, Thirteenth Infantry, U. S. Army, assistant executive officer and field astronomer; Second Lieut. Charles W. Whipple, Third Artillery, U. S. Army, assistant executive officer and field astronomer; H. C. Yarrow, acting assistant surgeon, U. S. Army, medical officer and zoological observer; J. T. Rothrock, acting assistant surgeon, U. S. Army, medical officer and botanical observer; Theo. V. Brown, hospital steward, U. S. Army, barometric observer, recorder, and computer; Dr. F. Kampf and John H. Clark, astronomical observers and computers; Louis Nell, Gilbert Thompson, F. O. Maxson, Fred. A. Clarke, J. C. Spiller, Frank Carpenter, E. J. Sommer, William A. Cowles, William H. Rowe, Robert J. Ainsworth, and William R Atkinson, geodetic and topographic assistants; Frank M Lee, Bernard Gilpin, B. W. Bates, Alston C Ladd, A. J. Tweed, and H. G. DuBois, barometric observers and recorders; J. B. Minnick and Irenez L. Chavez, barometric recorders; L. H. Hance, barometric recorder and collector; C. M. Morrison, barometric recorder; G. K. Gilbert, geological observer; Prof. E. D. Cope, paleontologist; Prof. C. A. White, paleontologist (office); Dr. Oscar Loew, mineralogical observer and chemist; H W. Henshaw, ornithological observer and collector; James M. Rutter, meteorological observer; Charles E. Aiken, ornithological collector; W. G. Shedd, collector; T. H. O'Sullivan, photographer; John E. Weyss, Charles Herman, and John C. Lang, draughtsmen (office); George M. Lockwook, Francis Klett, and W. D. Wheeler, clerks; Almont Barnes, general assistant.

The expedition of 1874 was unaccompanied by an escort. The requisite number of chief packers, cargadores, packers, herders, teamsters, and laborers were employed.

The field work of these parties completed the connection of the areas of New Mexico and Colorado, over which the surveyed portions were partially joined in 1873.

The Indians encountered this season are portions of the Ute, Apache and Navajoe tribes, and the Pueblos, none in large numbers. Except the latter, who live in villages and are agricultural and pastoral, they were not inclined to be specially friendly.

The mines visited are Rosita, in the Wet Mountains, those in Los Cerillos, and the San Juan; besides a new field which was being prospected with some success on the Alamosa.

One of the important discoveries this season was that of a new pass through the main divide of the Rocky Mountains, near the head of the main fork of Poncha Creek, just south of Hunt's Peak. It is lower than any pass across these mountains in Colorado, and will admit of a grade of not more than 212 feet to the mile for a road from Pueblo or Cañon City, on the Arkansas. By this pass 80 miles in distance can be saved to the Gunnison River and mines at its head. This pass (since used by the Denver and Rio Grande Railroad) has been named from its discover, Lieutenant Marshall.

The discoveries and collections in natural history were also important, and in several fields include new varieties and species. In the vicinity of San Ildefonso the discoveries embrace specimens of fish, of which quite a number of *Cyprenidæ* are new. Human remains of a tribe of which we have no history were found at a ruined fortified town at Abiquiu. In botany 9,000 specimens were collected. In ornithology, besides many varieties, six species were added to the known fauna of the United States.

An extensive series of deposits of the Eocene age was discovered in New Mexico, and its examination rewarded by the collection of remains of a considerable number of species of vertebrata, mostly mammalia, and among them four species of two new genera of *Toxodonita*, an order not previously identified as having existed on this continent. Many mineral springs were visited by the different parties; and vocabularies were made of four Indian languages.

The following is a summary of the field and office work during the year, viz:

Field.—Main telegraphic longitude stations, 5; latitudes determined, main stations 6, sextant stations 50; main triangulation stations occupied, 51; topographical stations occupied, 103; miles traveled, 11,440; main barometric stations occupied, 572; aneroid stations, 3,335; botanical specimens collected, 9,000; specimens of mammals, fish, reptiles, and insects, 20,155; specimens of birds, 1,227; other ornithologic specimens, 83; lots of geologic and mineralogic specimens, 497.

Office.—Astronomic positions computed, 55; sheets plotted, 15; cistern barometer altitudes computed, 872; aneroid barometer altitudes computed, 3,965. Atlas maps, 1 inch to 8 miles, published, 8; ready for publication, 3; partly completed, 2. Atlas sheets, 1 inch to 8 miles and 1 inch to 4 miles, in preparation, 13. Reports published, 5; in course of publication, 2; nearly ready for publication, 4. Maps distributed, 7,864.

Results obtained during the year of observations at Julesburg, which location was placed on some of the Government maps north of latitude 41° in Nebraska, show that it lies south of that latitude in Colorado. The astronomic co-ordinates of the main stations at Las Vegas and Cimmaron, N. Mex., Sidney Barracks and North Platte, Nebr., and Julesburg, Colo., were determined.

The astronomic instruments employed were similar to those of the preceding year with the addition of an automatic instrument for the determination of positive personal equation.

The additional implements of the geologists were picks and heavy chisels for collecting vertebrate fossils.

No special report of this survey was made except that which is contained in the regular annual report submitted by the officer in charge to the

Chief of Engineers, June 30, 1875, which is printed as Appendix LL to the Report of the Chief of Engineers for that year.

During this year's operations of the survey a number of topographic and geographic maps of the regular series were prepared and published.

EXPEDITION FOR GEOGRAPHICAL SURVEYS WEST OF THE ONE HUNDREDTH MERIDIAN IN COLORADO, NEW MEXICO, NEBRASKA, UTAH, CALIFORNIA, AND NEVADA, IN 1875.

The expedition was organized in two sections of three parties each, one to operate from Los Angeles, Cal., and the other from Pueblo, Colo., at initial points. The California division disbanded at Caliente, Cal., in November, 1875, and the Colorado section at West Las Animas, Colo., November 25.

The object of the survey, as in preceding years, was primarily the collection of data for the construction of detailed topographic maps, in pursuance of the systematic geographic and topographic survey of the western mountain region.

In addition, and to the extent practicable, investigations were conducted in geology, paleontology, mineralogy, and the several branches of zoology and botany. All mines and mining camps that could be reached were visited and examined, and mineral and thermal springs noted.

The systematic classification of the land hitherto begun received especial attention during this and subsequent seasons, becoming one of the most important incidentals to the main objects of the survey.

Careful and copious notes taken by the topographers of the several parties enable the areas entered to be divided into arable, grazing, timber, and desert, and also with reference to the presence of the precious and economic minerals at a trifling additional labor and expense.

The topographic maps serve as a basis for the delineation of these subdivisions in colors.

The area occupied was 39,169 square miles, including portions of southern Colorado, northern New Mexico, southern California, small sections in southwestern Nevada, and western Arizona.

The areas occupied during seasons of 1869–'71, 1873, and 1874 were again entered along certain lines with a view to perfect the triangulation and other connections of the areas of former years.

The personnel of this expedition was as follows: First Lieut. George M. Wheeler, Corps of Engineers, U. S. Army, in command, chief executive officer and field astronomer; First Lieut. William L. Marshall, Corps of Engineers, U. S. Army, assistant executive officer and field astronomer; First Lieut. Eric Bergland, Corps of Engineers, U. S. Army, assistant executive officer and field astronomer; First Lieut. William L. Carpenter, Ninth Infantry, U. S. Army, assistant executive officer; First Lieut. Rogers Birnie, jr., Thirteenth Infantry, U. S. Army, assistant executive officer and field astronomer; First. Lieut. Charles C. Morrison, Sixth Cavalry, U. S. Army, assistant executive officer and field astronomer; Second Lieut. Charles W. Whipple, Third Artillery, U. S. Army, assistant executive officer and field astronomer; H. C. Yarrow, acting assistant surgeon, U. S. Army, medical officer and zoological observer; J. T. Rothrock, acting assistant surgeon, U. S Army, medical officer and botanical observer; Theodore V. Brown, hospital steward, U. S. Army, barometric computer; Dr. F. Kampf, triangulation observer and computer; Louis Nell, Gilbert Thompson, F. O. Maxson, J. C. Spiller, Frederick A. Clark, Frank Carpenter, William A. Cowles, Anton Karl, and George H. Birnie, geodetic and topographic assistants; Frank M. Lee, William Sommers, William C. Niblack, George M. Dunn, John A. Hasson, Alston C. Ladd, and William Looram, barometric observers and recorders; Frank Holland and T. Von Brockdorff, barometric recorders; Prof. Jules Marcou, geological observer; Dr. Oscar Loew, geologic and mineralogic observer and chemist; Alfred R. Conkling, geological observer; Douglas A. Joy, geological assistant; H. W. Henshaw, zoological observer and collector; Charles F. Shoemaker, collector; Francis Klett and W. D. Wheeler, clerks (field); William H. Rideing, general assistant; John E. Weyss, Charles Herman, and John C. Lang, draughtsmen (office); Prof. F. W. Putnam, ethnologist (office); George M. Lockwood and J. D. McChesney, clerks (office).

The expedition was accompanied by two engineer soldiers and one sergeant and nine privates of the Twelfth Infantry; also the usual number of chief packers, cargadores, packers, herders, teamsters, laborers, etc.

Some of the work finished this year has permitted the completion and publication of maps of all those mountainous portions of the West of most intricate drainage areas, upon a scale of 1 inch to 4 miles, besides furnishing material for other maps, complete or in progress, on a scale of 1 inch to 8 miles, for the plateau and semi-desert regions.

Lieutenant Marshall, in charge of party No. 1, Colorado section, surveyed an area in south central Colorado, or that portion of the Platte and Arkansas divide between the southern edge of South Park and the Arkansas River.

The following is a general summary of important results of the season's work:

Sextant latitude stations	102
Bases measured	106
Triangles about bases measured	50
Main triangulation stations occupied	111
Secondary triangulation stations occupied	273
Three point stations occupied	436
Camps made	825
Miles meandered	9,463.3
Miles traversed not meandered	4,799.9
Stations on meanders	835
Magnetic variations observed	222
Monuments built	237
Cistern barometer stations occupied	707
Aneroid stations occupied	5,553
Mining camps visited	22
Mineral and thermal springs noted	21
Geological and mineralogical specimens collected	380
Paleontological specimens collected	107
Botanical specimens (species) collected	350
Mammals, specimens collected	90
Birds, specimens collected	710
Other ornithological specimens collected	57
Reptiles, lots collected	67
Fishes, lots collected	29
Insects, lots collected	325
Shells, lots collected	12
Crustacea, lots collected	11
Radiates, lots collected	5
Ethnological specimens collected	363

The only noteworthy change made this year in the instruments used by the survey was in the transit. An instrument subsequently known as "Young's Meander Transit" was devised from notes furnished by the topographers of the survey as the result of experience required, and has been adopted as combining in as great a degree as possible, strength, simplicity of design, and convenient size, with the necessary accuracy of results.

The pack-train of mules represented the only means of transportation for the working parties.

A report of the season's operations was made as Appendix J J of the Annual Report of the Chief of Engineers for 1876. This was subsequently repaged and published as Annual Report upon the Geographical Surveys West of the one-hundredth meredian.

This annual report contains, in addition to the executive and descriptive reports of the officers in charge of parties, a number of professional papers.

During the year two large quarto volumes (III and V) were issued from this office.

The archæological investigations about Santa Barbara resulted in the acquisition of a large amount of very valuable material in the shape of Indian utensils, implements, etc., which were exhumed under circumstances that proved, for some of them at least, a considerable antiquity.

Dr. Loew conducted a series of interesting experiments with reference to the determination of the physiological effects upon the human system of the hot climate of the Colorado Valley, where the temperature of the air rises above blood-heat for weeks in summer.

Upon studying the Indian vocabularies collected by himself in the West, Dr. Loew finds that certain Pah-Ute words show a resemblance to the Chinese and Japanese languages, this similarity not being noticed in any other tribe.

The result of Lieutenant Bergland's examination of the Colorado River, with reference to the practicability of its diversion for agricultural purposes, afforded a negative answer.

Mount Whitney, or Fisherman's Peak, the highest peak in the Southern Sierras, and presumably the highest in the range, was ascended by two parties, and its height found to be 14,470 feet.

Triangulation was carried forward this season in accordance with the general plan, and the system of points connected with the work of previous years.

As a result of the work of the season in the San Juan region, a special sheet was published on a scale of 1 inch to 2 miles.

The efficiency of method of the topographic work and the accuracy in its delineation showed a notable advance in this as during each of the previous seasons.

EXPEDITION FOR GEOGRAPHICAL SURVEYS WEST OF THE ONE-HUNDREDTH MERIDIAN, IN COLORADO, NEW MEXICO, CALIFORNIA, AND NEVADA, IN 1876.

The expedition was organized in two sections; the Colorado section, of two parties, at Fort Lyon, Colo., and the California section, of four parties, at Carson City, Nev.

These sections took the field during the month of August, and were disbanded late in November at the above-named points. The delay in organization was caused by the lateness of appropriations for work of the year.

The methods and objects of the survey were the same as during the previous year. The country examined and surveyed amounted to 21,044 square miles, situated in southeastern Colorado, northern and west central New Mexico, western Nevada, and eastern California. The areas that had been visited during the years 1871, 1873, 1874, and 1875 were again entered along certain lines when necessary to perfect the continuous belts of triangulation required to cover entirely the country under examination, which latter often enters connected areas likely to be occupied in ensuing years.

The following constituted the personnel: First Lieut. George M. Wheeler, Corps of Engineers, U. S. Army, in command, chief executive officer and field astronomer; First Lieut. Samuel E. Tillman, Corps of Engineers, U. S. Army, assistant executive officer and field astronomer; First Lieut Eric Bergland, Corps of Engineers, U. S. Army, assistant executive officer and field astronomer; Second Lieut. Thomas W. Symons, Corps of Engineers, U. S. Army, assistant executive officer and field astronomer; First Lieut. Rogers Birnie, jr., Thirteenth U. S. Infantry, assistant executive officer and field astronomer; First Lieut. Charles C. Morrison, Sixth U. S. Cavalry, assistant executive officer and field astronomer; Second Lieut. M. M. Macomb, Fourth U. S. Artillery, assistant executive officer and field astronomer; Dr. F. Kampf, triangulation observer and computer; Louis

Nell, Gilbert Thompson, F O. Maxson, J. C. Spiller, Frank Carpenter, Anton Karl, and William A. Cowles, geodetic and topographic assistants; Frank M. Lee, Louis Seckles, George M. Dunn, William C. Niblack, Alfred Du-Bois, and S. B. Cameron, barometric observers and recorders; Isaiah Brown, messenger and barometric recorder; Alfred R. Conkling, geological observer; H. W. Henshaw, zoological observer and collector; Francis Klett, property clerk; John E. Weyss, Charles Herman, and John C. Lang, draughtsmen (office); George M Lockwood, clerk (in charge of office during field season); J. D. McChesney, money clerk (office); C. D. Davis, quartermaster's clerk (office).

Two non-commissioned officers and five privates drawn from the Twelfth and Nineteenth Regiments of Infantry accompanied the expedition, and the usual number of cargadores, packers, herders, teamsters, laborers, etc.

The geology of the mountainous area about Lake Tahoe and near Carson City was studied by Mr. A. R. Conkling in connection with party No. 2, California section, while its zoology received attention at the hands of Mr. H. W. Henshaw.

The more prominent features of the field-work for the season are indicated in the following summary:

Sextant latitude stations	74
Bases measured	2
Triangles about bases measured	50
Main triangulation stations occupied	64
Secondary triangulation stations occupied	80
Stations on meanders	5,115
Three-point stations occupied	765
Camps made	317
Miles meandered	4,379.48
Magnetic variations observed	208
Monuments built	168
Cistern barometer stations occupied	749
Aneroid stations occupied	3,804
Mining camps visited	15
Mineral and thermal springs visited	16
Mammals, specimens collected	13
Birds, specimens collected	109
Reptiles, specimens collected	10
Fishes, specimens collected	9
Insects, lots collected	31
Shells, lots collected	2

Instruments.—These were practically the same as employed previously, with such slight modifications as had been suggested by experience, especially in regard to instruments used at main triangulation stations, the object had in view being to increase the portability without decreasing the value of the instrument for accurate work.

The transportation employed was entirely that of pack-trains, except that a light spring-wagon was used by the party engaged in the valley of the Carson for the safe transit of instruments.

Pack-train transportation has been necessary in all of the expeditions, as most of the routes were over regions where no roads or trails exist.

The usual report of the season's operations was made to the Chief of Engineers, and appears as Appendix NN of that officer's Annual Report for 1877. In addition to the main report and the customary executive and descriptive reports by the officers in charge of the several parties, it contains a number of accompanying papers and several atlas sheets.

The unusual shortness of the field season had its effect in limiting the amount of work accomplished. The special survey of Lake Tahoe inaugurated this season gave satisfactory results, and the data at hand warranted the production of a map of this extremely interesting lake region on a scale of 1 inch to 1 mile.

The requirements made upon the topographers and others by which their notes furnished information relating to the natural resources of the regions traversed, especially of the amounts of arable, timber, grazing, mineral, and arid lands, very satisfactorily met, and much further valuable data was thus secured.

EXPEDITION FOR GEOGRAPHICAL SURVEYS WEST OF THE ONE-HUNDREDTH MERIDIAN IN COLORADO, NEW MEXICO, UTAH, WYOMING, IDAHO, NEVADA, CALIFORNIA, AND OREGON IN 1877.

The expedition was organized in three divisions—one, of two parties, at Fort Lyon, Colo.; a second, of two parties, at Carson, Nev.; and a third, of two parties, at Ogden, Utah.

The several parties were disbanded between the dates of November 25 and December 10, at Carson, Nev.; Ogden, Utah; Fort Garland, Colo.; and Fort Union, N. Mex.

The general plan of the survey and its objects have been detailed under accounts of previous seasons.

The field of survey comprised 32,477 square miles, in west central Colorado, central New Mexico, northwestern Utah, southeastern Idaho, northeastern and east central California, and south central Oregon.

The areas embraced by the expeditions of 1873, 1874, 1875, and 1876, were again entered along certain lines when required to complete triangulation observations and topographic details.

The personnel was as follows: First Lieut. George M. Wheeler, Corps of Engineers, U. S. Army, in command, chief executive officer, field astronomer, and in charge of survey; First Lieut. Eric Bergland, Corps of Engineers, U. S. Army, assistant executive officer and field astronomer; First Lieut. Samuel E. Tillman, Corps of Engineers, U. S. Army, assistant executive officer and field astronomer; Second Lieut. Thomas W. Symons, Corps of Engineers, U. S. Army, assistant executive officer and field astronomer; First Lieut. Rogers Birnie, jr., Thirteenth Infantry, U. S. Army, assistant executive officer and field astronomer; First Lieut. Charles C. Morrison, Sixth Cavalry, U. S. Army, assistant executive officer and field astronomer; Second Lieut. M. M. Macomb, Fourth Artillery, U. S. Army, assistant executive officer and field astronomer; Dr. F. Kampf, triangulation observer and computer; Louis Nell, F. O. Maxson, Gilbert Thompson, Miles, Rock, C. J. Kintner, J. W. Ward, Alfred Downing, J. C. Spiller, William A. Cowles, Anton Karl, and E. T. Gunter, geodetic and topographic assistants; Frank M. Lee, Louis Seckels, George M. Dunn, William C. Niblack, Thomas W. Goad, John A. Hasson, Eugene L. Vail, J. M. Harris, C. D.

Davis, William Looram, F. E. McCrary, S. B. Cameron, T. H. Simpson, Jay Cooke, jr., and J. B. Callahan, barometric observers and recorders; Isaiah Brown, messenger and recorder; H. W. Henshaw, zoological observer and collector; John A. Church, mining observer; Alfred R. Conkling, geological observer; John E. Weyss, Charles Herman, and John C. Lang, draughtsmen (office); Francis Klett, clerk (field); J. D. McChesney, Gwyn A. Lyell, and C. D. Davis, clerks (office).

Four privates of the Fourteenth Infantry and one of Company D, Nineteenth Infantry, accompanied the expedition, with the usual number of cooks, packers, teamsters, and men of all work.

Five main base lines were measured at (1) Ogden and (2) Terrace, Utah; (3) Verdi and (4) Austin, Nev.; and (5) Bozeman, Mont.

The triangulation observations of this season were pushed with great vigor, the nets being extended over all the territory examined and connection made with prior years.

In addition to the several main parties, the special survey of the Lake Tahoe region was completed by a party organized by Lieutenant Wheeler, and with which he remained for a short time, consisting of Mr. John E. Weyss and others.

A special party under Lieutenant Wheeler operated from Ogden to the northward to the east of Cache Valley, in vicinity of Bear Lake, along Twin Creeks, and to the eastward in the Green River drainage, disbanding at Evanston, on the Union Pacific Railroad.

The examination of the Comstock Lode, begun by Mr. J. A. Church in June, was continued during the season, his attention being exclusively directed to the structure of the vein, the regimen of the mines and the high temperature encountered in the rocks.

Mr. A. R. Conkling continued his geological investigations, taking for his field a section of eastern California and western Nevada lying between latitude 38° and 39° 30′, and longitude 119° 15′ and 120° 54′.

Collections in the several departments of zoology were made by Mr. H. W. Henshaw, in the region from Carson, Nev., along the eastern base of the Sierras, into southern Oregon; special attention being directed to the ornithology.

The following mining districts were visited during the season and reported upon: Bodie, Meadow Lake, Placerville, Washington, Castle, Alpine, West Walker, Confidence, Monitor, and Silver Mountain in California, and the Iowa district in Idaho.

The following is a brief summary of certain important features of the work:

Sextant latitude stations	145
Bases measured	5
Triangles about bases measured	56
Azimuths about bases measured	13
Main triangulation stations occupied	106
Secondary triangulation stations occupied	264
Cross-sight stations observed	1,060
Three-point stations occupied	1,414
Stations on meanders	12,366
Miles measured	10,801
Cistern barometer stations occupied	1,447
Aneroid stations occupied	8,900
Magnetic variations observed	424
Rivers and creeks gauged	58
Camps made	761
Monuments built	367
Mining camps visited	19
Mineral and thermal springs noted	60
Minerals, fossils, and ores (specimens of) approximate	1,100
Mammals, specimens collected	14
Birds, specimens collected	228
Reptiles, lots collected	11
Fishes collected, lots	23
Fishes collected, specimens	200
Insects, lots collected	14
Shells, lots collected	8

No changes were made in the class of instruments used.

Reports, more or less in detail, of the routes followed by the several parties, and descriptive accounts of the areas examined, appear as Appendix NN in the Annual Report of the Chief of Engineers for 1878, accompanied by special reports and a number of atlas sheets.

This Appendix was repaged and printed separately as Annual Report upon the Geographical Surveys of the Territory of the United States West of the One-hundredth Meridian.

Volumes 2 and 4 of the quarto series were issued during the year.

The season of 1877 included a period of from six to seven months, and was an extremely successful one in almost all the several branches of the work, resulting in a very large accumulation of data.

Among other interesting matters may be mentioned the tracing of the Bonneville Beach, or outlines of the ancient fresh-water lake of the Great Basin, northward through Cache Valley and westward through Malade Valley. Sufficient additional information was obtained regarding this ancient lake to complete its outlines.

The collection of fishes of this season, though small, proved to be extremely interesting; besides containing two new species it illustrated several items of importance respecting the geographic range of previously known species.

EXPEDITION FOR GEOGRAPHICAL SURVEYS WEST OF THE 100TH MERIDIAN, IN COLORADO, NEW MEXICO, UTAH, CALIFORNIA, NEVADA, OREGON, AND WASHINGTON, IN 1878.

The expedition took the field in three divisions of three parties each. Of the Colorado division one party was organized at Fort Stanton, N. Mex., and two at Fort Garland, Colo. The two parties of the California division were organized respectively at Carson, Nev., and at Camp Bidwell, Cal., Ogden, Utah, was the initial point of the Utah section.

Owing to the lateness of the appropriation field work was not begun until the 1st of July.

The parties were disbanded after a season of about five months.

An area aggregating 25,550 square miles was occupied, situated chiefly in southwestern New Mexico, northern Utah, northern, central and southwestern California, western Nevada, and central Oregon.

Areas embraced during the seasons of 1873, 1874, 1875, 1876, and 1877 were again visited along certain lines when rendered necessary in perfecting triangulation and topographic details.

The following were the personnel: First Lieut. George M. Wheeler, Corps of Engineers, U. S. Army, in command, chief executive officer, field astronomer and in charge of survey; First Lieut. Samuel E. Tillman, Corps of Engineers, U. S. Army, assistant executive officer, field astronomer and triangulator; First Lieut. Thomas W. Symons, Corps of Engineers, U. S. Army, assistant executive officer, field astronomer and triangulator; Second Lieut. Willard Young, Corps of Engineers, U. S. Army, assistant executive officer, field astronomer and triangulator; Second Lieut. Eugene Griffin, Corps of Engineers, U. S. Army, assistant executive officer, field astronomer and triangulator; First Lieut. Rogers Birnie, jr., Ordnance Corps, U. S. Army, assistant executive officer, field astronomer and triangulator; Second Lieut. M. M. Macomb, Fourth U. S. Artillery, assistant executive officer, field astronomer and triangulator; Second Lieut. Henry H. Ludlow, Third U. S. Artillery, assistant executive officer and triangulation observer; Second Lieut. B. H. Randolph, Third U. S. Artillery, acting assistant quartermaster, acting assistant commissary of subsistence, and ordnance officer; Prof. T. H. Safford and Miles Rock, astronomic observers and computers; John H. Clark, astronomic observer; Louis Nell, Gilbert Thompson, F. O. Maxson, J. C. Spiller, Frank Carpenter, Anton Karl, James S. Polhemus, Charles P. Kahler, W. G. Walbridge, and Ed. Gillette, jr., geodetic and topographic assistants; Francis Klett, assistant topographer and clerk; Thomas W. Goad, George M. Dunn, Frederick W. Floyd, G. H. Schleicher, John A. Hasson, Louis Seckles, H. S. Wallace, William Hollis, John H. Morgan, Mark B. Kerr, and William L. Bailey, barometric observers and recorders; Sergt. Thomas Knight, Company F, Fourteenth Infantry, barometric observer; Isaiah Brown, barometric observer and messenger; R. Pitcher, Edward W. Lyon, John Bishop, W. A. Purington, W. A. Phillips, jr., and J. B. Callahan, odometer observers and recorders; Prof. J. J. Stevenson, geological observer; Israel C. Russel, assistant geological observer; H W. Henshaw, zoological assistant; Almont Barnes, general assistant and clerk; C. S. Chesney and C. D. Davis, clerks (office and field).

Office.—First Lieut. Charles C. Morrison, Sixth U. S. Cavalry, temporarily in charge; John D. McChesney, money clerk; John C. Lang, Charles Herman, and John E. Weyss, draughtsmen; Gwynn A. Lyell, draughtsman and clerk; Alfred Downing, draughtsman and computer; James M. Ewing, clerk.

The Army furnished one sergeant, one corporal, and two privates of the Fourteenth Infantry, and the usual quota of packers, laborers, etc., were hired.

In addition to the regular organizations covering contiguous and connected areas, the following special parties were sent out during this season:

A party in charge of Lieutenant Young was intrusted with the survey of Great Salt Lake. This included a meander of its shore line and of the islands, the gauging the amount of inflowing water, the determination of the amount of surface evaporation, and the rise and fall of the lake, as well as the topography of the country immediately bordering the lake and the islands. The Terrace-Lucin base-line previously measured was leveled and connected with the general triangulation system.

The detailed plane table contour survey of the Washoe mining region was completed and copies of the maps of all the underground workings kept up. Lieutenant Young visited several mining districts in southern California; Lieutenant Birnie others in New Mexico. (See Annual Report, 1879.)

Initial astronomical stations (with telegraphic determination of longitude) were concluded at (1) Fort Walla Walla, Wash.; (2) The Dalles, Oregon; (3) Fresno, Cal.; (4) Fort Bayard, N. Mex., and (5) Fort Bliss, near El Paso, Tex. Signals were sent from Fort Bayard Station to Ogden, Utah, by both an eastern and western circuit, thus affording independent determinations for comparison. Bases were measured at each of these points and developed connecting with the triangulation in every instance except at Walla Walla. An auxiliary basis was also measured near Austin, Nev.

The base line of 24 miles measured between Lucin and Terrace, Utah, was developed to connect with the triangulation work, the latter being carried, as was the custom, over the entire area surveyed in 1878 and where practicable extending it across to points lying in areas of prior years.

Prof. J. J. Stevenson continued his examination of the geology of certain areas in south central Colorado and north central New Mexico, which includes parts of the three great drainage areas—those of the Purgatory, the Canadian, and the Rio Grande.

Mr. H. W. Henshaw accompanied party No. 1, California section, and made zoological collections in the region traversed, with a special view to the study of its ornithology.

Fourteen mining districts were reported upon, viz: Ridge Bar, San Gabriel, San Antonio, Holcomb, Bear Valley, and Lone Valley, California; the Lone, Chloride, Mimbres, Pinos Altos, Aztec and Moreno, Los Cerillos, and Placer Districts, New Mexico; and the Las Animas District, Colorado.

The following table expresses certain of the prominent features of the field work:

Number of main astronomical stations	5
Sextant latitude stations	90
Bases measured	5
Triangles about bases measured	64
Main triangulation stations occupied	70
Secondary triangulation stations occupied	87
Three-point stations occupied	763
Stations on meander	15,936
Miles measured	10,299
Cistern barometer stations occupied	1,041
Aneroid stations occupied	7,057
Magnetic variations observed	197
Monuments built	156
Mining camps visited	15
Mineral and thermal springs noted	23
Minerals, fossils, and ores collected (approximate)	1,467
Mammals, specimens collected	11
Birds, specimens collected	243
Birds' eggs collected	12
Mammals (alcoholic) collected	3
Mammal crania collected	1
Bird crania collected	7
Fishes, specimens	200
Fishes, lots	12
Snakes, specimens	25
Snakes, lots	16
Lizards, specimens	25
Lizards, lots	7
Batrachians, specimens	50
Batrachians, lots	11
Hemiptera collected	1
Orthoptera, specimens	200
Orthoptera, lots	6
Shells, specimens	25
Shells, lots	3
Crustaceans, specimens	12
Crustaceans, lots	1
Fossil leaves, specimens	72

The field instruments employed were those given in description of "methods."

A report of the season's results appeared as Appendix OO of the Chief of Engineers Annual Report of 1879. A repaged edition was issued as the annual report of the survey, Vol. VI, Botany, of the quarto series issued from the press during the year.

With the report was a progress map and an outline map of the Comstock Lode. Accompanying the report, but in separate covers, were seven quarter atlas sheets.

The results of the season of 1878, while presenting no especially novel features as contrasted with previous years, are yet notable in a general way for the great amount of work accomplished and the value of the data gathered bearing on the several subjects of inquiry. In this respect this, the latest field season, exceeds in the aggregate of its results any previous year. While this gratifying showing is in part due to the large working force employed, no small amount of the credit should be attributed to the improved methods of work, and to the experience in their several departments gained by the members of the survey. Experience in extended surveys is especially necessary. In fact nowhere is the value of a skilled personnel more apparent than in a survey of the far West, where new problems and unforeseen contingencies are continually arising that tax ingenuity, patience, and forethought to their utmost.

GEOGRAPHICAL SURVEY PARTIES FOR THE SEASON OF 1879, IN COLORADO, CALIFORNIA, AND UTAH.

No funds for *field* operations being available after June 30, comparatively little work was accomplished during the field season of 1879. Several small parties were, however, sent out to complete details in certain areas entered during the years 1873, 1875, 1877, and 1878.

A party under Lieutenant Young continued the hydrographic and topographic survey of Great Salt Lake, occupying the interval between April 22 and June 30.

A second party, with Lieutenant Macomb as executive officer, took up the survey of the area in east central California, as left by his division at the close of the field season of 1878, and finished important details. This party was in the field from May 16 to June 27.

A party under Louis Nell was engaged in triangulation observations in central Colorado; it localized a number of new mining camps, as Silver Cliff, Leadville, Ten Mile, Carbonate, Frying Pan Gulch, Monarch, and the new discoveries in the basin of the Gunnison.

Professor Stevenson again entered, for a brief interval, the scene of his previous year's labors, and filled in certain gaps in the work. He also visited and examined the mines of the Placer Mountains and of Los Cerillos near Galisteo Creek.

Reports by Lieutenants Young and Macomb on the work intrusted to them, and a preliminary report by Professor Stevenson on the section examined by him, will be found in the annual report for 1879, as cited above.

The personnel was as follows: Capt. George M. Wheeler, Corps of Engineers, U. S. Army, in command; First Lieut. B. H. Randolph, Third Artillery, U. S. Army, field quartermaster, ordnance officer, and commissary; Second Lieut. Willard Young, Corps of Engineers, U S. Army, chief of party and field astronomer; First Lieut. M M. Macomb, Fourth Artillery, U. S. Army, chief of party and field astronomer; Louis Nell, chief of party, triangulation and topographic observer; F. O. Maxson, field triangulation and topographic observer; Prof. John J. Stevenson, chief of party and geological observer; Francis Klett, topographer and surveyor; E. Gillette, jr., assistant topographer; Louis Seckles, barometric observer and recorder; C. D. Davis, clerk; Isaiah Brown, barometric recorder and messenger; Sergt. Thomas Knight, Company F, Fourteenth Infantry, U. S. Army, barometric observer and recorder; Corp. Joseph T. Hill, Company I, Fourteenth Infantry, U. S. Army, odometer recorder.

Office, July 1, 1879.—First Lieut. Samuel E. Tillman, Corps of Engineers, U. S. Army, temporarily in charge; John D. McChesney, money clerk; H. W. Henshaw, clerk in charge of reports and publications; Miles Rock, astronomic and geodetic computer; Fred. W. Floyd, computer; Charles P. Kahler, J. S Polhemus, J. C. Spiller, Gilbert Thompson, and Anton Karl, topographic assistants; Charles Herman, John C. Lang, John E. Weyss, and Albert Noerr, draughtsmen; James M. Ewing and Mark B. Kerr, clerks; John W. Irwin, jr., general assistant.

Subsequent to July 1, with all available means and assistants, the various reports and maps were brought as near as possible to completion (see list of reports and maps in this volume), while finally the office closed for lack of funds, February 28, 1884; since which, as circumstances have permitted, the volume on geographic positions, etc., the Venice report, and the present and final volume have been issued, as also a number of maps.

The mountainous part of the total area of 1,443,360 square miles west of the one-hundredth meridian is 993,360 square miles, of which 359,065 square miles were surveyed topographically and otherwise examined during the expeditions above noticed. A summary of results in the several branches appears on pages 137 to 146 of the volume herewith. The manner of conducting the survey operations (observations and reductions) will be found as Appendix C of this volume.*

Of necessity much material and many records, incompletely reduced, were transferred to the Engineer Department, U. S. Army, as were all original field and manuscript records of the astronomic, geodetic, trigonometric, topographic, hypsometric, and magnetic departments, including original triangulation sheets (unpublished); original platting sheets (published); original platting sheets (unpublished), and original finished topographic sheets (published).

Nothing was elsewhere or otherwise transferred. Numerical results for latitudes, longitudes, and altitudes will be found distributed through the annual, special, and main quarto reports.

The following is a tabulated list of maps and reports:

MAPS.

1. Topographic maps, atlas sheet series (scales, 1 inch to 8 miles, 1 inch to 4 miles, and 1 inch to 2 miles, including five preliminary sheets)	55
2. Land classification sheets based on above (scale 1 inch to 4 miles)	30
3. Geologic sheets based on above (scales 1 inch to 8 miles, 1 inch to 4 miles, including two preliminary sheets)	13
4. Maps of all kinds, bound with reports	54
5. Special and miscellaneous maps (scales from 1 inch to 12 miles to 1 inch to 1,500 feet)	12
Total	164

REPORTS.

1. Regular quarto volumes	8
2. Miscellaneous quarto volumes	7
3. Annual reports, separately published	12
4. Special reports, folio and royal octavo	3
5. Miscellaneous pamphlet reports, octavo and duodecimo	11
Total	41

*The project presented in 1872 for a connected and continuous survey, approved by act of June 10, 1872, estimated a cost of $2,500,000, spread over an interval of 15 years. Had not the appropriation been stopped in 1879 the field work for the whole area west of one-hundredth meridian could easily have been completed by 1887, if not earlier.

LAKE SURVEY.

While the admirable work of this office has been within areas east of the Mississippi, yet it has also successfully co-operated with certain western parties, in the establishment of telegraphic longitudes, results from which appear on page 763 *et seq.* (Professional Papers, Corps of Engineers, U. S. Army, No. 24; Primary Triangulation of the U. S. Lake Survey; Comstock, 1882.)

The observers at Detroit were Capt. H. M. Adams and Lieut. P. M. Price, U. S. Engineers, and assistants O. B. Wheeler and A. R. Flint. The latitudes and longitudes of twelve points are given: Four in Dakota, Wyoming, and Nebraska (Capt. W. S. Stanton, U. S. Engineers, observer); one in Nevada (Capt. W. A. Jones, U. S. Engineers, observer); one in Utah (Dr. F. Kampf, U. S. Geographical Survey, observer); one in Kansas (Lieut. E. H. Ruffner, U. S. Engineers, observer); and five in Texas (Lieut. William Hoffman, U. S. Army, observer).

In 1876 the duty of making a survey of the Mississippi River was placed upon the Lake Survey, which was commenced at Cairo, Ill., during the winter of 1876–'77, and base measuring triangulation, topographic, hydrographic, and precise leveling work was continued also from Memphis southward during two succeeding winters.

All of these results were availed of by the Mississippi River Commission Survey, including complete maps (topographic and hydrographic) of 40 miles of the river southward from Memphis.

MISSISSIPPI RIVER COMMISSION SURVEY.

This Commission, constituted by act of June 28, 1879, instituted a system of surveys not useful only to the proximate ends in view, but also in connection with the wider ultimate range of inquiry when necessary.

The U. S. Lake Survey, during the winter of 1876–'77, began a special survey of the Mississippi River (topographic and hydrographic) in the vicinity of Cairo, which was continued during the winters of 1877–'78 and 1878–'79, at and below Memphis, all of the work of which was availed of by the Mississippi River Commission.

It consisted of a developed line of secondary triangulation, resting upon secondary bases when necessary, principally from Cairo to the head of the Passes, about 1,100 miles. The triangulation at Cairo connects and depends upon a secondary base of the U. S. Lake Survey. Co-operation was extended during 1880 and 1881 by triangulation and hydrographic parties of the Coast and Geodetic Survey, as appears from the reports of this office and also that of the Commission.

Tertiary triangulation was availed of along certain reaches.

All existing survey data was utilized* and co-operation had with the Coast Survey as to the triangulation and precise leveling, which was carried from a beach point at the Gulf along the banks of the river northward to Fulton, Ill., and from thence to the level of Lake Michigan, at Chicago, where it is joined to the line of precise levels brought by the Lake Survey from tidewater at New York City.

The average closure of the triangles ranged from 2 to 6 seconds.

Topography consists of developing the shore line of the actual river, with its banks, tow-heads, chutes, islands, etc., also levees, elevations of banks, water surfaces, cross-sections of levees, etc., all resting upon the triangulation, with five-foot contours depending on numerous elevations (sketched) carried back an average distance of three-fourths of a mile each side.

All topographic work intermediate between △ stations was determined by stadia measurements frequently checked.

Nine principal trans-alluvial level lines were run to obtain information as to the alluvial bottom lands and their reservoir capacity; also similar levels over 160 miles between Lower Red River and the Atchafalaya.

Elevations by vertical angles (by circle or telescope level), all creeks and lakes, between bluffs and the river located.

Collections were made of reliable high-water marks of 1883.

The topography includes outlines of bluffs, old river lakes, and bayous, the Red River, and Cut-off Bayou to the main stream; also sloughs, swamps, fields, woods, and houses.

---

*In 1879 the Coast Survey had published charts of the river between Point Houmas (72 miles above New Orleans) and the Gulf, showing depths and marginal topography.

Measurements made of caving and changes in sliding banks, with bank line, cross-section, and reliable elevations of old and new river banks. Difference of elevation determined between top and bottom of bluffs, with heights of tops above mean water surface; also connections with county and State lines and with township and section corners of public lands. The precise levels were run in duplicate, in opposite directions, with permanent beach marks every 3 miles.

Hydrography.—Soundings in boats for cross-sections of the river and its approaches for about every half mile, with intermediate lines across base. Cross-sections were repeated near the principal crevasses after the flood of 1882.

Profile of water surface for low water of 1883 from St. Louis to New Orleans was determined. Special hydrographic surveys made in vicinity of crevasses.

Resurvey made to determine the enlargement of the Atchafalaya. Besides normal sections in 1882 soundings were taken (1882) along the line of deepest water. In 1884 special surveys made above, below, and through cut-offs.

Observations made of flood escapes through crevasses; correct data obtained as to depths of bad bars at low water.

Longitudinal lines sounded along the thread of deepest water from Island No. 1 to Donaldson's Point, also 98 miles north of Caruthersville.

Physical inquiries extending to all the recognized phenomena likely to have a bearing upon problems of improvement were instituted.

Physical examinations of selected reaches, presenting locally and relatively the most widely contrasted elements of width, depth, and curvature, were made.

Stations for recording river elevations were maintained and increased where necessary, so as to trace the progress of floods and the principal features of the river slopes.*

The trigonometric stations have been marked by stones 3 feet long, dressed 6 by 6 inches at one end; balance rough, with top projecting a few inches from the ground.

* Twenty gauges have been maintained continuously on the main river and its tributaries.

The precise level stations were marked by flat stones 18 inches square and 4 inches thick, with hole in center, into which a copper bolt is leaded. This is incased by a cast-iron 4-inch pipe 5 feet long, with elevations of top of pipe and stone both determined.

Computations.—The computations were usually made by angle adjustments by least squares for quadrilaterals and pentagons, with computations of lengths, and azimuths of the sides, and formation of equations of condition and their solutions.

Instruments.—The instruments employed were as follows: Triangulation, Troughton & Sims 12-inch and Gambey 10-inch theodolites, Repsold 12-inch and Pistor & Martins 5-inch universal instruments, Wurdemann-Gambey 10-inch and 6-inch transit theodolites, and ordinary transits. There were also Stackpole and Kern Y levels, with rods, ordinary and pocket sextants, chronometers, stadias, standard meter, iron standard bars, steel tapes, prismatic compasses, pedometers, and hand levels.

The cost of certain parts of the completed survey is stated at $169 per lineal mile and at $57 per square mile for topography alone, exclusive of the cost of all other branches.

Geographic co-ordinates (latitudes and longitudes) results of the triangulation may be found published in progress report, 1881, being Senate Executive Document No. 10, Forty-seventh Congress, first session; Appendix SS, Part III, Annual Report Chief of Engineers, 1883, pages 2158 *et seq.;* and Appendix TT, Part III, Annual Report Chief of Engineers, 1884, pages 2445 *et seq.*

Maps—The map publications consist of detailed contour charts (3 feet and 5 feet intervals), scale 1 to 10,000; including outline and topographic maps, and those of the river lakes, the same reduced to 1 to 20,000; preliminary maps, 1 to 63,360; with a general map of the whole alluvial basin from Cape Girardeau to the Gulf (see tabular list of maps).

The Progress and Annual Reports have usually been published first as executive documents, appearing during the sittings of Congress, which have afterwards been incorporated in the Annual Report of the Chief of Engineers, as follows: Appendices SS, 1881; RR, 1882; SS, 1883; TT, 1884; WW and WW_2, 1885. The Annual Report for 1886 appears as

House Executive Document No. 30, Forty-ninth Congress, second session.

The survey is considered complete below Cairo; above Cairo the triangulation is carried to Keokuk, Iowa, the detailed field survey being complete for 25 miles above Cairo.

The first extension when made will be to complete topography and hydrography upward as far as the mouth of the Missouri, it being in contemplation finally to continue it as far as St. Paul, Minn.

MISSOURI RIVER COMMISSION.

Prior to 1884, commencing in 1878, the surveys on the Missouri River consisted of an accurate delineation of the shore line, islands, and sand bars, the general topographic features of the valley, and the line of bluffs bordering the same, the whole checked by a system of triangulation carried along the river banks.

Soundings were made, on lines normal to the current, from 500 to 1,500 feet apart; carefully checked levels were carried from Pierre to the mouth.

The results have been reduced and published as photolithographs, scale 1 inch to 1 mile. The Missouri River Commission commenced in 1884 a secondary triangulation of the river, to be carried from bluff to bluff, marked by permanent monuments and the establishments of permanent bench-marks, all to be connected with former surveys.

The monuments marking the triangulation points consisted of a stone 18 by 18 by 4 inches placed 3 feet 4 inches in the ground, in which was placed a 4-inch gas-pipe 3 feet long, the top covered with a cast iron cap, secured by a bolt and nut. (See Appendix XX, Annual Report Chief of Engineers, 1885, Part IV, pages 3015 *et seq.*)

SURVEYS FOR RIVER AND HARBOR IMPROVEMENTS.

These have been conducted at numerous points throughout the whole country, including frequent reaches of navigable rivers, also harbors and their approaches, but being for Engineers' purposes solely have been directed to the physical relations of channels and water-ways, within the purview of the improvements, and hence have been made with an eye single to these improvements. Immeeiate results have always been required, and hence, while often possessed of much topographic and hydrographic detail, are possessed of no geographic connection (no latitudes, or latitudes being established as a rule) and are valuable more particularly in preliminary compilation. The plats are either published with the Annual Reports of the Chief of Engineers, in executive documents, or held as original drawings at the Engineer Department.

MAPS, ENGINEER DEPARTMENT.

The recompilation of the Western Territory Map, originally constructed and compiled at close of the Pacific Railroad surveys by Lieut. Warren, commencing in 1867, was the only general topographic map of this territory until a new compilation (scale 1 to 500,000) was begun in 1876, and published in 1879 as a photolithograph (scale 1 to 2,000,000). The compilation of a new outline map of our territory west of the Mississippi was commenced in 1880, the compilation completed in 1882, the same engraved and published in 1884 in outline, and in 1885 with hill work in color.

Special photolithographed maps (1 to 1,500,000) were issued in 1880, separately, as follows: Colorado, Oregon, Washington and Idaho, New Mexico and Arizona, California and Nevada.

A new map covering the entire territory of the United States, designed both for military and geographic purposes, had in 1869 been compiled and engraved. This was revised in 1874, and a new edition printed. This was further revised, and in 1877 again re-issued.

In 1882 a new outline map of the United States was commenced, and in 1885 engraved and issued.

In 1886 a new outline map of the United States (scale 1 to 2,000,000) was commenced, as also a compiled map of Central America (scale 1 to 1,250,000).

In 1881 an outline map of the United States (scale 1 inch to 52½ miles) showing location of works and surveys for rivers and harbors was issued.

From time to time many military topographic and geographic maps of various scales, usually prepared at the headquarters of military divisions and departments, have been published and issued either at the Engineer Department or at the above offices, as appears from the several Annual Reports of the Chief of Engineers. It has been impossible, for want of data, to name all of them, and it may be said that these are such current compilations, demanded by the commanding general, as means permit.

INTERIOR DEPARTMENT.

GEOLOGICAL EXAMINATION IN NEBRASKA, BY PROF. F. V. HAYDEN, 1867.

In 1867, when Nebraska was admitted as a State, Congress set apart the unexpended balance ($5,000) of the appropriation for legislative expenses of the Territory for a geological survey of the new State.

The examination was conducted by Dr. F. V. Hayden, who was assisted by Prof. F. B. Meek, and by Mr. James Stevenson as business agent. The sale, for a party of ten, from the subsistence stores of the Army was authorized.

The report of the work was made to the Commissioner of the General Land Office, and was devoted to the geological structure of Nebraska.

GEOLOGICAL EXPLORATION OF WYOMING, BY PROF. F. V. HAYDEN, 1868.

In 1868 $5,000 was appropriated to continue the work of geological exploration in Wyoming Territory.

The party consisted of nine persons and was organized at Cheyenne, Wyo.

The field work extended westward to Greene River. The geological structure along the line of the Union Pacific Railroad and along the Overland Stage Route was examined.

The Laramie Plains and North Park were visited and described.

The report of this work was also made to the Commissioner of the General Land Office.

GEOLOGICAL SURVEY OF THE TERRITORIES, BY PROF. F. V. HAYDEN, 1869.

In 1869 the work was placed under the supervision of the Secretary of the Interior, and an appropriation of $10,000 was made for a geological examination of Colorado and New Mexico.

This may be regarded as the proper commencement of the survey.

The field party consisted of eleven persons in all, including, besides Dr. Hayden, Mr. James Stevenson, managing director; Mr. Persifor Frazer, jr., mining engineer; Prof. Cyrus Thomas, entomologist and botanist, and Henry W. Elliott, artist.

The greater part of the outfit was furnished by the Quartermaster's Department, and such aid as was needed was supplied at the military posts en route.

The field labors commenced in the latter part of June at Cheyenne, Wyo., from which point a reconnaissance was made along the eastern edge of the Rocky Mountains via Denver, Central City, and Cañon City to Santa Fe, N. Mex.

Trips were made to the mines at the head of the Cache la Poudre River, the coal mines at South Boulder, the silver mines of Georgetown, the gold mines of Central City and Middle Park.

From Santa Fe the return was made via the Rio Grande through San Luis Valley, Poncho Pass, Arkansas Valley, and South Park to Denver.

The resulting report and all those thereafter were made to the Secretary of the Interior.

EXAMINATION OF 1870.

In 1870 the appropriation was $25,000.

The area explored comprised a portion of Wyoming Territory.

A reconnaissance was made from Cheyenne northward along the eastern base of the Laramie Range via the Chugwater, North Platte, and Sweetwater Rivers to South Pass.

Frequent excursions were made on each side of the route of travel, and the Sweetwater mines and the southern portions of the Wind River Mountains were visited.

From South Pass the party passed down the Little and Big Sandy Creeks to Green River, and thence by way of Church Buttes to Fort Bridger.

A permanent camp was established at the latter point, from which numerous excursions were made, especially to the Uintah Mountains, the northern slopes of which were explored.

From Fort Bridger the course was southward to Henry's Fork and via that stream to Green River City, on the Union Pacific Railroad.

From the latter place the old stage road was followed up Bitter Creek, over Bridger's Pass and the Medicine Bow Mountains, across the Laramie Plains, and through the Laramie Range via Cheyenne Pass to Cheyenne, the point of departure.

The party in the field in 1870 consisted of twenty persons, with Dr. F. V. Hayden in charge; James Stevenson, assistant; Henry W. Elliott, artist; Prof. Cyrus Thomas, agriculturist; William H. Jackson, photographer; John W. Beaman, meteorologist; Charles T. Turnbull, secretary; Arthur L. Ford, mineralogist; C. P. Carrington, zoologist; Henry D. Schmidt, naturalist, and L. A. Bartlett, general assistant.

Outfits and equipments were furnished by the Quartermaster's Department and assistance "by the military authorities of the west," which caused a "great saving to the appropriation."

EXAMINATION OF 1871.

In 1871 it was decided to carry on topographic work in connection with the geological explorations.

The plan adopted was that of a topographic reconnaissance—the reconnaissance of the immediate line of march, with the country in sight from it controlled by courses and distances, the former measured by compass, the latter by odometer, and the whole checked by sextant latitudes.

The party organized as follows, at Cheyenne, Wyo.: Dr. F. V. Hayden, geologist, in charge; James Stevenson, assistant; Henry W. Elliott, artist; Prof. Cyrus Thomas, agricultural statistician and entomologist; Anton Shouborn, chief topographer; A. J. Smith, assistant; William H. Jackson, photographer; George B. Dixon, assistant; J. W. Beaman, meteorologist; Prof. G. N. Allen, botanist; Robert Adams, jr., assistant; Dr. A. C. Peale, mineralogist; Dr. A. C. Turnbull, physician; with a number of general assistants, the entire field party numbering about thirty-six persons. The greater portion of the outfit (including horses, mules, wagons, and other equipments) were furnished from the Army, and aid, where possible, by the military authorities. Commissary stores were purchased at cost price, with the cost of transportation added. One company, Second Cavalry, under Captain Tyler and Lieutenant Grugan, was a joint escort to this party and those of Captains Barlow and Heap, U. S. Engineers. The escort officers were replaced at Yellowstone Lake by Lieutenant Doane.

The party proceeded by rail from Cheyenne to Ogden, in Utah, whence a reconnaissance was made with a wagon train northward via Cache Valley, Snake River Plains, and the Madison Valley, through Utah and Idaho into Montana as far north as Bozeman, in the Gallatin Valley. and thence to Boteler's ranch, on the Yellowstone River.

From the latter point a trip of some six weeks' duration was made with a pack-train to Yellowstone Lake and the geysers and hot springs on the Fire Hole or Upper Madison River (a portion of which region was afterwards set aside by Congress as the Yellowstone National Park).

The return trip was made along the Jefferson Fork of the Missouri and across the Snake River Valley to Fort Hall, in Idaho, and thence via Bear Lake Valley and Bear Lake to Evanston, Wyo., where the party disbanded for the season.

The amount appropriated was $40,000.

EXAMINATION OF 1872.

In 1872 two well-equipped parties were put in the field. The topographic work was improved by the addition of a running system of triangulation, which, in conjunction with the observations for latitude, were used in correcting the work.

The first, or Yellowstone division, was under the immediate charge of Dr. F. V. Hayden, with the following members: Adolf Burck, chief topographer; Henry Gannett, astronomer; A. E. Brown, assistant topographer; E. B. Wakefield meteorologist; Dr. A. C. Peale, mineralogist; W. H. Holmes, artist; Walter B. Platt, naturalist; W. B. Logan, secretary; and three general assistants.

The rendezvous for this division was at Fort Ellis, in Montana, from which point the trip to the Yellowstone Park was taken. The headwaters of the Yellowstone, Madison, and Gallatin Rivers were explored in much greater detail than during the previous year. The same assistance as that of the previous year was rendered by the military authorities.

The second, or Snake River division, was in charge of Mr. James Stevenson, and was constituted as follows: Prof. Frank H. Bradley, chief geologist; W. R. Taggart, assistant geologist; Gustavus R. Bechler, chief topographer; Rudolph Hering and Thomas W. Jaycox, assistant topographers; William Nicholson, meteorologist; John M. Coulter, botanist; Dr. Josiah Curtis, surgeon and microscopist; C. Hart Merriam, ornithologist; Campbell Carrington, naturalist; Robert Adams, jr., and others, general assistants. The superintendent of the Yellowstone National Park also accompanied the party. This division, starting from Fort Hall, in Idaho Territory, made a reconnaissance of the country between that post and the Yellowstone Park, including the sources of Snake River, and the Teton Mountains and the southern portion of the Park.

The appropriation for the year was $75,000.

UNITED STATES GEOLOGICAL AND GEOGRAPHICAL SURVEY OF THE TERRITORIES.

SEASON OF 1873.

In 1873 the field of work was transferred, and fuller and more detailed topographic observations, in charge of James T. Gardner, carried on in conjunction with the geological examination.

A connected survey, covering uniformly the whole country, controlled by a triangulation, took the place of the route reconnaissance of the previous years.

At the beginning of the work a base line was carefully measured near Denver, and the system of triangulation was expanded by well conditioned triangles. The triangulation was controlled by connection with stations at Denver, Colorado Springs, and Trinidad, the latitude and longitude of which were determined by the United States Coast Survey. The angles were measured with 8-inch theodolites, reading to ten seconds of arc. The mean error of closure of the triangles measured in 1873 is 10′ 3″.

The secondary triangulation was carried on by the topographers coincidently with the topographic work. The angles were measured with a 4-inch theodolite reading to minutes. The mean error of closure is about two minutes.

The topographic observations were made from commanding points, mainly from the stations in the secondary triangulation susceptible of location and were fixed in position by the intersections. All important streams were meandered. Heights were measured by the cistern barometer, and by vertical angles. The base barometer stations were so distributed, horizontally and in height, that any hypsometric work could be referred to a base in no case more than 50 miles distant nor differing in height more than 2,000 feet. All the high mountain peaks were carefully connected by vertical angles, and all barometric readings taken on them, were reduced to a common point, and then referred to the observations taken on the summits of Mount Lincoln or Pike's Peak as a base.

The work in Colorado began in 1873 with an appropriation of $75,000.

The principal triangulation party was in charge of James T. Gardner.

The eastern portion of the mountainous part of the State was embraced topographically and geologically by three divisions, which covered in all some 23,000 square miles. The first or Middle Park division was directed by Mr. A R. Marvine, geologist, with G. R. Bechler as topographer and S. B. Ladd topographical assistant.

The area surveyed by this division was approximately a rectangular belt, the eastern end of which rested on the plains near Denver. This belt extended westward across the main chain of the Rocky Mountains to and including the Middle Park.

The second or South Park division was in charge of Mr. Henry Gannett, topographer, with Dr. A. C. Peale as division geologist, and Mr. W. R. Taggart as assistant. The area surveyed by them extended westward from the plains to the Elk Mountains.

The third or San Luis division was directed by Mr. A. D. Wilson, topographer. Mr. George B. Chittenden was assistant topographer, and Dr. F. M. Endlich division geologist.

The field occupied by this division was the southern portion of the eastern mountainous part of the State.

Besides the division just enumerated, there was a party of supervision, under Dr. F. V. Hayden, with Mr. W. H. Holmes as geological artist, and Mr W. H. Jackson photographer, and various assistants and collectors.

Second Lieut. William L. Carpenter, Ninth U. S. Infantry, accompanied the expedition as naturalist.

The same assistance as hitherto was afforded by the military authorities.

SEASON OF 1874.

In 1874 Congress appropriated $75,000 for the continuation of the work in Colorado, and the work was extended westward and southwestward, covering an area of 13,000 square miles. The divisions were late in reaching the field and were constituted as follows: Party of general supervision—Dr. F. V. Hayden, geologist in charge; W. H. Holmes, assistant geologist and artist; Mr. George B. Chittenden, topographer. This party was occupied mainly with the examination and mapping of the moraines of the Upper Arkansas Valley and the detailed examination of the Elk Mountains.

First division, A. R. Marvine, division geologist in charge; S. B. Ladd, topographer.

This division continued their work of 1873 westward.

Second division, Henry Gannett, topographer in charge; Dr. A. C. Peale, geologist. The area surveyed was that lying west of the Elk Mountains between the Grand and Gunnison Rivers.

Third division, A. D. Wilson, topographer in charge; Dr. F. M. Endlich, geologist. The work of the preceding year was extended westward and southward.

The party of primary triangulation was in charge of Mr. James T. Gardner, and measured a base in San Luis Valley, carrying also the triangulation over the southern part of the State.

The photographic and naturalist's division was under the supervision of Mr. W. H. Jackson, photographer. Mr. Ernest Ingersoll was naturalist.

Middle Park and the San Juan region were visited and particular attention paid to the cave dwellings and other ruins in southern Colorado.

Dr. Elliott Coues, surgeon U. S. Army, rendered valuable assistance in and contributions to the publications, commencing with this year.

SEASON OF 1875.

The appropriation for 1875 was $75,000, and work was resumed in the western part of Colorado. An area of 24,000 square miles was surveyed by the following divisions of the survey:

First or southern division, A. D. Wilson, topographer in charge; Dr. F. M. Endlich, geologist. This division was in the southern part of Colorado, mainly in the Sangre de Christo Range and the adjacent country.

Second or southwestern division, W. H. Holmes directing, with George B. Chittenden as topographer, continued the work of Mr. A. D. Wilson of 1874 to the westward. Mr. Holmes made also a special observation regarding the prehistoric remains of southwestern Colorado.

Third or Grand River division, with Henry Gannett, topographer, as director, and Dr. A. C. Peale as geologist, extended westward their work of the previous year.

Fourth division, in charge of G. R. Bechler, topographer, worked in the eastern part of the State, connecting by meanders and triangulation of several isolated areas surveyed during the previous years.

The principal triangulation was under the supervision of James T. Gardner.

The photographic and naturalists party was directed by W. H. Jackson, with Ernest Ingersoll as naturalist. They spent most of the season in southwestern Colorado investigating the extent and distribution of the ruins in that region. Their field was extended also to include the Moquis Pueblos.

SEASON OF 1876.

In 1876 an appropriation of $65,000 was made to complete the survey of Colorado, of which about 10,000 square miles remained to be examined. The field season was short, but the work was accomplished.

The primary triangulation was completed by Mr. A. D. Wilson, who was accompanied by Mr. W. H. Holmes, for the purpose of taking a general view (for comparison) of the two great plain belts that lie one along the east and the other along the west base of the Rocky Mountains.

The first or Grand River division, directed by Henry Gannett, with Dr. A. C. Peale, geologist, completed the western central portion of the State, and also surveyed a small area lying north of Grand River.

The second or White River division was in charge of George B Chittenden, topographer, accompanied by Dr. F. M. Endlich as geologist, and worked south of White River, extending the survey over into Utah.

The third or Yampah division was directed by G. R. Bechler; Dr. C. A. White was the geologist. The field of work was the extreme northwestern portion of Colorado, lying between the Yampah and White Rivers, which area was satisfactorily completed.

SEASON OF 1877.

Examinations were carried northward into Wyoming and Idaho Territories, beginning at the northern line of the work of the exploration of the 40th parallel. During the season 30,000 square miles, embracing parts of Wyoming, Idaho, and Utah, were covered. The following parties were put in the field:

First, party of primary triangulation, in charge of A. D. Wilson, chief topographer.

Second, Green River division, in charge of Henry Gannett, topographer, with Dr. A. C. Peale, geologist. The area surveyed was the Green River Basin and the country westward of the Portneuf River.

Third, Sweetwater division. in charge of George B. Chittenden, topographer, with Dr. F. M Endlich as geologist. This division surveyed the area east of the Green River Basin lying between the Union Pacific Railroad and the Wind River and Sweetwater Mountains, including the latter range and a part of the former

Fourth, Teton division, in charge of G. R. Bechler, topographer, with Orestes St. John, geologist. The region surveyed by this division was directly north of that occupied by the Green River division, and included the Teton Mountains and a portion of the Snake River Plains.

There were also several special parties in the field, and among them one for critical paleontologic work, under Dr. C. A. White, who examined the geological formations that lie on both sides of the Rocky Mountains and on the north and south of the Uintah Mountains.

Mr. W. H. Jackson, with the photographic division, made a tour through the northern part of New Mexico and the northeastern part of Arizona, securing material for the illustration of methods of building employed by the Pueblos or town-building Indians.

On account of office work—superintending publications—Dr. Coues, surgeon U. S. Army, could not perform extended field work.

SEASON OF 1878.

In 1878 the work of the preceding year was extended northward, and included the Yellowstone National Park. The total area comprised was 7,000 square miles.

The appropriation for the year was $75,000, and four parties were put in the field, so constituted that they could be divided as the work required. They were made up as follows:

First, party of primary triangulation; A. D. Wilson, chief topographer, in charge.

Second, Yellowstone Park division; Henry Gannett, topographer, in charge. W. H. Holmes was geologist of the division, and investigated the general geological structures of the Park. Dr. A. C. Peale was also a member of the division, and made a special examination of the hot springs and geysers of the Park.

Third, Teton division; F. A. Clark, topographer in charge; O. St. John, geologist. This division surveyed the northern end of the Wind River Mountains, the Gros Ventres, Shoshone, and Owl Creek Ranges, and a part of the Snake River Valley.

Fourth, photographic division; W. H. Jackson, photographer, in charge. This party was occupied in the Park and in the Wind River Mountains.

Nine maps (pocket form) accompanied the Annual Report of 1878, as follows:

No. 1. Economic map of portions of Wyoming, Idaho, and Utah. Scale, 1 inch to 8 miles.

No. 2. Geologic map of portions of Wyoming, Idaho, and Utah. Scale, 1 inch to 8 miles.

No. 3. Geologic map of part of central Wyoming. Scale, 1 inch to 4 miles.

No. 4. Geologic map of parts of western Wyoming and southeast Idaho. Scale, 1 inch to 4 miles.

No. 5. Geologic map of parts of western Wyoming, southeast Idaho, and northeast Utah. Scale, 1 inch to 4 miles.

No. 6. Geologic map of Yellowstone National Park. Scale, 1 inch to 2 miles.

No. 7. Topographic map of central Wyoming. Scale, 1 inch to 4 miles (contours, 200 feet).

No. 8. Topographic map of part of western Wyoming and southeast Idaho. Scale, 1 inch to 4 miles (contours, 200 feet).

No. 9. Topographic map of part of western Wyoming, southeast Idaho, and northeast Utah. Scale, 1 inch to 4 miles (contours, 200 feet).

PUBLICATIONS.

The publications of the Geological and Geographical Survey of the Territories may be grouped under the following:

Annual reports (octavo).—There are twelve regular, beginning with 1867 and ending with 1878. There is also a report of the first three in one volume, and also two preliminary reports (viz, those for 1877 and 1878) and a supplement to the fifth annual, making in all sixteen publications of this class.

Bulletins (octavo).—There are six volumes of the Bulletin, which include twenty-seven bulletins issued separately.

Miscellaneous publications (octavo).—There are twelve of these publications, independent of each other but forming a regular series, numbered from I to XII, consecutively. As there are three editions of No. I and two of No. V, the total number is fifteen.

Monographs (quarto).—The quarto series of final reports already published includes eleven volumes. These are as follows: Vol. I, Fossil Vertebrates, Leidy, 1873. Vol. II, Cretaceous Vertebrata, Cope, 1875. Vol. III, Book I, Tertiary Vertebrata, 1884. Vol. IV, Miocene Vertebrata, Cope, (unpublished), 1887. Vol. V, Zoology, Thomas, 1873. Vol. VI, Cretaceous Flora, Lesquereux, 1874. Vol. VII, Tertiary Flora, Lesquereux, 1878. Vol. VIII, The Cretaceous and Tertiary Floras, Lesquereux, 1883. Vol. IX, Invertebrate Paleontology, Meek, 1875. Vol. X, Geometrical Moths, Packard, 1876. Vol. XI, North American Rodentia, Coues & Allen, 1877. Vol. XII, Fresh Water Rhizopods, Leidy, 1879; and Vol. XIII, Fossil Insects, Scudder (unpublished), 1887.

Unclassified publications.—This class does not form any regular series, and numbers fifteen in all, ranging in size from 18° to folio.

Maps.—Some of the published maps form parts of the various reports, while others were issued separately. Of the latter, some of the principal ones are as follows:

1871.—General map in colors, scale 1 inch to 10 miles, of portions of Idaho, Montana, and Wyoming, compiled, including work of that year.

1872.—Map of vicinity of headwaters of Snake River (Idaho, Wyoming, and Montana), scale 1 inch to 5 miles, brush work for hills; and map of Madison, Gallatin, and Upper Yellowstone drainage basins, scale 1 inch to 4 miles, sketchy contours, approximating 100 feet. Both colored, and issued as geological maps. General geologic map of the area explored and mapped * * * 1869 to 1880, scale 1 inch to 41.03 miles, was also issued. The principal map publication, however, was an atlas of Colorado (double folio), in 1878, consisting of 20 sheets, i. e., engraved title page, and legend sheets; four general sheets, 1 inch to 12 miles each, covering all of Colorado, (1) Triangulation, (2) Drainage, (3) Economic, and (4) General Geologic; six detailed topographic sheets, 1 inch to 4 miles, upon which are based six geologic sheets in colors, each sheet embracing 2½ degrees of longitude and 1¼ degrees of latitude; also, two sheets of geologic sections and two of panoramic views.

The whole presents the results of the field work from 1873 to 1876, inclusive, and, besides Colorado, embraces small adjacent portions of Utah, Arizona, and New Mexico.

A brief partial list of publications of this work is found in its catalogue of publications, second edition (revised to December 31, 1876); also House Executive Document No. 81, Forty-fifth Congress, second session (1878).

A reference to the methods employed to secure the topographic field data upon which to base a topographic map to receive the geologic and other colors, in and subsequent to 1873, will be found in Annual Report, 1873 (p. 627 *et seq.*), by James T. Gardner, and Annual Report, 1876 (p. 275 *et seq.*), by A. D. Wilson.

Commencing in 1867, the object of the observations by and under Dr. Hayden were the collection of data possible in a rapid geologic reconnaissance, supplemented by topographic reconnaissance data commencing in 1871, and subsequently more ample topographic details, referred to a field triangulation, graphically reduced, the whole resting on initial check points determined astronomically by the Coast Survey and quite similar to the work prosecuted in the fortieth parallel geological exploration.

The principal instruments used when the topographic work reached its best stage were 8-inch Wurdemann theodolites graduated to 10 minutes and reading to 5-seconds, gradientas, steel tapes, compasses and odometers, cistern and aneroid barometers with hygrometers.

Connection was made with Coast Survey astronomic stations at Denver, Colorado Springs, and Trinidad, Colorado. Six readings were taken for main triangulation stations and azimuths; with 10″.3, stated as error of closure for these triangles and 2′ for those subsidiary.

Determinations of position for the Colorado work are found in the Annual Report for 1876, p. 285 *et seq.*, and for that in Wyoming, Idaho, and Utah in the Annual Report for 1877, p. 661. The elevations determined by this survey (since compiled into the Dictionary of Altitudes, by Gannett) are referred to by volume and page in the following list. Only the first pages of continuous references are given: 1871, p. 521 *et seq.*; 1872, p. 799 *et seq.*, 813 *et seq.*; 1873, p. 657 *et seq.*, 667, 675, and 678.; 1874, p. 429 *et seq.*, 441, 446, and 492.; 1875, p. 299, 300, 342, 362 *et seq.*, 388, 408, 418, 440; 1876, p. 336 *et seq.*, 357 *et seq.*, 377; 1877, p. 681 *et seq.*; 1878, p. 459 *et seq.*

The total area reported by Hayden as having been covered topographically is 107,000 square miles, of which 37,000 square miles lie north and 70,000 square miles south of the Union Pacific Railroad.

The last field season was that of 1878, subsequent to which office reductions were continued, while it would appear from the following that in the main any unfinished results were transferred to the Geological Survey.

In the prefatory note to Vol. VIII, Floras (Lesquereux), the Director of the Geological Survey states that "on the 27th of September, 1882, at the request of Dr. F. V. Hayden, the completion of the publication of the U. S. Geological and Geographical Survey of the Territories, formerly under his charge, was committed to the Director of the Geological Survey," by an order of the honorable the Secretary of the Interior.

The volumes thus referred to would appear to be Vols. III (except Book I) and IV, Vertebrata; and Vol. XIII, Fossil Insects.

The Director further states that "a portion of the unpublished materials of the Hayden Survey" was transferred to the Geological Survey, and that "all the field-notes and the manuscript notes" were thus transferred, and that "the present Geological Survey inherited all the unfinished topographic work of the Hayden Survey, but it did not inherit its natural history work and some of its work in paleontology."

He further states that the Hayden Survey abandoned the unfinished part of their work not germane to the present Geological Survey; i. e., the natural history part.

The following is a condensed list of maps and reports resulting from this exploration:

MAPS.

		Number.
1. General maps		3
2. Atlas of Colorado (scale 1 inch to 12 miles and 1 inch to 4 miles):		
1.	2	
2. Geology	4	
3. Population	6	
4. Geology	6	
5.	2	
		20
3. General, special, and sketch maps bound with reports		53
Total		76

REPORTS.

1. Annual reports, octavo	12
2. Bulletins, octavo	27
3. Miscellaneous, octavo	12
4. Monographs, quarto	11
5. Unclassified	15
Total	77

GEOLOGICAL AND GEOGRAPHICAL SURVEY OF THE ROCKY MOUNTAIN REGION.

Mr. J. W. Powell states (see House of Representatives Report, No. 612, Forty-third Congress, first session, pp. 46 and 48) that in the years 1867,* 1868, and 1869, he was exploring in western Colorado and eastern Utah, about the source of the Grand, White, and Yampah Rivers, under the auspices of the Smithsonian Institution and certain scientific societies.

In 1869 he made the descent of the Colorado River from Green River Station, Union Pacific Railroad, through and including the Grand Cañon to the mouth of the Rio Virgin. In 1871 his work relating to the exploration of the basin of the Colorado River was placed under the Secretary of the Interior.

The object of the examination, beginning with a general exploration, seems to have been developed to embrace more or less definitely the branches of geology, topography, natural history, including ethnology—patterning somewhat after the geologico-topographic reconnaissance inaugurated by Clarence King in the exploration of the fortieth parallel.

In the later years of the work a classification of lands was attempted, to determine the position and extent of the irrigable, timber, mineral, and waste lands †

The total area explored, examined, or surveyed, suitable for publication in map form, by and under the direction of Mr. Powell, from the time of taking the field in 1867 to the close of the field duties of this expedition in 1878 (data from which is now being utilized by the Geological Survey), is stated by him (page 47, Senate Miscellaneous Document No. 82, first session Forty-ninth Congress) at 67,000 square miles.

* During 1867, by authority, rations for twelve men were purchased from the Army Subsistence Department. Subsequently they were furnished for twenty-five men at the expense of the War Department.

† One sheet of the atlas of the Uintah Mountains shows classification colors for small detached areas.

SEASON OF 1870.

Mr. Powell states that the total area explored and surveyed during this season, in northern Arizona and southern Utah, was 6,000 square miles, and that the professional personnel were: J. W. Powell, geologist, in charge; A. H. Thompson, geographer; F. M. Bishop and W. H. Graves, topographers; also one chief packer, one teamster, three employés, and from two to ten others, temporarily, as guides and hunters. In pursuance of joint resolution approved June 11, 1868, rations were issued by the commissary branch of the War Department for twenty-five men for the years commencing 1868 and ending in 1878.

The instruments used were, as found stated in the several reports, zenith telescopes, theodolites, sextants, gradientas, wooden rods, steel tapes, compasses, barometers, and hygrometers, part of which were borrowed from the Engineer Department.

The route of the reconnaissance extended from Salt Lake City to the Cañons of the Colorado, thence eastward to the Moqui villages, disbanding at Old Fort Defiance December 5, 1870.

SEASON OF 1871.

Professional personnel: J. W. Powell, geologist, in charge; J. F. Stewart, assistant geologist; A. H. Thompson, geographer; F. M. Bishop, F. S. Dellenbaugh, and S. V. Jones, topographers; E. O. Beaman, photographer; J. K. Hillers, assistant photographer; also W. C. Powell, F. A. Richardson, and A. J. Hatten as general assistants, with one chief packer, 13 temporary employés, and a number of Indians as guides, hunters, and messengers

Area explored and surveyed in southern Wyoming, Utah, and Arizona, 12,000 square miles.

The routes pursued were by boat, leaving Green River May 22, descending the Colorado to the mouth of the Paria, with land work for a narrow belt on either side, thus gathering material for a reconnaissance map.

A preliminary report to the end of 1871 appears as House Mis. Doc. No. 173, Forty-second Congress, second session (1872).

SEASON OF 1872.

Professional personnel: J. W. Powell, geologist, in charge; A. H. Thompson, geographer; S. V. Jones and F. S. Dellenbaugh, topographers; J. K. Hillers, photographer; also W. C. Powell, A. J. Hatten, George Adair, Jacob Hamlin, George Riley, Nathan Adams, John Renshawe as general assistants, 18 temporary employés, with from 2 to 20 Indians as guides, hunters, and messengers.

Area surveyed in Utah and Arizona, 8,000 square miles.

The principal work for the year was in the Henry Mountains and vicinity.

A partial report, of July 17, 1873, appears as House Mis. Doc. No. 76, Forty-second Congress, third session (1873).

SEASON OF 1873.

Professional personnel: J. W. Powell, geologist, in charge; A. H. Thompson, geographer; J. H. Renshawe, topographer; J. K. Hillers, photographer; also, Nathan Adams, Joseph Haycock, George Adair, and Jacob Hamlin as general assistants, with temporary employés and a number of Indians.

Area surveyed in southern Utah and northern Arizona, 6,000 square miles.

A third preliminary report was submitted to the Secretary of the Smithsonian Institution and by him to the House of Representatives (8°, pp. 36, Washington: Government Printing Office. 1874), containing a summary of all work then executed.

SEASON OF 1874.

Professional personnel: J. W. Powell, geologist, in charge; Edwin E. Howell, assistant geologist; A. H. Thompson, geographer; J. H. Renshawe, W. H. Graves, and H. C. DeMotte, topographers; O. D. Wheeler, assistant topographer; J. K. Hillers, photographer.

Area surveyed in Wyoming, Utah, and Arizona, 15,000 square miles.

SEASON OF 1875.

Professional personnel: J. W. Powell, geologist, in charge; G. K. Gilbert, Capt. C. E. Dutton (U. S. Army), and C. A. White, assistant geologists;

A. H. Thompson, geographer; Robert Bell, J. H. Renshawe, and W. H. Graves, topographers; O. D. Wheeler, assistant topographer; J. K. Hillers, photographer.

Area surveyed in Wyoming, Utah, and Arizona, 10,000 square miles.

SEASON OF 1876.

Professional personnel: J. W. Powell, geologist, in charge; G. K. Gilbert, Capt. C. E. Dutton (U. S. Army), and C. A. White, assistant geologists; A. H. Thompson, geographer; J. H. Renshawe and W. H. Graves, topographers; O. D. Wheeler, assistant topographer; J. K. Hillers, photographer.

Area surveyed in Wyoming and Utah, 10,000 square miles.

This area is situated between the Wahsatch Mountains on the west and the Green and Colorado Rivers on the east and southeast.

SEASON OF 1877.

Professional personnel: J. W. Powell, geologist, in charge; G. K. Gilbert and Capt. C. E. Dutton (U. S. Army), assistant geologists; A. H. Thompson, geographer; J. H. Renshawe and W. H Graves, topographers; O. D. Wheeler, assistant topographer.

Area surveyed in Utah, 10,000 square miles.

This work, in common with the greater share of all that executed by this expedition, is situated in the basin of the Colorado of the West, above the mouth of the Grand Cañon.

A brief report of operations for 1876 and 1877 was submitted November 25, 1877, to the Secretary of the Interior (8°, pp. 19, Washington: Government Printing Office, 1877), in which reference to ethnologic work, afterwards merged into the Bureau of Ethnology, is made.

SEASON OF 1878.

Professional personnel: J. W. Powell, geologist, in charge; G. K. Gilbert and Capt. C. E. Dutton (U. S. Army), assistant geologists; S. H. Bodfish, J. H. Renshawe, and O. D Wheeler, topographers; P. B. Wright, W. A. Phillips, —— Tipton, and F. P. Morgan, assistant topographers; J. K. Hillers, photographer.

Area surveyed in Utah and Arizona, 10,000 square miles.

The above was the final season of field work for this expedition.

A communication regarding the continuation of ethnologic researches appears as House Miscellaneous Document No. 35, second session Forty-sixth Congress (1880).

Independent of the progress reports already mentioned the following quartos were issued:

Exploration of the Colorado River of the West, Powell, 1875, pp. 291, with 2 maps; Geology of the Uintah Mountains, Powell, 1876, pp. 218, with folio atlas; Geology of the Henry Mountains, Gilbert, 1877, pp. 160, with 5 plates and maps, second edition 1880; Lands of the Arid Region, Powell, 1878, pp. 195, with 3 maps, second edition 1879; and also Geology of the High Plateaus of Utah, Dutton, 1880, pp. 264, with folio atlas.

In 1880 three quarto volumes had issued from the ethnological branch, which later became a separate office, with its annual and other reports; but these results are not germane to this memoir, which for its main object has the analysis of the geographical foundation of national or Government maps, which, to be intelligible and homogeneous, should have sifted from it all the natural history portions, and remain more as an exponent of the mathematical field and office parts of topography and geography and their artistic delineation, and publication. Other than the maps accompanying reports, six preliminary sheets were issued; also four relief maps and two stereograms of the Grand Cañon, High Plateaus, and Henry Mountains were prepared for distribution to colleges and libraries.

A part of the topographic work was published in the atlas accompanying the report upon the Uintah Mountains and that upon the High Plateaus.

Mr. Gannett states, with regard to the topography, that "it has been republished entire by the present survey," *i. e.*, the Geological Survey.*

So far as can be ascertained no geographic positions (latitudes and longitudes) were published by this office. The same may be said with regard to altitudes, except such as appear on published maps.

A general reference to progress and results of the work may be found in House Executive Document No. 80, Forty-ninth Congress, second session.

---

* Of the eighty-seven topographic base maps issued (April, 1887) for geologic purposes twenty-three are referred to on the face of each sheet as having been supplied in part or whole from the above work.

Tabulated list of maps and reports.

MAPS.			No.
1. Preliminary sheets		......	6
2. Accompanying reports:	1. Topographic	1	
	2. Geologic	14	
	3. Economic	2	
Scale 1 to 1,000,000, 1 inch	4. Miscellaneous and sections	19	
to 16 miles, and 1 inch	5. Maps and plates	5	
to 4 miles (principally).			41
Total		......	47

REPORTS.	
1. Annual and Progress	5
2. Quartos	5
3. Miscellaneous pamphlets	2
Total	12

(Also six volumes on ethnological subjects.)

Upon the close of this work, as stated by Mr. Powell in his letter of May 21, 1886, to Senator Allison, "all of the material, embracing collections of fossils, minerals, and rocks, and all field-notes of the geologist, and all topographic manuscript maps, together with the field-notes, computations, etc.," were transferred to the U. S. Geological Survey.

GEOLOGICAL EXAMINATION OF THE BLACK HILLS OF DAKOTA, BY W. P. JENNEY, E. M., AND H. NEWTON, E. M., 1875.

The parties conducting this examination left Cheyenne, Wyo., for the northward May 27, 1875. The object of the expedition, in accordance with letter of instructions of Commissioner of Indian Affairs of March 27, 1875, was "to obtain, pending certain negotiations for the cession of the Black Hills by the Sioux Indians, the true facts regarding the nature and value of the mineral deposits" having been lately discovered in that region.

The route to Fort Laramie (where the escort was joined) was by the usual traveled road from Cheyenne, the former point being left on May 24. The Hills were reached via Raw-Hide Butte and Old Woman's Fork.

Camp was made on the East Fork of the Beaver on June 3, from which point the instrumental work was begun, a permanent camp being at once established on French Creek, from whence operations were carried on by two parties. Succeeding bases of supplies were established as the work proceeded to the northward until the examination embraced the entire area of the Black Hills between the forks of the Cheyenne.

The routes within the Hills do not appear in detail. The area of the Black Hills, as stated by Mr. Newton in his report, aggregates 5,000 square miles.

The object of the expedition having been accomplished, the parties rendezvoused at the mouth of Rapid Creek, on the South Fork of the Cheyenne, preparatory to return march to Fort Laramie (via White River and Spotted Tail and Red Cloud Agencies), which point was reached on October 14, after an absence of four months and twenty days.

The professional work was carried on by W. P. Jenney, E. M., geologist, in charge, assisted by H. Newton, E. M., geologist; V. T. McGillycuddy, M. D., photographer; Capt H. P. Tuttle, astronomer; and W. F. Patrick, E. M., together with eleven miners and laborers.

The party was accompanied by a military escort of fully four hundred men, with a train of seventy-five wagons, in command of Lieut. Col. R. J. Dodge, Twenty-third Infantry, with Lieut. M. F. Trout, Ninth Infantry, as adjutant; Lieut. J. F. Trout, Twenty-third Infantry, as acting assistant quartermaster; Lieut. J. G. Bourke, Third Cavalry, topographer; and Assistant Surgeons Jaquette and Kane. The above escort consisted of two companies of the Ninth Infantry, under Capts. A. H. Bowman and S. Munson and Lieut. H. De Lany; two companies of the Second Cavalry, under Capt. E. J. Spaulding and Lieuts. C. T. Hall, J. H. Coale, and F. W. Kingsbury; four companies of the Third Cavalry, under Capts. W. Hawley, G. Russell, and H. W. Wessells and Lieuts. A. D. King, R. E. Whitman, James Lawson, J. E. H. Foster, and C. Morton.

Thanks are rendered in the final report for the hearty co-operation of the several officers, as well as a recognization of topographic assistance by Lieutenants Morton and Foster.

The instruments used were one transit theodolite, one surveyor's transit, one sextant, two marine and one pocket chronometers, two mountain and five aneroid barometers and thermometers. These (except the chronometers) were transported while in the Hills upon pack animals.

Topographic observations were made by the reconnaissance method, distances being estimated by time, courses, and topographic features observed with a prismatic compass.

Longitude was determined by chronometric differences,* and sextant observations were made for latitude. Triangulation, starting from an astronomic base (there being no measured base), was made to include the principal peaks.

A preliminary report, accompanied by a small preliminary map by Dr. McGillicuddy, was made by Mr. Jenney to the Office of Indian Affairs, and appeared on page 181 of the Annual Report of the Commissioner (1875).

A subsequent report by Mr. Jenney to the Indian Office, entitled: "The Mineral Wealth, Climate and Rain-fall, and Natural Resources of the Black Hills," appears as Senate Ex Doc. No 51, Forty-fourth Congress, first session (1876), with same map as in preliminary report (scale 1 inch to 8 miles).

A preliminary report on the paleontology of the Black Hills, by R. P. Whitfield, was printed as a pamphlet in July, 1877, by the Geological and Geographical Survey of the Rocky Mountain region.

The final report in quarto form, edited by Mr. G. K. Gilbert, on the geology and resources of the Black Hills of Dakota, by H. Newton, E. M., and W. P. Jenney, E. M., with an atlas, was published in 1880, under the auspices of the Geological and Geographical Survey of the Rocky Mountain Region. This volume contains, besides the contributions of Newton revised and edited by Mr. Gilbert, and that of Jenney substantially as found in his earlier report, others in the following order: On paleontology, by R P. Whitfield; on microscopic petrography, by John H. Caswell; on botany, by Prof. Asa Gray; and on astronomy and barometric hypsometry, by H. P. Tuttle. On May 28, 1879, the results of this exploration were transferred to the survey of the Rocky Mountain region, by direction of the Secretary of the Interior.

Mr. Newton revisited the Black Hills in 1877, to repeat certain of his observations and record the results of the rapidly developing mining in-

* The errors of the longitudes were afterwards corrected by a reference to points established on the eastern boundary of Wyoming, near "Camp Jenney" of the expedition; finally, by telegraphic longitudes of Deadwood and other points within the Hills, determined by Captain Stanton, Corps of Engineers, in 1877.

dustry, where he died from typhoid fever, at Deadwood, August 5, 1877; hence the revision of his manuscript by Mr. Gilbert as stated.

Maps.—The following are the maps known to have been separately issued:

LIST OF MAPS RESULTING FROM THE GEOLOGICAL EXPLORATION OF THE BLACK HILLS.

Title.	Author.	Date.	Scale.	No. of sheets.	Size within border.	Area in sq. ms. Approx.	Hill work. How represented.	Mode of reproduction.
Topographical map of the Black Hills.	Jenney and others.	1875	1″=8 ms.	1	17½″ x 15½″	9,300	Hachures.	Lithography.
The same..........	....do	1875	1″=4 ms.	1	35″ x 31″	9,300	....do	Do.
Black Hills of Dakota (to accompany report of Henry Newton, E. M., etc.).*								
1 sheet, bird's-eye view of the Black Hills.*	....	1875	....	3	27¼″ x 19½″	......	....	Colored lithograph.
1 sheet, Black Hills of Dakota.*	....	......	1″=4 ms.	...	35″ x 28″	9,216	Hachures.	Photolithograph.
1 sheet, Black Hills of Dakota (geologically colored).*	....	......	1″=4 ms.	...	35″ x 28″	9,216	Contours.	Colored photolithograph.

* In atlas.

RÉSUMÉ.

The topographic map (scale 1 inch to 4 miles) shows this class of observations to have extended over part, if not all, of an area of 9,300 square miles. The geological map (based upon the above) embraces an area of 9,216 square miles. The results, independent of those shown in the report of Newton on geology, Jenney on resources, and Whitfield, Caswell, and Gray on the natural history collections made, and the triangulation and topographic detail for the maps by Dr. McGillicuddy, as shown in report of Mr. Tuttle, are, longitudes 24,* latitudes 97, altitudes 93, and variations 13 in number.

These longitudes were found by Mr. Tuttle in 1877, by reference to points on eastern boundary of Wyoming, to be 4′ 47″ too far east; a further correction was introduced by a reference to telegraphic longitudes, established the same year by Stanton at Deadwood and other points within the Hills.

Chapters on the Dakota Indians by Mr. Newton were reserved for publication by the Bureau of Ethnology.

The following was expended in field work (see House Ex. Doc. No. 80, Forty-fifth Congress, second session): By direct appropriation, $14,000; indirect appropriation (allotted from "beneficial object fund for certain tribes of Northern Sioux"), $11,000; total, $25,000.

Wagons, camp equipage, and horses were loaned by the Quartermaster's Department, arms were loaned by the Ordnance Department, and rations purchased from the Commissary Department at cost. The cost of the escort was purely a military expense.

SUBDIVISION OF THE PUBLIC LANDS.

Of the 971,174,878 acres reported by the Land Office as having been subdivided June 30, 1886, 724,529,431 acres lie west of the Mississippi, while of the 844,329,269 acres then remaining unsurveyed all except 7,252,857 acres (Florida) belongs to the same territory, including, however, 369,529,600 acres (estimated) for Alaska, where these surveys have not yet been commenced. It appears that the law requires the establishment of no latitudes, longitudes, or altitudes in connection with these surveys, neither has it been the custom to conduct systematic topography, the latter being simply planimetric without a geographic basis; hence the results of the Land Office surveys, so far as relates to their uses in the compilation of general topographic and geographic maps, are but preliminary, on account of the above deficiencies, the available data being only such minor details as can be adjustetd to known geographic co-ordinates. For preliminary field and subsequent office plats they have, however, furnished valuable information.

BOUNDARIES OF STATES AND TERRITORIES.

These lines, when bounding States cut out of the public domain west of the Mississippi, were for a number of years run and marked by officers of Topographical Engineers, but immediately prior and subsequent to the late war they have been demarked under the General Land Office by contractors who have secured the services of competent astronomers and surveyors, employed under the authority of the Secretary of the Interior.

The following is a tabulated list of certain of these boundaries furnished by the Commissioner of the General Land Office:

State and Territorial boundaries surveyed under the direction of the General Land Office, between 1857 *and* 1880.

Boundary.	Names of surveyors and astronomers.	Date of survey.	Length of line measured.			Cost of survey.
			mls.	*chs.*	*lks.*	
West boundary of Minnesota.*	Chauncey H. Snow and Henry Hutton ..	1859	128	33	91	$5,000.00
Washington and Oregon.	Daniel G. Major (F. G. Hesse and John Major, assistants).	1864	96	57	00	4,500.00
North boundary of California.	Daniel G. Major (John J. Major, assistant).	1868-'69	212	40	00	12,750.00
Oregon and Idaho .	Daniel G. Major	1867	124	17	02	7,452.77
North boundary of New Mexico.	Ehud N. Darling (J. Weissner and Alonzo Mace, assistants).	1868	331	60	00	19,000.00
West boundary of Nebraska.	O. N. Chaffee	1869	207	22	26	7,804.48 (both)
South boundary of Nebraska.†	O. N. Chaffee	1869	104	72	07	
East boundary of Nevada.	Isaac E. James (J. T. Gardner, assistant).	1870	401	50	56	10,625.00
Utah and Idaho....	Daniel G. Major (John J. Major, assistant).	1871	153	56	00	6,480.00
East boundary of California.	Alexander W. Von Schmidt	1872-'73	611	75	77	40,750.32
West boundary of Kansas.	John J. Major	1872	207	26	00	8,293.00
North boundary of Nevada.	Daniel G. Major (John J. Major, assistant).	1872-'73	304	62	00	15,401.11
South boundary of Wyoming.	Alonzo V. Richards (T. H. Safford and A. MacConnel, assistants).	1873	367	48	81	22,056.61
West boundary of Wyoming.	Alonzo V. Richards (Augustus MacConnel, assistant).	1874	277	72	66	13,850.00
Part south boundary of Colorado.‡	John J. Major	1873-'74	57	04	50	2,282.25
Part east boundary of New Mexico.§	John J. Major	1873-'74	34	40	00	1,380.00
North boundary of Nebraska.	Chauncey Wiltse (E. P. Austin, assistant).	1874	224	12	20	8,069.49
Washington and Idaho.‖	Rollin J. Reeves and C. S. Denison	1873	176	40	00	10,590.00
Arizona and New Mexico.	Chandler Robbins (John H. Clark, assistant).	1875-'76	390	48	31	27,342.27
Arkansas and Indian Territory.	Henry E. McKee............................	1877	196	75	83	11,805.48
Wyoming and Dakota.	Rollin J. Reeves (Horace P. Tuttle, assistant).	1877	138	32	00	7,000.00
Colorado and Utah.	Rollin J. Reeves (Horace P. Tuttle, assistant).	1878-'79	276	51	66	15,000.00
North boundary of Wyoming.	R. J. Reeves (H. P. Tuttle and C. M. Stephens, assistants).	1879-'80	346	43	00	20,000.00

* This survey included only that part of the line not marked by natural boundaries.

† 41° north latitude, from 25° to 27° longitude west from Washington. A survey of the boundary between Kansas and Nebraska was made between November 16 and December 5, 1854, by John P. Johnson, surveyor (result not available); the initial point being the intersection of the 40th parallel with the Missouri River, having been previously determined in 1854 by Capt. Thomas J. Lee, Topographical Engineers.

‡ 37° north latitude, from 25° west from Washington to 103° west from Greenwich.

§ 103° west from Greenwich, from 36° 30′ north latitude to 37° north latitude.

‖ From confluence of Snake and Clearwater Rivers, north to 49° north latitude. Survey abandoned 2 miles south of 49° north latitude.

NOTE.—All the reports of the above boundary surveys are in manuscript only.

The western boundary of Missouri, from the Missouri River at the mouth of the Kansas in a straight line to the southern boundary of Missouri (177 miles), was run in 1824 by Joseph C. Brown. The boundary between Missouri and Iowa, being parallel of 49° 44′ 06″ N. latitude between Des Moines and the Mississippi Rivers, was established in 1837 (length 203 miles); in 1847 the boundary between Arkansas and Missouri—being the parallel of 36° N. latitude from the Mississippi to the St. Francis (36 miles 49.88 chains) and the parallel of 36° 30′ N. latitude from the St. Francis to the western boundary of Missouri (247 miles 44.41 chains).

That part of the eastern boundary of Colorado lying on the 25th meridian west from Washington, from latitude 40° to 41° N. (69 miles) was run in 1870 by O. N. Chaffee, surveyor.

The boundary between Dakota and Montana, being that part of the 27th meridian west of Washington between latitudes 45° and 49° N. (276 miles 26 chains) was determined in 1877 by Daniel G. Major, astronomer.

The two last above-named were under the auspices of the General Land Office, where it is presumed that the original records are to be found. The locus of the original records of the three others above is not known. It is believed that all of the original records of boundaries west of the Mississippi will be found either at the General Land Office or at the Engineer Department.

No data has been found available for the boundaries between Louisiana and Arkansas, Iowa and Minnesota, Minnesota and Wisconsin, and of the eastern line of the public land strip. It is believed that the boundaries between Arizona and Utah, and Montana and Idaho, have not yet been demarked, nor that part of northern Colorado adjoining Nebraska.

The survey of the 98th meridian west longitude from the Red to the Canadian River was made by Messrs. A. H. Jones and H. M. C. Brown (Daniel G. Major, astronomer), under a contract with the acting Commissioner of Indian Affairs, dated October 13, 1857. The length of the measured line was 93 miles and 38 chains. The record of the observations and results of the astronomer are believed to be in the Indian Bureau.

That part of the 100th meridian west longitude which lies between the southern boundary of the Cherokee country and the Red River was measured in 1859 by Messrs. A. H. Jones and H. M. C. Brown (Daniel G. Major, astronomer), under contract with the Indian Office. The original field-notes, showing that the survey was begun April 22 and completed May 11, 1859, the length of the measured line to be 109 miles 56.59 chains, and the reductions of the astronomer, are of record in the Indian Bureau. The above was adopted and made a part of the official boundary survey between the United States and Texas. (See Senate Ex. Doc. No. 70, Forty-seventh Congress, first session.)

Special surveys of Indian lands have been made by Daniel and John J. Major in the eastern Ute reservation of Colorado in 1881, with an initial point at Gunnison, and of boundaries of Indian reservations, and in the subdivision of Indian lands, but data there upon it has not been practicable to obtain.

UNITED STATES GEOLOGICAL SURVEY.

This office was created by appropriation act of March 3, 1879, and placed under a director, who "shall have the direction of the Geological Survey and the classification of the public lands, and examination of the geological structure, mineral resources and products of the national domain." Under this act a geologic-topographic reconnaissance work similar to that pursued by King in the geologic exploration of the 40th parallel, and also to some extent by Hayden and Powell, was begun west of the Mississippi River; while the words of an appropriation act of 1882 "to continue the preparation of a geological map of the United States" have been interpreted to authorize field work east of the Mississippi River, since which date similar operations have been conducted largely within that territory. The memoir herewith was intended only to bring a reference to the works down to January 1, 1880, and time and means alike forbid a tracing of this office, then but just begun, but now grown to large proportions. However, from the testimony of the Director (Mr. J. W. Powell, who succeeded Mr. Clarence King),* and the Annual Reports of the Survey, certain information regarding field operations and office results will be herewith found.†

* See Senate Mis. Doc. No. 82, Forty-ninth Congress, first session.

† The progress of field triangulation to year ending June 30, 1886, will be found in report by Henry Gannett, in the Seventh Annual Report from this office, pp. 45 *et seq.*

Following the scope given to geology by this office, it appears that a survey of the whole United States, consisting of a geologic examination, for the graphic illustration of which topographic maps as a base are specially produced, has been inaugurated.

These are not published as topographic maps for general distribution* (there being no authority therefor), but are to be issued, as prepared, with the geologic colors added. The Director states a considerable area as covered by the original observations of this office, but as regards results germane to the scope of this memoir of later works, i. e., astronomic, geodetic, trigonometric, topographic, and hypsometric, nothing yet published regarding results seems to define the exact value or extent of the latitudes, longitudes, and altitudes or the mathematical basis of the work.

The publications are more purely geologic, or of an allied character.

The results can much better be traced, grouped, analyzed, and compared when further publications shall admit of determining the above mentioned principal branches.†

It appears, as stated by the Director, that all of the unreduced and unpublished results of the geologic and geographic survey of the Rocky Mountain region were transferred to this Survey, and likewise all of the similar material from the geologic and geographic survey of the Territories, except the natural history and a part of the paleontology.

Nothing whatever, either as to personnel, instruments, material, or supplies, professional or other records, published or unpublished maps and reports, or data of any sort, was transferred from the office of the United States Geographic Survey west of the 100th meridian, all the records of which were deposited in the archives of the Engineer Department, War Department, as heretofore stated.

---

* At this writing (April 20, 1889) a number of topographic sheets—53 full degree (scale 1 to 250,000), 127 quarter-degree (1 to 125,000), and 101 one-sixteenth degree (1 to 62,500)—have been engraved and issued prior to the geologic work proper, but not for general distribution and use as topographic maps. Of the above, 53 full degree (about one-half from prior surveys), 70 quarter degree, and 2 of one-sixteenth degree are found west of the Mississippi (data furnished by Henry Gannett, in charge of Division of Geography, U. S. Geological Survey).

† No publication upon geographic co-ordinates has so far been mentioned in any of the "advertisement" prospectuses of the publications of this office, with the single exception of Bulletin No. 49, "On the latitudes and longitudes of certain points in Missouri, Kansas, and New Mexico, by R. S. Woodward," announced as in press March 1, 1889. (April 20, 1889.) Stated as published in Bulletin of July 1, 1889.

STATE DEPARTMENT.

UNITED STATES NORTHERN BOUNDARY COMMISSION.—LAKE OF THE WOODS TO THE SUMMIT OF THE ROCKY MOUNTAINS (49TH PARALLEL), 1872-'74.

The United States Boundary Commission, having for its object "to determine and mark the boundary line between the United States and British Possessions, as defined in the second article of the convention between the United States and Great Britain, of October 20, 1818," this line being the 49th parallel from the meridian of the northwest corner of the Lake of the Woods to the summit of the Rocky Mountains, was authorized by act of Congress, approved March 19, 1872, and commenced field operations at Pembina, September 1, 1872. Besides marking the boundary line, an accurate survey of all topographic features in a belt 5 miles wide on the United States side and of the shore of the Lake of the Woods from the 49th parallel to the mouth of Rainy River, was made and consolidated on a series of maps, as also reconnaissance surveys of all routes traveled by the geodetic and astronomic parties.*

The work of the Commission divides itself into astronomic and geodetic, which will be given separately.

First, Astronomic.—1872. In this year two astronomical stations were observed, thus determining the "northwest point" of the Lake of the Woods and the initial point or the west bank of the Red River of the North, Capt. W. J. Twining being the observer.

1873. Captain Twining observed at Pointe Michel, 20 miles west of Red River, at Turtle Mountain, west side, and at west of Rivière des Lacs, 237 miles west of Red River.

---

* The United States Commission was organized with Archibald Campbell, Commissioner, and Maj. F. M. Farquhar, Corps of Engineers, chief astronomer; Capt. W. J. Twining, First Lieut. J. F. Gregory, and Second Lieut. F. V. Greene, Corps of Engineers, being detailed as assistants. In the spring of 1872, Major Farquhar having been relieved at his own request, Captain Twining was appointed and thereafter continued chief astronomer.

The 49th parallel was determined as follows: Astronomical stations were established alternately by the British and United States Commissions at approximate distances apart of 20 miles, and these were connected by tangents checked by azimuths at each end. The offsets to the parallel from these tangents were corrected proportionately, the astronomical determinations being considered absolute. The latitudes were. determined by zenith telescope, the longitudes by chained distances from Red River (the initial point). These longitudes were to have been checked by telegraphic comparisons and determinations through Fort Shaw, Mont., to Corinne, Utah, which proved impossible because communication was broken during the period of operations. Iron monuments, one mile apart, were planted to mark the line from longitude 96° to 99° west, with usually stone pyramids for the more westerly portions.

Capt. J. F. Gregory observed at Pembina Mountains, east side, at Long River, at South Antler Creek, at Mouse River, at Mid Coteau, at Bully Spring, and at Four-hundred-and-eight-and-a-half-mile Point.

Assistant Lewis Boss observed at Pembina Mountains, west side.

1874. Captain Gregory observed this year at Frenchman's Creek, Pool on Prairie, East Fork Milk River, Milk River Lakes, East Butte, Red River, North Fork Milk River, and at Chief Mountain Lake The line was completed from longitude 106° 12′ to the summit of the Rocky Mountains, where the survey connected with that part of the northwestern boundary heretofore established (1859).

In 1872 Capt. and Bvt. Lieut. Col. F. M. Farquhar, Capt. and Bvt. Maj. W. J. Twining, and Lieut. J. F. Gregory, all of the Corps of Engineers, were the astronomical observers.

The escort in 1872 was a part of Capt. A. A. Harbach's company, Twentieth Infantry; in 1873 two companies of the Seventh Cavalry and Captain Harbach's company, Twentieth Infantry, all under command of Maj. M. A. Reno, Seventh Cavalry; and in 1874 two companies of the Seventh Cavalry and five companies of the Sixth Infantry, under Major Reno.

The instruments used were zenith telescopes Nos. 7, 11, and 20, by Wurdemann; Nos. 7 and 11 were of 25 inches focal length, damaged by use; No. 20, of 32 inches focal length, in good condition. The chronometers, three in number, were by Negus, of New York, and Bond, of Boston. The sextants, two in number, were by Stackpole & Bro., New York. Astronomical transits in 1873, No. 30, and in 1874, No. 4; both by Wurdemann.

Second, Geodetic.—Lieut. F. V. Greene was placed in charge of the tracing of the line and of the topographic work in the years 1872, 1873, 1874, and 1875. The methods of work in these branches will be found described by Lieutenant Greene (pp. 341–369), Appendix B, of the main report, which is published as Senate Ex. Doc. No. 41, Forty-fourth Congress, second session, and contains reports of the Commissioner, Archibald Campbell; of Captain Twining, Captain Gregory, Lieutenant Greene; and the maps, except the preliminary and final series.

The original plats of this survey were transferred to the archives of the Engineer Department.

Capt. J. F. Gregory, U. S. Engineers, in connection with the Northern Boundary Survey during the first field season of 1872, was in charge of the geodetic and topographic work with Lieut. F. V. Greene and Mr. F. Von Schrader (now Lieutenant, Twelfth Infantry), as assistants. Work this season was confined to topographic surveys in vicinity of the boundary line, the Red and Pembina Rivers, the establishment of the northwest angle of the Lake of the Woods, and surveys in that vicinity of the boundary.

In 1873 he was in charge of an astronomical party with Mr. E. L. Mack and Mr. O. S. Wilson as assistants.

Observations for latitude were made at seven stations and the parallels marked with large stone mounds. A part of the sextant work was done by Mr. Wilson.

Reconnaissance was made from the second crossing of the boundary line (in longitude 102° approximate) to Fort Totten, Dakota, and thence to Fort Seward, crossing Mouse River at the mouth of Willow Creek.

Lieut. (now Captain) C. O. Bradley, Twentieth Infantry, commanded the escort, beginning with fourteen enlisted men, afterwards increased to twenty-six in number.

1874. Had charge of an astronomical party with Mr. Lewis Boss and A. J. Egerton as assistants. Dr. Elliott Coues, surgeon U. S. Army, accompanied the party as naturalist.

Eight astronomical stations along the 49th parallel were determined and marked, carrying the work to its western limit on Chief Mountain Lake, of the Pacific water-shed.

Reconnaissance surveys of the trails were made by compass and odometer. Also observed for latitude of Fort Buford with zenith telescope, and made reconnaissance from the mouth of Polar River to west bank of Frenchman's Creek, and to the boundary line about longitude 107° 24′.

Observations for time and latitude en route were made by Mr. Boss. Longitudes and latitudes were determined by sextant and chronometer of the trail, from Station Thirteen to Fort Buford.

Mr. Boss made a reconnaissance of the route from the termination of tne boundary to Fort Benton.

The escort consisted of Company D, Sixth Infantry, about forty men and three Indian scouts, commanded by Capt. M. Byrant, Sixth Infantry (now Major, Fourteenth Infantry), and Lieut. F. W. Thibaut, Sixth Infantry, second in command.

1875. Set the cast-iron pillars* east and west of Red River, at even mile intervals, and made special surveys at the northwest angle, Lake of the Woods.

The escort consisted of twelve enlisted men commanded by Lieut. C. H. Low, Twentieth Infantry. The last astronomical station was established on Chief Mountain Lake, a special geodetic and topographic survey of which and the neighboring mountain region was made by Assistant Boss.

RECONNAISSANCES AND SURVEYS BY LIEUT. F. V GREENE, CORPS OF ENGINEERS, IN CONNECTION WITH THE UNITED STATES NORTHERN BOUNDARY COMMISSION (1872-'75).

Lieutenant Greene, acting under general instructions from Major Farquhar, United States Engineers, in 1872, and subsequently from Captain Twining, United States Engineers, chief astronomer Northern Boundary Commission, commenced September 5, 1872, at latitude 49° on Red River.

The field work intrusted to him comprised the immediate charge and direction of the parties engaged upon geodetic and topographic operations, and the making of reconnaissance surveys of all routes passed over by these parties, outside of the belt of more accurate surveys. It was accomplished within the following dates:

1872. September 5 to November 12. From Red River eastward to Roseau River, 33 miles. Topographic survey by theodolite and chain of Red River near the boundary. Escort, Company K, Twentieth Infantry, Capt. A. A. Harback; civil assistant, F. Von Schrader.

1873. June 8 to October 25. From Red River westward to Poplar River, 384 miles. Assistants: Computer, L. Chauvenet; topographers, F.

* These pillars were "hollow iron castings, three-eighths of an inch in thickness, in the form of a truncated pyramid, 8 feet high, 8 inches square at bottom, 4 inches square at top with solid pyramidal cap, and an octagonal flange, one inch in thickness at bottom," with an average weight of 285 pounds. A list of all the monuments, some few of which were stone pillars and cairns and earth-mounds, are given on pp. 35-40 of the report.

Von Schrader, A. Downing, C. L. Doolittle. The escort, from September 11 to October 15, was a detachment of twenty-five cavalry under command of Lieut. R. H. L. Alexander.

1873-'74. October 25 to February 16. From Red River to Lake of the Woods, 88 miles; thence to Rainy River. No escort. Assistants: Computer, O. S. Wilson, C. E.; topographers, C. L. Doolittle, A. Downing.

1874. June 21 to October 1. From Poplar River to the summit of the Rocky Mountains, 380 miles. Escort, two companies Sixth Infantry and twelve Indian scouts, Capt. E. R. Ames, Sixth Infantry, in command. Assistants: Computer, O. S. Wilson, C. E., topographers, C. L. Doolittle, V. T. McGillicuddy, B. Vitzthum.

In 1873-'74 the escorts were parts of a general escort under command of Maj. M. A. Reno, Seventh Cavalry.

1874. First, a reconnaissance from Frenchman's Creek on the Missouri, in longitude 104° 54′ along Poplar River and its branches to the 49th parallel, made as above, with three astronomic camps. Second, a reconnaissance from astronomical station 24 to astronomic station 25 by way of Fort Turney on Frenchman's Creek; one astronomic camp. Third, a reconnaissance of the trail made by the wagon train while Lieutenant Greene was running the meridian line to Fort Shaw; two latitude camps. Fourth, a reconnaissance along the "Riplinger Road," skirting the base of the Rocky Mountains from the 49th parallel to Fort Shaw, by C. L. Doolittle; four latitude camps. Fifth, a reconnaissance from Fort Shaw to Fort Benton; one astronomic camp. Sixth, boat survey of the Missouri River from Fort Benton to Bismarck, September 10 to October 1. This was based on the astronomic determination of 17 points on the river, by sextant for latitude and time, and by the mean of six chronometers, compared daily, and with well deduced traveling rates for longitude—the longitude of Fort Benton being determined by chronometers transported from the boundary, and that of Bismarck by telegraph by Major Barlow. Between these points courses were kept with 6-inch vernier compasses by Doolittle and McGillicuddy, and distances estimated by time and the speed of the current. In reducing the computed co-ordinates, compass notes were adjusted to the astronomic observations.

1875. July 1 to September 13. Lieutenant Greene proceeded to Fort Shaw, connected the meridian line with the flagstaff and with the principal meridian of the land office, but was unable to obtain a telegraphic longitude of the fort.

The topographical information gained by these surveys was compiled under the supervision of Captain Twining into the following maps:

(1) A preliminary series in an index and forty-five sheets, on a scale of 1 inch to 1 mile,* which show the topography of the 5-mile belt. These were photolithographed at once upon completion, and furnished the British Commission.

(2) A final series of joint maps in an index and twenty-four sheets, on a scale of 1 inch to 2 miles, which take in the topography for 4 miles on the British side of the line, and have been reduced from the British and United States preliminary series. Of these final sheets twelve were executed by the British Commission and twelve by the United States. In both series the polyconic projection was used.

Draughtsmen employed: A. A. Aquirre, E. Mahlo, E Collet, A. Von Hoake, and A. Downing.

In addition to the above the following reconnaissances were made by Lieutenant Greene:

1873. October 15–25. From the second crossing of Mouse River (latitude 49° longitude 101° 54′ 58″), along Mouse River on its southern bend to near the mouth of Wintering River; thence direct to Fort Totten. Trail was kept by C. L. Doolittle with vernier compass, odometer, and flags. Seven camps were located astronomically by sextant; latitudes and longitudes by two Negus box chronometers, with traveling rates well deduced from observations at Mouse River crossing and at Pembina, both well established points.

The notes of these reconnaissances were compiled into a series of "reconnaissance maps," a profile and six maps, on a scale of 1 inch to 8 miles, which show the general features of the country from latitude 47° 30′ to 49°, and from longitude 94° 30′ to 114° 05′ (projection polyconic).

---

*The topographic field plots were reduced on scale of 1 to 30,000, at once, or immediately upon reaching the office.

The positions of the following military posts were determined: Fort Pembina, Dak., latitude 48° 56′ 45″.1, longitude 97° 13′ 47″.4; Fort Buford, Dak., latitude 47° 59′ 22″.19, longitude 103° 58′ 20″; Fort Totten, Dak., latitude 47° 58′ 40″, longitude 99° 01′ 38″; Fort Shaw, Mont., latitude 47° 30′ 33″.2, longitude 111° 48′ 19″.5; Fort Stevenson, Dak., latitude 47° 34′ 20″, longitude 101° 26′ 40″.

Lieutenant Greene, though always with detached and independent parties, acted subsequent to 1872 under general instructions from Captain Twining, chief astronomer of the Commission.

The British Commission consisted of Capt. D. R. Cameron, R. A., Commissioner, and Capt. S. Anderson, R. E., chief astronomer.

The Commissions worked in harmony throughout, establishing jointly the initial and other necessary points, and agreeing upon the boundary as the astronomical rather than the mean parallel of latitude 49° north.

Dr. Elliott Coues, surgeon, U. S. Army, accompanied the Commission as surgeon and naturalist, making field observations and collections, which latter was also done to the extent that circumstances would permit.

The results of the observed and computed latitudes of principal stations are found on pages 96 to 169; those for astronomical stations, with probable errors, are tabulated on page 95, and a list of latitudes and longitudes with altitudes added, on pages 198–199, with British latitudes on page 198; longitudes, pages 349 to 355, and on page 298 a summary of results with probable errors.

TREASURY DEPARTMENT.

COAST AND GEODETIC SURVEY.

Prior to the commencement of operations by the Coast Survey on the Pacific, only two nations (Spain and Russia) had had anything like a permanent establishment for the exploration of the west coast.

It might be said that the English had a principal center of exploration founded in 1824 at Fort Vancouver, from which many exploring expeditions, by sea and land, were sent out.

Instructions for the extension of the Coast Survey to the Pacific were issued by the Treasury Department in 1848, when the work, then consisting of a general reconnaissance of the whole coast, was placed under the charge of Lieutenant MacArthur, of the Navy.

Since the above date the field and office work has gradually developed through the necessary preliminary and formative stages, culminating in a hydrographic and topographic survey of the regular standard order of value of this work, done on the eastern coast, which, for our possessions from the Mexican boundary to Fuca Straits with Puget's Sound, was, at the close of the season of 1884, about three-fifths done, and the publication of charts, sailing directions, and tide tables proportionately advanced.

Nothing less than an inspection of the several Annual Reports since 1849 will give anything like an adequate view of the work.

The following table, kindly furnished from the office of the Coast Survey, relates to the results for the eastern gulf and west coasts:

U. S. Coast and Geodetic Survey.—Astronomical, Geodetic, and Magnetic Statistics.

Operations and Items—Results.	Total to July, 1885.
Reconnaissance (both exterior and interior):	
Area in square statute miles	377,960
Base lines:	
Primary, number of, measured and computed	14
Primary, length of, in statute miles	90
Subordinate, number of, measured and computed	130
Subordinate and beach measures, length of	476
Triangulation:	
Area in square statute miles (exterior and interior)	199,864
No. of stations occupied for horizontal measures	11,080
No. of (observed computed) geographical positions determined	21,105
No. of stations occupied for vertical measures	762
No. of elevations determined trigonometrically	1,915
No. of heights of bench-marks by spirit leveling	3,014
Lines of spirit leveling, length of, in statute miles	3,330
Astronomical work:	
No. of azimuth stations	190
No. of latitude stations	318
No. of longitude stations, telegraphic	127
No. of longitude stations, chronometric or lunar	110
Magnetic work:	
No. of stations occupied	693

NOTE.—The above statistics are necessarily approximated; at the time they are prepared the field records may not be all in; the triangulation sketches are not ready for use, and the computations not made to allow of accurate counting.

It was found impossible to separate the numbers for the Atlantic, the Gulf, and the Pacific coasts and Alaska.

No separation could be made between the primary, secondary, and tertiary triangulation, since they shade into each other by degrees, and interlace interminably. No area is counted twice, nor any station, though re-surveys may have been made.

Late information from the office of this Survey indicates that "more than 5,500" of the above are "geodetic positions;" to none of the latter, however, can any final value be assigned at present for the very obvious reason, viz, the incompleteness of the primary or main triangulation designed to connect them. These positions are therefore neither on uniform data, nor as yet properly supported, and consequently the time for their publication has not arrived.

Instruments.—The following are among the principal field instruments now being used by this office:

Reconnaissance: Gradientas, sextants, prismatic compasses, and tape lines.

Geodesy: Primary 6-meter compensating base apparatuses, 4-meter secondary base apparatuses, 16 and 8 inch theodolites, reconnoitering telescopes, heliotropes, gradienters, and signal lamps for night observations.

Astronomy: (1) Zenith telescopes for latitude; (2) 46-inch transits, adapted for time and latitude; (3) prismatic transits for time and latitude; (4) electric chronographs for registering time observations; (5) telegraphic key-boards; (6) personal-equation apparatuses.

Topography: Plane tables complete, with a telemeter rod.

Hydrography: Sextants, optical densimeters, deep-sea thermometers, and self-registering tide-gauges.

Miscellaneous: Pendulums, geodesic levels, tide-predicting machines, maximum and minimum thermometers, and a stoppered level.*

Mr. F. H. Hassler was Superintendent from 1807 to 1818, and from 1832 to 1843; Prof. A. D. Bache from 1843 to 1867; Prof. Benj. Peirce from 1867 to 1874; Carlile P. Patterson from 1874 to 1881; Julius E. Hilgard till 1885; and at present Mr. F. M. Thorn.

According to a statement of the Superintendent, of March 11, 1884, there were 63 field and 114 office civilian assistants, while in August, 1884, there were 58 naval officers and 340 seamen of the Navy engaged. The total number of the field parties (1884–'85) is given as fifty-eight. The total personnel (civilians, naval officers, and seamen) aggregated 575 in all.

The salaries and allowances to the normal force, with names, will be found on page 764 *et seq.* Senate Mis. Doc. No. 82, Forty-ninth Congress, first session.

Army officers were employed on this work up to the war of the rebellion, since which date none have been so employed.

The objects of the Coast and Geodetic Survey will be found on page 525 *et seq.* House Ex. Doc. No. 270, Forty-eighth Congress, second session,

* Short descriptions of these instruments are given in a pamphlet at the exhibit of the Survey at New Orleans, 1884–'85, and are referred to in Appendix No. 18, Coast Survey Report, 1884.

under the head of "Functions," which show that its practical results in the main are as an aid to navigation and commerce, while the classes of work prosecuted may be said to be generally astronomic, base measuring, trigonometric, topographic, hydrographic, tidal, magnetic, deep-sea soundings, and sea-current observations, in the field, and their subsequent office reductions, with publication in a series of annual reports and charts.

The field work of the Survey is divided in twelve sections for the coast proper, to which four others have been added for transcontinental work and the aid rendered State surveys.

The work as a whole has been mainly hydrographic, the topography usually extending inland from 1 to 3 miles from the shore line, of which Nos. IX, X, XI, XII, XV, and XVI, are the divisions prosecuting field work west of the Mississippi River. (See Annual Report, 1885.)

At the end of 1885 the topography had embraced an area of 3,364 square miles.*

Likewise the inside hydrography had embraced 3,500 square miles, and the outside hydrography 5,740 square miles.†

Until within a few years the explorations in Alaska were carried on without system, scattered along the whole coast.

In 1883 regular reconnaissance work, comprising topography and hydrography preliminary in character, was begun, and had progressed (end of 1885) over an area of 3,500 square miles.

Off-shore and deep-sea soundings (including Commander Belknap's soundings in the *Tuscarora*) have been made in the Santa Barbara channel, and in the approaches to San Francisco, over an area of about 4,250 square miles.

The transcontinental triangulation in vicinity of 39th parallel was reported at end of 1885 as about three-fifths done, the gaps west of the Mississippi being between Kansas City, Mo., and Mount Carson, Colo., about 8° longitude (450 miles), and between Pike's Peak, Colorado, and

---

*As a rule the topography extends 1 to 3 miles from the shore line; in special cases much further, in others less.

†The inside hydrography comprises the general coast line, and includes all bays, sounds, and rivers. The outside hydrography comprises the close surveys outside the coast line, including open bays, averaging 15 miles in width, with ranges from 5 to 30 miles.

Salt Lake City, Utah, about 70° longitude (375 miles). Levels of precision have only extended a few miles west of St. Louis.

Tidal observations were commenced by the Coast Survey about 1834, and have been made at over one thousand stations, mainly on our own coasts.

They are usually prosecuted primarily for hydrographic purposes while some are series recorded by self-registering tide-guages, with a view to tidal predictions, tidal tables based on which are issued annually.

Of the latter there are now six of nineteen years or more, and twenty-nine ranging from one to nineteen years.

The tidal tables of 1887 contain the predicted times and heights of high and low waters for every day in the year, at four principal and ninety-two subordinate (or derivative) stations on the Pacific coast.

Gravity determinations are reported at San Francisco, and magnetic observations and compilations have always been undertaken in conjunction with the regular work, the latter made general for the whole United States.

Longitudes, as determined by the electric telegraph between 1846 and 1885, appear as Appendix No. 11, Annual Report, 1884.

Certain late longitudes, latitudes, azimuths appear as Appendix No. 9, Annual Report, 1885, and heights of stations in Appendix No. 10, Annual Report, 1884.

Lists of geographical positions may be found in the following Coast Survey Annual Reports: Appendix 12, 1851, pp. 162–442; Appendix 7, 1853, pp. 14–42; Appendix 8, 1855, pp. 119–148; Appendix 25, 1857, pp. 264–301; Appendix 20, 1859, pp. 216–267; Appendix 15, 1864, pp. 144–182; Appendix 9, 1865, pp. 99–136; Appendix 10, 1865, pp. 137; Appendix 13, 1868, pp. 171–242; Appendix 6, 1874, pp. 62–65; Appendix 11, 1874, p. 134, and Appendix 8, 1885, pp. 285–439, including points established by the Borden Survey of Massachusetts. A list of heights of trigonometric stations appears in Appendix 9, 1870, pp. 90–91. A description of bench-marks at tidal stations is found as Appendix 10, 1870, pp. 92–97.

An exploration and discussion of the field and office methods now in vogue in this work, together with the construction of maps, will mainly be found in the following Annual Reports:

Bases.—Appendix 11, 1883, pp. 277–288, and Appendix 8, 1882, pp. 139–149.

Triangulation.—Appendix 17, 1875, pp 279–292; Appendix 20, 1876, pp. 391–399; Appendix 9, 1882, pp. 151–197, and Appendix 9, 1885, pp. 441–467.

Latitude.—Appendix 10, 1866, pp. 72–85.

Longitude.—Appendix 6, 1880, pp. 81–92.

Time, longitude, latitude, and azimuth—Appendix 14, 1880, pp. 201–286; Appendix 7, Annual Report, 1884, pp. 323–375.

Geodesic leveling.—Appendix 11, 1882, pp. 517–556.

Plane tables.—Appendix 13, 1880, pp. 172–200.

Ellipticity.—Appendix 15, 1881, pp. 442–456.

Magnetic dip and intensity.—Appendix 6, Annual Report, 1885, pp. 129–274.

Topographic and hydrographic delineation.—Appendix 20, 1860, pp. 216–229.

Projections.—Appendix 15, 1880, pp. 287–296, and Appendix 6, 1884, pp. 135–321.

Topographic drawings.—Appendix 14, 1883, pp. 367–368.

Computations, formula, and factor.—Appendix 7, 1884, pp. 323–375, and index to scientific papers; Appendix 6, 1881, pp. 91–123.

The publications of the Coast Survey consist of "Annual Reports," "Charts," "Coast Pilots," "Tide-Tables," and professional and scientific papers, the latter usually appearing as appendixes to the "Annual Reports."*

The latter have appeared from 1853 to date, in quarto form; prior to which they formed a part of the regular executive document series.

The charts are classed as "finished" and "preliminary." The former are printed from engraved plates, and include all details; the latter are issued as soon as possible after the survey to meet the most pressing needs of navigation, and are either engraved or photolithographed.

The general character of the charts is as follows:

---

*A general index of scientific papers, methods, and results, found in the appendixes to the several Annual Reports, appears as Appendix 6, Annual Report, 1881, and a descriptive catalogue of publications forms Appendix 6, Annual Report, 1883.

1. Sailing charts, scale 1 to 1,200,000, exhibiting the approaches to a large extent of coast, and giving offshore soundings.

2. General charts of the coast, scales 1 to 400,000 and 1 to 200,000, especially intended for coastwise navigation, showing configuration of the shore, the positions of islands, rocks, and shoals, the light-houses, life-saving stations, and other natural and artificial landmarks.

3. Coast charts, scale 1 to 80,000, from which may be recognized the beacons, buoys, light-houses, etc., while entering channels to bays and harbors.

4. Harbor charts, in large scales for needs of local navigation. The total number of charts of all kinds issued, as shown by official catalogue of 1886, is 402, distributed as follows:

Locality.	Engraved.		Photo-lithographed.	Total.
	Finished.	Preliminary.	Preliminary.	
Atlantic and Gulf coasts......	209	19	59	287
Pacific coast..................	26	24	22	72
Alaska.........................	....	....	43	43
Total..................	235	43	124	402

Thirty-eight miscellaneous maps and plans, not adapted for the use of navigators, have also been issued. (See catalogue.)

A compilation for a general map of the United States (scale 1 inch to 10 miles) was begun in 1883 and continued while a small appropriation was available. (See Appendix 4, Annual Report, 1883.)

An elaborate model, in plaster, of the Atlantic Basin and Gulf of Mexico, has been constructed.

UNITED STATES NAVAL OBSERVATORY.

When practicable this office has co-operated with survey parties in the West, and has also established independent astronomic latitudes and longitudes, to be found mentioned in the following volumes, published by the Naval Observatory:

Washington astronomical and meteorological observations, Vol. XIV, 1869, Appendix II, report of Professor Newcomb, U. S. Navy, page 13.

Vol. XIV, 1869, Appendix II, report of Prof. William Harkness, U. S. Navy, page 40.

Vol. XIV, 1869, Appendix II, report of Prof. William Harkness, U. S. Navy, page 49.

Vol. XIV, 1869, Appendix II, report of Prof. William Harkness, U. S. Navy, page 59.

Vol. XVII, 1870, Appendix I, page 39.

Vol. XIX, 1872, Appendix II, pages 15, 19, and 21.

Vol. XXI, 1874, Appendix II, page 10.

Vol. XXIII, 1876, Part II, Appendix III, pages 43, 48, 116, 138, 139, 175, 186, 253, 334, 348, and 408.

Vol. XXIV, 1877, Appendix V, page 15.

It has been ascertained that the Nautical Almanac Office published a special report by Prof. A. C. Coffin, U. S. Navy, in 1869 (pp. 69–71), upon the total solar eclipse, containing independent determinations of astronomic latitudes and longitudes west of the Mississippi.

MISCELLANEOUS.

Survey operations, including one or more of triangulation, topographic, geologic, or cartographic factors, have been conducted by several States, but it is not the province of this memoir to indicate their scope or results.* As to the latter, the geographic co-ordinates of but few points have been determined. Of all railroad surveys that one projected and partially completed by the Northern Pacific has been the most comprehensive and refined. The progress and results of all works of survey not prosecuted directly by the General Government should be currently secured and availed of at a permanent bureau, as herein mentioned.

MAPS.

Although the present volume has not been printed until 1889, yet circumstances have prevented the continuation in detail of the works and results of the several expeditions and surveys west of the Mississippi River since 1880, yet it has been possible to add a reference to the existing topo-

* A brief reference to State surveys then existing between 1875 and 1881, will be found on page 59 *et seq.* House Ex. Doc. No. 270, Forty-eighth Congress, second session.

graphic maps of a general character, the outgrowth of the several offices and organizations, that have contributed each its quota to our general knowledge of the topography and geography of the interior of our country. The following list is believed to be complete at date of its compilation (March 31, 1887):

MISCELLANEOUS, TOPOGRAPHIC, AND OTHER GOVERNMENT MAPS, INCLUDING GEOLOGIC.

UNITED STATES.

Description or name of map.	Scale.	No. of sheets when complete.	Total issued.	By whom issued.	Administration.	Remarks.
Outline map of the United States.	$\frac{1}{5000000}$	4	4	Engineer Department, U. S. Army.	War Department.	Prepared in the Office of the Chief of Engineers, U. S. Army, 1885. Military posts shown by colored flags.
Outline map of the United States, showing location of works and surveys for river and harbor improvements.	$\frac{1}{3326400}$	4	4	... do	.. do	Compiled for the index to Report of Chief of Engineers, 1879. Printed in black.
Land Office map of the United States.	$\frac{1}{2534400}$	4	4	General Land Office.	Interior Department.	Compiled and printed in black and five colors, 1884. A new map of the United States has been compiled on same scale (1 inch to 40 miles), and issued in 6 sheets.
Topographical Atlas of territory of the United States west of the 100th meridian.*	$\frac{4}{253440}$	....	35	Office of Geographical Surveys under Engineer Department.	War Department.	Thirty sheets issued with land classification. Topography based on initial astronomic points and trigonometric net. Natural objects, means of communication, artificial and economic features prominent according to importance. Geology and natural history incidental to main purpose, *i. e.*, Topography.
	$\frac{1}{506880}$	95	15			
Geological Atlas of territory of the United States west of the 100th meridian.	$\frac{1}{506880}$	95	11	....do	... do	Colors superposed directly upon topographic sheets of same scale.
Atlas of geological exploration of 40th parallel (special topographic sheets).	$\frac{1}{253440}$	5	5	Engineer Department, U. S. Army.	... do	Topography from a geological standpoint, *i. e.*, natural features prominent, communications less so, in artificial and economic details deficient. Outlines engraved, hill work in crayon, shading based on plotted contours.
Atlas of geological exploration of 40th parallel (special geological sheets).	$\frac{1}{253440}$	5	5	....do	....do	Outlines engraved. Elevations in contours. Geological formations in colors, superposed on the topographic map as a base. Also 1 sheet of geologic sections and an index map, 1 inch to 6 miles.
Outline map of territory of the United States west of the Mississippi River.	$\frac{1}{2000000}$	4	4	....do	....do	Prepared in the Office of the Chief of Engineers, U. S. Army. Printed in black; printed also in hachures in color.

MISCELLANEOUS, TOPOGRAPHIC, AND OTHER GOVERNMENT MAPS, ETC.—Continued.

UNITED STATES—Continued.

Description or name of map.	Scale.	No. of sheets when complete.	Total issued.	By whom issued.	Administration.	Remarks.
Part of atlas of Colorado.	$\frac{1}{253440}$	6	6	Geological Survey of the Territories.	Interior Department.	Topography from a geological standpoint. Natural features most prominent, communications less so, artificial features still less.
Part of geological atlas of Colorado.	$\frac{1}{253440}$	6	6	....do	.. do	Result of color directly superposed upon topographic map of same scale. This atlas also contains 4 sheets, each scale 1 inch to 12 miles, embracing the State, showing triangulation, drainage, land classification, and general geology; also geologic sections and panoramic views.
Charts of the survey of northern and northwestern lakes.	$\frac{1}{5000}$, $\frac{1}{8000}$, $\frac{1}{10000}$, $\frac{1}{15000}$, $\frac{1}{16000}$, $\frac{1}{20000}$, $\frac{1}{25000}$, $\frac{1}{30000}$, $\frac{1}{32000}$, $\frac{1}{40000}$, $\frac{1}{50000}$, $\frac{1}{80000}$, $\frac{1}{120000}$, $\frac{1}{400000}$, $\frac{1}{600000}$	79	79	Engineer Department, U. S. Army.	War Department.	Work begun 1841; completed 1881. Re-edition of 69 charts being issued, printed in black. Elevations on older charts in hachures; on others by contours, 20 feet and 60 feet intervals, and hachures. Copper engraved; preliminary edition of 34 sheets by photo-lithography. For use of lake vessels and as an aid to river and harbor improvements.
Survey of part of Mississippi River.	$\frac{1}{10000}$	229	16	Mississippi River Commission.	....do	Photo-lithographed. Printed in black; elevation by contours at 3 feet and 5 feet intervals. From Cairo to Wolf Island and Memphis to Commerce Cut-off, from field data by Lake Survey (Comstock), the balance in MS. only and not to be published; 50 in outline; 137 with full topography, which with 16 published embrace the river from Cairo to Donaldsonville, below which are charts by Coast Survey; also 26 lake charts (5 feet contours).
Do...............	$\frac{1}{20000}$	69	9	....do	....	Reduction from $\frac{1}{10000}$ by photolithography combining several sheets in one.
Maps of part of Mississippi River.	$\frac{1}{63360}$	32	32	....do	....do	These include the river from Cairo to the head of the Passes; also 3 index charts and 2 of titles and notes, surveys by Mississippi River Commission.
Alluvial Valley of the Mississippi.	$\frac{1}{316800}$	8	....	....do	....do	Shows area overflowed, existing levees, cross sections, etc., compiled from all existing surveys from Cape Girardeau to the Gulf, including the several subdivisions of the lower river.

* For publications issued by this work, see "List of Reports and Maps of the United States Geographical Surveys west of the 100th Meridian," 2d edition, 1881; also, Annual Reports, Chief of Engineers, 1872 to 1885.

The General Land Office of the Interior Department issues compiled planimetric maps of the United States, as also of the States and Territories wherein remain unsold public lands, in black and two colors, except for Florida and Arizona, which are in three colors. Ohio and Indiana, scale 1 inch to 10 miles; Alabama, Arkansas, Florida, Iowa, Mississippi, Wisconsin, Indian Territory, and Dakota, scale 1 inch to 12 miles; Illinois, Louisiana, and Missouri, scale 1 inch to 14 miles; Colorado, Kansas, Minnesota, Nebraska, Oregon, Arizona, Utah, Washington Territory, and Wyoming, scale 1 inch to 15 miles; Michigan, Nevada, Idaho. and New Mexico, scale 1 inch to 16 miles; and California and Montana, scale 1 inch to 18 miles.

The Post-Office Department has, since the year 1869, issued twenty-five separately compiled planimetric maps, aggregating sixty-three sheets, each embracing a single or a number of States, on scales of 1 inch to 6 miles for the largest, and 1 inch to 15 miles for the smallest (issued bi-monthly).

The Coast Survey commenced the compilation of a general map of the United States, scale 1 inch to 10 miles (engraving and publishing the plate showing New Jersey and adjoining territory), the appropriation for which, however, is now suspended.

Of the regular hydrographic charts of the Coast Survey, 402 have been issued, on forty-sever different scales, from 1 : 3000 to 1 : 3500000. (See catalogue, 1886.)

Certain preliminary maps and those prepared to accompany reports were issued by the geological exploration of the Colorado River, and the geological and geographical survey of the Rocky Mountain region under J. W. Powell.

The geological explorations of the Black Hills published one topographic and one geological map of the Black Hills, each scale 1 inch to 4 miles. The relief of the topographic sheet is by contours and hachures, with drainage in blue; that for geologic purposes with contours and drainage in black.

The present Geological Survey has also issued three sheets embracing territory in northeastern Arizona and northwestern New Mexico; and there have also been printed by this office fifty-three sheets, scale 1 inch to 4 miles, for areas west of the Mississippi River, each representing one degree of latitude and one of longitude (about one-half from prior surveys) as a topographic base for field purposes and upon which to delineate and subsequently publish, in colors, the geological formations. Also seventy quarter degree and two one-sixteenth degree sheets.

Various compiled maps, especially of western areas, prepared at the Engineer Office, headquarters military divisions and departments, have been published, when possible, as currently required. (See Annual Reports, Corps of Engineers, to date.)

Material now exists from which the compilation of a general military topographic atlas of the United States,* including Alaska, could be begun, resulting from various works, and found distributed among the following Government offices:

WAR DEPARTMENT.

In the Engineer Department are lodged original and other results from the following: (1) United States Lake Survey (northern lakes and part of

* See also essay by Lieut. M. M. Macomb on "The necessity for a fixed policy in the War Department in regard to * * * the construction of a general military atlas of the United States."

St. Lawrence River); (2) United States geographical surveys; (3) geological exploration of the 40th parallel; (4) river and harbor surveys; (5) fortification surveys (in manuscript only); (6) Pacific Railroad surveys; (7) bureau of exploration and surveys, including military and geographical surveys west of the Mississippi; (8) exploration and reconnaissance headquarters of military divisions and departments, including surveys of military reservations; (9) certain international boundary surveys; (10) exploration of Yukon River, Alaska.

In the War Department proper may be found explorations in Alaska (Allen), and notes, maps, etc., at the various engineers' offices, headquarters divisions and departments.

The Mississippi and Missouri River Commissions retain in their offices manuscript material of special topographic and hydrographic surveys made under their auspices.

TREASURY DEPARTMENT.

Office of the Coast and Geodetic Survey for topography of the Atlantic, Gulf, and Pacific coasts; also Alaska, transcontinental triangulation, and that in aid of State surveys, including Mississippi River to head of tidal influence and precise levelings.

INTERIOR DEPARTMENT.

The General Land Office for its subdivision plats; boundaries between States and Territories; surveys of private land claims and Indian reservations; topography of the United States geological survey of the Territories; the geological and geographical survey of the Rocky Mountain region; the geological exploration of the Black Hills, and the United States geological survey.

STATE DEPARTMENT.

Records of the Texas, Northeast, Northwest. Northern and Mexican boundaries.

NAVY DEPARTMENT.

Latitudes and longitudes by the Naval Observatory and Nautical Almanac.

There are also results from all State boundaries; the subdivision surveys in Texas; triangulation and topography by the State surveys of Massachusetts and New York; topography of State geologic surveys of New Hampshire, New York, New Jersey, Pennsylvania, Ohio, North Carolina, Georgia, Michigan, Missouri, and California; of surveys for railroads, including trans-continental survey, and canals, for turnpike, toll, and other wagon-roads, for counties, towns; also, by private or corporate parties, including the utilization of all manuscript and published data from all of these surveys, decided as available after competent inspection.

Systematic compilation, based upon the above, should be constantly prosecuted independently of whatever field-work may be carried forward.

Imperfect as it is feared the foregoing memoir may prove, resulting in part from want of assistance and ill health during its preparation, one trusts that it will serve to perpetuate in authentic form an official record of those organizations, officers, and others that as a whole have contributed to the aggregate of our present critical geographic knowledge of that portion of our territory west of the Mississippi up to 1880.*

* There does not yet exist a published list of the principal latitudes and longitudes established by the several Government surveys, gathered in a single tabulated view, and all known separately-published lists are in a measure fragmentary. Such a list, compiled under competent jurisdiction, accurately weighted as to precision, and classified, with description of monuments, and careful bibliographical references, although a matter of no little labor, would nevertheless prove of great permanent value.

www.ingramcontent.com/pod-product-compliance
Lightning Source LLC
LaVergne TN
LVHW010238110826
845151LV00004B/1329

9781425524708